Storming Zion

Storming Zion

Government Raids on Religious Communities

STUART A. WRIGHT

AND

SUSAN J. PALMER

OXFORD
UNIVERSITY PRESS

OXFORD

UNIVERSITY PRESS

Oxford University Press is a department of the University of Oxford.
It furthers the University's objective of excellence in research, scholarship,
and education by publishing worldwide. Oxford is a registered trade mark
of Oxford University Press in the UK and in certain other countries

Published in the United States of America by
Oxford University Press
198 Madison Avenue, New York, NY 10016,
United States of America

© Oxford University Press 2016

Library of Congress Cataloging-in-Publication Data
Wright, Stuart A.
Storming Zion : government raids on religious communities / Stuart A. Wright
and Susan J. Palmer.
p.   cm.
Includes bibliographical references and index.
ISBN 978-0-19-539889-2 (cloth : alk. paper) — ISBN 978-0-19-539890-8
(pbk. : alk. paper) 1. Religion and state. 2. Cults. I. Title.
BL65.S8W75 2015
322'.1—dc23
2015009978

1 3 5 7 9 8 6 4 2

Printed by Courier Digital Solutions, USA

Contents

Preface and Acknowledgments

RAIDS ARE BY no means a recent phenomenon. The word *rade* can be found in Middle English, as in a riding, or a road. In Old English, rād meant "the act of riding" or "the act of riding with a hostile intent." This noun (or verb) seems to belong to more primitive, lawless cultures of the past; for example, the *creach* (Gaelic for plunder, pillage, rob) in the 16th-century Highlands, where cattle rustling among the MacGregors and other rival clans was a common practice. In the 18th century we find the term used to refer to the killing and scalping of French settlers in Nova Scotia by native militias from the Wabanaki Confederacy. In the mid-19th century, *razzia* (Arabic for raids or military attacks) were carried out by Moorish slave hunters in North Africa. Sir Walter Scott, in his 1817 novel *Rob Roy*, uses the term "raid" to describe a military expedition on horseback.

"Religious raids"—raids on minority religions deemed pagan, infidel, or heretical—have often marked the turning points in national histories. In France, one can find a reference to a raid in the slaughter of the Cathars at Carcassonne in 1209. In Greece, Mount Athos has been a target of frequent raids over the centuries, attacked by pirates, Saracens, and Russian fleets. From 1307 to 1309, the mercenaries of the Catalan Grand Company raided Mount Athos, sacking its monasteries and plundering its treasures. Recently, in 2013, the Greek government sent riot police to storm Mount Athos, in a futile attempt to forcibly remove a group of monks from Esphigmenou monastery. The monks threw stones and Molotov cocktails at police and judicial officials as they attempted to climb the steep heights of the monastery. The conflict began in 2002 when Patriarch Bartholomew of Constantinople declared the monks of Esphigmenou an illegal brotherhood and ordered their eviction (Bernardelli, 2013). In the German Reformation the most famous raids ended in the 1535 siege of Münster, where John of Leiden reigned over his "New Jerusalem" commune (Williams, 2000).

It seems surprising to us today that this primitive and draconian method of quelling dissident religious communities is still in use, and is actually waxing in frequency and becoming more militarized. This book is a study of contemporary raids on new or nontraditional religious communities in 17 countries, but focusing on those in the United States and France. We became aware of these raids through our research in the field of new or nontraditional religious movements (NRMs). In 1990, Susan Palmer received a three-year Canadian federal grant (SSHRC) to study the role of children in NRMs.[1] She observed that many of the groups she chose to research (The Family International, the Twelve Tribes, the United Nuwaubian Nation—groups that were millenarian and communal and interesting because of their radical, religiously-based, and highly developed alternative gender and family patterns) all experienced raids by authorities attempting to "rescue" their children. Again, when she was researching Quebec's *nouvelles religions* she found that a few of them, such as the Apostles of Infinite Love, had been raided. Palmer also came across a surprising number of raids in her study of NRMs (known as *"sectes"*) in France. She even found herself in the midst of a raid by the Gendarmerie during one of her research visits to Tabitha's Place in 1997. We will address some of these raids at length in this book.[2]

Stuart Wright's interest in government raids on NRMs peaked in 1993 following the disastrous federal siege of the Branch Davidian community outside Waco, Texas, where 86 people died. Wright found that a number of other minority religious communities had been targeted for government raids in the early 1990s. Indeed, the decade of the nineties proved to be a watershed in the history of raided religious groups as we discovered in our study.

Initially, the subject of government raids arose during a conversation at a scholarly conference. We were both intrigued and baffled by the frequency and ferocity of the raid phenomenon. These dramatic NRM-state confrontations generated many exciting media reports and several journalistic studies (Freedberg, 1994; Kaihla and Laver, 1993; Lee, 2003). However, only a handful of scholarly studies had emerged and these were exclusively case studies focusing on specific communities. There were no systematic overarching or comparative studies of government raids on new or nontraditional religions of which we were aware. Yet this seemed to be critically important given some of the patterns we were witnessing in various raids. It was out of this discussion that we eventually devised the book project.

Our research involved several stages. First, we collected data on raids through reading local news reports, legal documents, organizational newsletters, police reports (i.e., the FBI reports via the FOIA), files collected by human rights organizations and educational centers, and searching the Internet (including both NRM and anticult websites). We also used our contacts with other scholars in different countries and with researchers who had covered raids on NRMs previously. Through the standard methods of field research, interviews, and participant observation, we gathered personal accounts of raid experiences, historical details on the conflicts that preceded the raids, and ethnographic data on the groups' membership, beliefs, and practices. Through triangulation or cross-verification of different sources (religious leaders, their cultural opponents, and various secular authorities such as lawyers, zoning officials, law enforcement officers, etc.) we were able to compare and analyze the data.

It is our hope that this book will shed some light on the social and ideological factors which contributed to (and continue to provoke) these dramatic NRM-state conflicts. This cross-national investigation of the social, political, and countermovement forces behind government raids and their legal repercussions should provide a rich source of material for those seeking to understand the public management of religious minorities in Western democratic countries. We also hope that the results of this study will be of interest to the media, civil liberties groups, legislators, policy-makers, regulatory officials, law enforcement, human rights organizations, and other public-minded groups in the event of future raids.

We wish to acknowledge generous support from grants for this research. Stuart Wright received a Jack Shand Travel Grant from the Society for the Scientific Study of Religion (SSSR) to support research abroad on raided communities. Susan Palmer received a Standard Research Grant from the Social Sciences and Humanities Research Council (SSHRC) funded by the Federal Government of Canada, 2011–2015.[3] The funding and support for this project enabled us to travel to some very remote places in order to visit raided communities, conduct interviews, and collect data. In 2009, we spent the better part of the summer in Europe carrying out our research. We want to thank Michael York for allowing us to use his apartment in Paris as our home base. We put 6,000 kilometers on a rent car visiting these religious communities stretching from Belgium, to the south of France, to the Piedmont Valley in Italy. We have some very fond memories, meeting a number of kind and gracious people who hosted us for a day or two, observing firsthand their daily routines and interactions, taking a few side trips to places such as the Shrine of Our Lady of Roca-madour, and also getting lost in the French Alps several times and trying to get directions to our next meeting place.

Several human rights and educational organizations were critical to our research. In particular we want to acknowledge the assistance of Willy Fautré of Human Rights Without Frontiers (HRWF), based in Brussels, for his help in compiling information on government raids in Europe. He and his staff were essential in helping us to make contact with and gain access to some of the religious communities, as well as with key scholars and attorneys representing the raided groups. The staff at the Center of Information and Counseling on New Spiritualities (CICNS) in Montpezat de Quercy, France was also very helpful in the course of our project. The London-based INFORM Center and the Italian-based CESNUR assisted us in providing documentation on lesser-known raided groups.

We also wish to acknowledge the invaluable help of practitioners and spokespersons from the new religions we researched: Vishti of Manda-rom; Danielle Gounord and Eric Roux of Scientology; Shomer, Havah, and Hakam of the Twelve Tribes; Claire Borowick and Lonnie Davis of The Family International; Clive Doyle and Sheila Martin of the Branch Davidians; and Dowayne Barlow of the FLDS. We found that face-to-face interactions with members of these communities served to humanize the conflicts and tragedies that befell them.

We would also like to thank Bernard Doherty for assistance in re-searching government raids in Australia and Adam Klin-Orin for help in researching state raids on NRMs in Israel. David Bromley and Jim Rich-ardson served as reviewers and provided invaluable insights and com-ments, especially in the formative stages of the book.

Finally, we want to acknowledge our editor, Cynthia Read, for recognizing the importance of this project for OUP. We appreciate her commitment to the book as it extended beyond the anticipated deadline by several years. We also want to thank Assistant Editor, Marcela Maxfield, for guiding us through the completion of the manuscript and Senior Project Manager, B. Gogulanathan, for his thorough fact-checking and copyediting by Brendan Frost. The edito-rial staff at Oxford was patient, meticulous, and supportive to the end.

Of course, we would be remiss not acknowledge the support and un-derstanding of our significant others, Nancy and Doug. From start to finish, this project covered more than five years. We think they are proba-bly the only two people happier than the authors that this book was finally finished.

Storming Zion

I

Government Raids on Religious Communities

ON SEPTEMBER 5, 2013, German police conducted a massive raid on an American-based sect, the Twelve Tribes, in Klosterzimmern and Wornitz, Bavaria. The raid team included an estimated 100 police and 60 social workers in a predawn raid. Authorities seized 40 children from 60 families and drove off in 25 vans. The raid was predicated on allegations of physical child abuse. When examined by state doctors, however, no evidence of child abuse was found. Nonetheless, the *Jugendamt* (Youth Services) obtained a court order for protective custody. The parents were allowed very little contact with the children; most parents did not see their children for four months after the raid. Three nursing mothers were permitted to stay with their infants and four older children in an institution. But on December 9, there was a second raid, much to the surprise of the institution's caregivers, when all the infants and children were seized.

This sect-state dispute centered on the practice of spanking children. The religious community had already been raided in 2002, following a dispute over homeschooling. This may still have been in the minds of officials after the new law was passed in 2000 that established a child's right to a "nonviolent education."[1] Even by German standards, however, the 2013 raid was exceptional. Normally, when abuse is suspected, the *Jugendamt* is required by law to send social workers to assist individual families in resolving problems. Only in the most extreme cases are children taken by the state. In this case, an emergency action was claimed necessary because authorities were concerned that the *Sekt* would flee. But a careful analysis suggests that the government's actions were more likely linked to pressure by well-organized anti-*Sekt* opponents (Palmer and Frisk, 2014).[2]

The raids in Germany on the Twelve Tribes raise questions not only about the discretion of state officials in taking these extreme measures but also about their similarity to other state raids we have witnessed over the years. To wit, when we thought about the wide range of government raids on new or nontraditional religious movements (NRMs) with which we were familiar, we noticed a striking similarity in raid patterns. At the very least, the similarities included aggressive claims-making by detractors and the types of claims made (Wright, 1995a); the navigation of a "dispute-broadening" process by opponents (Bromley, 1998a); the formation of oppositional alliances among apostates, anticult organizations and actors, and concerned relatives (Hall, 1995; Hall and Schuyler, 1998; Palmer, 1998; Wright, 1995a); the successful coalition-building of allied opponents with state agents and media (Hall and Schuyler, 1998); and a rapid mobilization of an oppositional coalition leading up to the government raid (Bromley, 1998b; Palmer, 1998, 2011a; Wiseman, 2011; Wright, 2011; Wright and Fagan, 2011).

In order to examine our ideas more systematically, we set about to compile a comprehensive list of state raids on NRMs. We assumed that such a list could be culled with some modest research efforts. We were wrong. The task of compiling a raid list became a major undertaking. The number of government raids on NRMs proved to be much larger than we anticipated. Using Internet searches, personal records and archives, our contacts with NRMs, and the assistance of colleagues in North America and Europe, as well as human rights organizations like Human Rights Without Frontiers International in Brussels and organizations dedicated to the rights of minority faiths such as the Coordination des Associations et Particuliers pour la Liberté de Conscience (CAP) and the Le Centre d'information et de conseil des nouvelles spiritualités (CICNS) in France, we were able to track down a sizeable number of state raids conducted abroad. We have spent more than four years assembling this list, and though we make no claims that the list is exhaustive, we are confident that it is the most complete compilation by anyone to date. Of course, there are no reliable means to determine the parameters of our population and we continue to come across new raid cases in our investigation. We have imposed some parameters on the list ourselves so as to make the project more manageable. The list does not include any cases from Eastern Europe, Russia, or the former Soviet bloc states. It does not include cases from Asia (except Japan) or Africa. The list focuses on North and South America, Australia, Israel, and Western Europe. We decided we could live with these limitations. For now we leave it to other researchers in the future to add to this list or expand the list to the countries we have excluded.

Since there has been no large-scale comparative study of government raids to our knowledge, the research presented some very interesting possibilities. Both of us have studied new or alternative religious movements for over 30 years and have published extensively in this field. We have conducted research on dozens of raided groups, explored the claims of detractors, studied the criminal allegations of authorities, and followed the court cases and legal outcomes, not to mention the impacts on these raided communities. But these efforts have invariably been case studies. While the case study method has its merits, by focusing on isolated cases of raids, or on raids targeting a specific group, we may have failed to grasp the larger picture. To get a different perspective, we step back from examining only individual cases and ask broader questions. What might we gain in terms of sociological knowledge if we studied raids in the aggregate? What can we learn about the dynamics of the conflict between sect and state if we focus on raids solely as our unit of analysis? How common are government raids on NRMs? Has the number of government raids remained more or less constant over time? Or have state raids been increasing in recent years, as appears to be the case? And if so, why?

Why Raids?

Before proceeding to a discussion of raid patterns, we should define what we mean by a state raid. A state or government raid is defined here as a sudden incursion or surprise attack by a well-armed division (or divisions) of law enforcement agents, accompanied possibly by other state personnel (e.g., child protection officials, state social workers, emergency medical personnel, etc.). We want to emphasize that raids constitute an extreme and high-risk form of law enforcement action by the state. The raid tactic is typically designed for critical incidents involving groups or individuals that police believe pose an imminent danger or the threat of violence. Thus raids are most often used against groups which are believed to be armed and may offer violent resistance, such as gangs, terrorists, or drug traffickers. In some instances, we have been told, raids may be conducted to gain an element of surprise in order to search a property before the evidence is destroyed. But in such cases, it is often impossible to separate the element-of-surprise rationale by police from those that are simply driven by the emergent "war model" (Kraska, 2001a) or "military model" of crime control (Skolnick and Fyfe, 1993:113–116). Also referred to as "paramilitary policing" (Kraska and Kappeler, 1996), this model of crime control has had a transformative effect on law enforcement culture and organizational structure significantly in the last 30 years (Balko, 2013; Haggerty and Ericson, 2001; Kraska, 2001a; Kraska and Kappeler, 1996; Skolnick and Fyfe, 1993). Transformations of police culture have been documented by sociologists and criminologists most frequently in the language and attitudinal perspective denoted by the prevalence of a "martial rhetoric" embodied in the "war mentality." It has transposed the culture and identity of police by socializing officers to think of themselves as "soldiers" and treating suspected criminals as "enemies of the state." Changes in organizational structure have produced new role expectations and status sets from the adoption of a military command structure and discipline, and police academies following close-order drill and military-like protocols (Skolnick and Fyfe, 1993:113). There are certainly appropriate case-specific uses for paramilitary policing, but much of the criminological research shows it has suffered from "mission creep," extending well beyond its designed purpose (Kraska and Cubellis, 1997; Kraska, 2001b).[3] In cases involving new or alternative religious communities, the rationale for using raids is severely weakened for reasons we discuss below.

Raids entail high-risk operations; they are more likely to result in injury or death for police, alleged criminals, and innocent bystanders. As such, the raid tactic has to be weighed carefully against the risks incurred and the availability of other less dangerous options. Use-of-force operations can be deadly, as we witnessed in the federal raid on the Branch Davidians outside Waco, Texas, in 1993. It is well understood in law enforcement training and protocols that the use of force is a means of last resort, not the first option. But that appears not to be the case in many of the raids we have studied. We find that raid tactics have been used routinely against NRMs, at least since the late 1980s or early 1990s, even when other options were available. In many cases, investigations preceding the raids were poorly conducted and less violent means of enforcement were eschewed in favor of "dynamic entries" or predawn surprise attacks. Use-of-force operations were deployed even though the religious communities in the vast majority of cases had no history of violence or criminality. Despite the lack of physical threat to police, agents stormed residences with automatic weapons, outfitted in full military gear or black uniforms, complete with flak jackets, combat boots, Kevlar helmets, and stun grenades. Sometimes they were accompanied by helicopters, combat engineering vehicles (CEVs), and snipers. In many cases, the residences housed young children and infants. How is this aggressive overreach by the state explained?

Historically, police officers are sworn to "protect and serve" and expected to uphold the rights of the accused. There are constitutional protections, legislative guarantees, and traditions enjoyed by citizens in a democratic society that are designed to restrain police in the use of unnecessary or excessive force. All of the state raids in this study took place in Western democracies where these kinds of rights are constitutionally enshrined and protected.

Given the risks and legal issues associated with raids as a strategy in law enforcement and the targets for which they were designed, when is a raid on a religious community ever appropriate? What are the conditions to be met in order to qualify for the raid tactic? Is there a *threat assessment* made to determine the use of a raid? If so, how reliable is the threat assessment? Who makes the threat assessment, what sources are consulted, and what accountability measures are implemented to ensure responsible decisions? These are important questions that pertain to state raids targeting minority religious communities, and in many of the cases we have examined, the answers or explanations offered are often inadequate, at best.

We argue here that in overwhelming majority of cases the investigations into claims or charges made against the religious groups in question could have been conducted in less violent and dramatic fashion, through ordinary or routine investigative procedures. The bulk of the claims in cases against minority religions involve allegations such as child abuse, sexual abuse, polygamy, forced servitude, undue influence ("brainwashing"), and medical or financial fraud. The types of alleged violations listed here merit investigation when there is sufficient evidence, but they do not rise to the level of a high-risk response; they certainly do not require armies of police or SWAT teams in paramilitary gear descending on residences or communities as if they are terrorists. That this kind of government overreach appears to be common is deeply disturbing. While not all state raids on new or unconventional religions have been paramilitary raids, this extreme enforcement tactic has been used on NRMs frequently in recent years. This holds true despite the fact that there is often no evidence that the religious communities are armed, possess even the capability of resistance, or pose any imminent threat to the safety of its members or police investigators. Yet these new or minority religions are regularly treated like gangs, drug cartels, or narcoterrorists.

Features of State Raids on NRMs

When government raids are examined in the aggregate we make several important discoveries. First, there are far more government raids on NRMs than we imagined and that anything in the research literature has suggested heretofore. Our study has documented 116 state raids on NRMs over the last five to six decades in 17 different countries (see Table 1.1). There may be others we have not been able to locate as the list is continually updated.[4] Most scholars will likely be surprised at this number, even among those who are quite knowledgeable and well informed. There is a reason for this, we surmise. Most government raids have been carried out against relatively small and obscure religious groups without much media attention or fanfare. In most cases, the group is known only to local populations and does not rise to the level of a regional or national story. Highly publicized cases, such as the federal raids on the Waco Branch Davidians in 1993 or the FLDS in 2008 in the United States, or the Japanese raid on Aum Shinrikyo in 1995, are exceptions likely because they involve extraordinary circumstances such as extensive violence, injury, or death, or in the FLDS case, the historically unprecedented action taken by Texas officials to seize 439 sect children and place them into state protective custody. It is probably safe to assume that few people outside specialized academic circles or local populations where a raid occurs are aware of such state incursions involving other little-known groups like Church of the Firstborn, the Apostles of Infinite Love, Ogyen Kunzang Choling, the community of Horus (also known as the International Center of Parapsychology and Scientific Research of the New Age), or Damanhur. These circumstances likely explain why in the past the higher incidence rate of state raids has not been widely known.

The second discovery from our research concerns the sharp rise in the rate or number of government raids. Historically, the number of government raids remained low for decades until the 1990s and then rose sharply. For the four decades prior to the 1990s, there were on average 6.5 government raids on new or nontraditional religious movements per decade. But something happened in the late 1980s and early 1990s setting the stage for a dramatic shift.

Between 1990 and 1999, the number of government raids on NRMs jumped to 54, nearly a nine-fold increase. After 2000, the number of raids remained high ($N = 35$), though falling off somewhat from the previous decade. Figure 1 provides a line graph of the rate of state raids over time.

Table 1.1 List of State Raids on New or Nontraditional Religious
Communities

Group Targeted	Year(s)	No. of Raids
1. FLDS (United States)	1944, 1953, 2008	(3)
2. Doukhobors (Canada)	1953–1957	(3)
3. Pinnacle Rastafari (Jamaica)	1957	(1)
4. Scientology (United States, Canada, Australia, France, Belgium, Italy, Greece)	1963, 1965, 1971, 1977, 1983, 1990–1995, 1998–1999, 2000, 2002, 2009	(31)
5. Apostles of Infinite Love (Canada)	1966, 1967, 1978, 1999	(4)
6. Raelians (France)	1973, 1979, 1991, 2001	(4)
7. The Family (Argentina, France, Spain, Australia Mexico, Italy, United Kingdom)	1978, 1979, 1989–1993	(12)
8. Twelve Tribes (United States, Nova Scotia, France, Germany)	1984, 1987, 1994–1997, 2002, 2013	(8)
9. ISKCON (France, Belgium, Germany)	1974, 1987, 2005	(3)
10. Alamo Foundation (United States)	1988, 1991, 2008	(3)
11. Longo Mai (France)	1989	(1)
12. Nation of Yahweh (United States)	1990	(1)
13. Damanhur (Italy)	1991, 1992	(2)
14. Mandarom (France)	1994–1995, 2001	(4)
15. Branch Davidians (United States)	1993	(1)
16. Aum Shinrikyo (Japan)	1995	(1)
17. Church of Bible Understanding (United States)	1995	(1)
18. Ogyen Kunzang Choling (France, Belgium)	1997	(2)
19. Horus (France)	1991–1997	(6)
20. Rudolph Steiner/Waldorf Schools (France)	1999	(6)
21. Terranova (France)	2000	(1)
22. Le Patriarche/Dianova (France)	2001	(1)
23. Nuwaubians (United States)	2002	(1)
24. Order of St. Charbel (Australia)	2002	(1)
25. Aleph (Japan)	2006	(1)
26. Hikari no Wa (Japan)	2007	(1)
27. Kigenkai (Japan)	2007	(1)

(*continued*)

Table 1.1 (continued)

Group Targeted	Year(s)	No. of Raids
28. Les Gens de Bernard (France)	2007	(1)
29. Communaute des Beatitudes (France)	2008	(1)
30. Sikhs (Belgium)	2009	(1)
31. Church of the Firstborn (United States)	2009	(1)
32. Domaine de Chardenoux/Terre du Ciel (France)	2010	(1)
33. Goel Ratzon (Israel)	2010	(1)
34. Agape Ministries (Australia)	2010–2011	(2)
35. Bratslav Sect (Israel)	2011	(1)
36. Centre de Biodynamisme (France)	2011	(1)
37. Academy for Future Health (Dominican Republic)	2012	(1)
38. Amour et Misericorde (France)	2012	(1)
		Total 116

The data reveal that 77 percent of government raids on NRMs have occurred since 1990. Or stated differently, only 23 percent of government raids over the last 60-plus years took place before 1990. How is this sharp increase in the rate of state raids explained?

An astute observer might point out that the decade prior to the new millennium generated a wave of apocalyptic fervor among religious movements and sects that posed a unique problem for law enforcement, which, in turn, produced more scrutiny by authorities and hence the increase in government raids. In the 1990s, there was substantial public attention focused on Y2K and related issues of millennial concern among Christian evangelical and fundamentalist sects (Cowan, 2003), as well as trumpeted fears of "doomsday cults."[5] In October 1999, for example, the FBI issued warnings to law enforcement agencies and disseminated a report called *Project Megiddo*, advising of possible violence on the eve of the millennium by "apocalyptic cults" and other extremist groups.[6] The FBI also worked with its Israeli counterparts in formulating a threat assessment of millennial religious groups. Israeli authorities expelled members of two

Christian millennial groups, House of Prayer and Solomon's Temple, and denied entry to a third group, the Denver-based Concerned Christians, citing suspicions of violence or possible mass suicide. Monte Kim Miller, the leader of Concerned Christians, apparently claimed to be one of the "witnesses" described in the Book of Revelation who would die on the streets of Jerusalem prior to the Second Coming of Christ. Authorities were afraid Miller might create a violent confrontation with police in order to trigger an apocalyptic end to the millennium. For all the apprehensions and fears, however, Armageddon did not materialize and the millennium passed without incident.

Heightened apocalyptic fervor during the decade of the nineties may have contributed in part to the sharp rise in government raids. But this argument is less than persuasive with respect to the data for several reasons. First, increased pre-millennial apocalyptic fervor fails to explain why the rate of government raids remained relatively high *after* the turn of the millennium. Government raids since 2000 have continued at a much higher rate than pre-1990 levels and do not appear to be returning to the previous baseline. With the passing of the millennial date and the accompanying scores of failed predictions of the Endtime, the eschatological urgency of the doomsday event dissipated (Cowan, 2003), essentially undermining the apocalyptic-fervor rationale for government raids. Second, increased pre-millennial apocalyptic fervor does not explain why nonapocalyptic NRMs were raided at a higher rate during the 1990s. Of the 54 raids conducted in the 1990s, only eight targeted apocalyptic groups.[7]

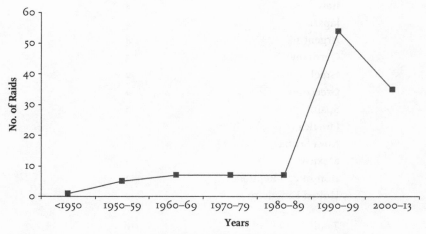

FIGURE 1.1 Government Raids on New or Nontraditional Religions

Roughly 85 percent of these raids were carried out against *non-apocalyptic* sects or NRMs. The same holds true of government raids after 2000. Of the 35 raids conducted after the turn of the millennium, only four (11 percent) were carried out against apocalyptic sects or movements.[8] Given these patterns, we conclude that there must be other forces driving the sudden rise and sustained higher rate of government raids on NRMs over the last few decades.

The third significant finding from our data on governments raids is the distribution, or rather, the uneven distribution of cases. While these raids spread across seventeen different countries, the largest concentration of raids has occurred in France. Nearly half of the 116 government raids on NRMs ($N = 57$) has taken place in France. Table 1.2 shows the distribution of government raids on NRMs by country. France has launched four times as many raids as the second country on the list, the United States, which has executed 14 raids. Australia is third on the list with nine government raids. France, the United States, Australia, and Canada

Table 1.2 State Raids on NRMs by Country

Country	No. of Raids
France	57
United States	14
Australia	9
Canada	8
Belgium	4
Italy	4
Japan	4
Argentina	4
Germany	3
Israel	2
Greece	1
Spain	1
Jamaica	1
Nova Scotia	1
Mexico	1
Dominican Republic	1
United Kingdom	1
Total	116

together account for 76 percent of all the state raids on NRMs. So clearly, the government raids are concentrated unevenly.

However, we contend that the distribution of raids has less to do with geography than with the development of what social movement theorists, particularly those applying the "contentious politics" analytical framework, understand as mechanisms of movement formation—strategic framing, attribution of opportunities or threats, and social appropriation of social sites or bases for mobilization (see McAdam, 1999; McAdam, Tarrow, and Tilly, 2001; Snow et al., 1986; Tarrow, 1994; Tilly, 1978). By "framing" we refer to the process by which movement organizations and actors actively engage in "meaning work" or "signification" in the struggle over the production and maintenance of ideas (Snow and Benford, 1992:136). By "attribution of opportunities or threats" we refer to the capacity of movement entrepreneurs to recognize and take advantage of political opportunities (openings in or increased access to political elites) or exploit perceived threats to a group's interest. Opportunity and threat are often inextricably tied together. For example, what scholars call the anticult movement (ACM) has been centered on the perceived and inflated threat of "cults" and the alleged harms they impose on their members (Bromley and Shupe, 1994; Shupe and Bromley, 1980; Shupe and Darnell, 2006). Yet the success of the ACM, as we shall see, has also been dependent on the ability of movement activists to gain access to government officials, to persuade them of their framing of the problem ("destructive cults," brainwashing, child abuse, etc.), and to effectively pressure authorities to take action. By "social appropriation" we refer to the ability of movement actors to mobilize preexisting organizations and associational networks, thereby building coalitions and forging alliances to leverage movement objectives (McAdam, Tarrow, and Tilly, 2001:47–48).

The origin of the transnational linkage described above begins in the United States with the formation and development of the American anticult movement. In order to understand the patterns of increased government raids, we must first understand the history and expansion of this critical countermovement. By applying a social movement/contentious politics framework to the analysis, we hope to show how new movement organizations and actors emerged though opposition and reaction, defined a perceived threat to the social order, formed coalitions with like-minded actors, and forged alliances with state agents and media to shape the trajectory of contention, culminating in government raids on disfavored and marginal religious communities.

History and Background of Anticult Movement

The American anticult movement first formed in the 1970s in response to
youth conversion to new religious movements. With the relative success of
NRMs in the late 1960s and 1970s, a distinct secular anticult movement
(ACM) arose as a counterpart to the Christian countercult movement
(CCM); it comprised family and relatives of converts allied with social
workers, psychologists, mental health specialists, and disgruntled or dis-
illusioned ex-members (Introvigne, 1995). Shupe and Darnell (2006) contend that several developments converged simultaneously to facilitate the
formation and growth of the ACM. As family-based groups began to form
in opposition to sons and daughters becoming involved in NRMs, social
and behavioral scientists (sympathetic and unsympathetic) begin paying
attention; post–Korean War research on POW indoctrination was resur-
rected (and misinterpreted) to explain conversion by a few select behavioral scientists; and Theodore "Ted" Patrick developed a method of forced
deconversion (deprogramming) which he offered to distraught families
of NRM converts (for a substantial fee), inspiring a "cottage industry
of self-proclaimed health experts who engaged in copy-cat vigilantism"
(Shupe and Darnell, 2006:28).

The cornerstone of ACM ideology was drawn from the post–Korean
War research on "brainwashing," or what investigators called "thought
reform" (re-education) or "coercive persuasion" (Lifton, 1961; Schein,
1961). These methods of indoctrination were used by the Chinese on
American POWs in an effort to force confessions of war crimes, compel
denunciations of the United States, and declare loyalty to Communism.
Of course, the model of "cult brainwashing," predicated on the alleged
success of indoctrination techniques employed during the Korean War,
was highly problematic from the outset. The journalist Edward Hunter,
who first popularized the term "brainwashing," was a CIA operative, and
his book, *Brainwashing in China*, was used as a propaganda tool at the
height of the Cold War (Bromley and Richardson, 1983). Concerned about
the disturbing claims of the Chinese to re-educate American POWs, the
U.S. government funded research by psychiatrists Lawrence Hinkle and
Harold Wolff in 1956 to study brainwashing. The researchers had full
access to the secret files of the CIA as well as some former Communist
interrogators and their prisoners. Their findings refute the effectiveness
of brainwashing claims. First, only 21 of 351 POWs subjected to thought
reform programs claimed conversion. Second, Hinkle and Wolff found

that in cases where indoctrination techniques appeared effective, observers were only witnessing behavioral compliance produced through threats, physical abuse, and torture (see Anthony and Robbins, 1994:460--461).

Nonetheless, ACM leaders believed they had uncovered the real reason American youth were inexplicably joining exotic and unconventional religious groups. It was believed that so-called cult leaders, particularly those from Asian countries (Sun Myung Moon, Swami Bhaktivedanti, Guru Maharaji, Parmahansa Yogananda, Bhagwan Shree Rajneesh), had learned to apply the techniques of thought reform in more subtle ways, *without* using torture or physical coercion. In effect, cult leaders had mastered a form of purely *psychological* brainwashing, using the commanding power of religion to lure youth into their domain and achieve control over converts. *Psychological* control allegedly was accomplished through "trance-induction techniques" such as chanting, meditation, prayer, and speaking in tongues (glossalalia). *Social* control was accomplished through heightened group pressure, mutual confession, "love-bombing," exhaustion/fatigue, deficient diet, information control, and social isolation (Hassan, 1988; Langone, 1993a; Ross and Langone, 1988; Singer, 1995; Tobias and Lalich, 1994). With the active promotion of the brainwashing model by some psychologists, counselors, and mental health specialists during the early stages of the movement, the anticult framing of the issue became widely disseminated and firmly entrenched in the popular press and in public opinion (Beckford, 1985; Bromley and Breschel, 1992; Robbins, 1988; Olsen, 2006).

The first ACM organization was founded in opposition to a NRM called the Children of God (COG). In 1972, concerned relatives of members in COG organized in San Diego to form Free the Children of God or FREECOG. The formation of FREECOG coincided with the emergent practice of deprogramming. In the beginning, deprogramming often involved the abduction and forced detention of NRM members in order to execute the involuntary deconversion program. The architect of this practice, Ted Patrick, encouraged distraught parents to form FREECOG (Shupe and Bromley, 1980:90; Shupe and Darnell, 2006:34), with whom he benefitted financially from referrals by the organization. Indeed, Mr. Patrick's first clients were parents of members of COG (Patrick and Dulack, 1977). The development of the anticult movement beginning with FREECOG has been chronicled elsewhere by scholars (Shupe and Bromley, 1980:88–119; Shupe and Darnell, 2006:34–37). FREECOG experienced numerous obstacles and setbacks in the early years. But as the organization learned from its mistakes and expanded its focus beyond just the Children of God to a broad range of NRMs, it began to find some success. In 1974, the director of FREECOG, William Rambur, organized a national meeting to recalibrate its methods and goals and announce its renaming as the Citizens Freedom Foundation (CFF), along with a new board of directors. Shupe and Bromley (1980:92) note that these actions were taken with "the intent to establish a nationwide countermovement."

Between 1974 and 1976, a number of ACM grassroots organizations were founded. These included the Citizens Organized for the Public Awareness of Cults, Return to Personal Choice, Love Our Children, Free Minds, and Citizens Engaged in Reuniting Families. Some of these organizations persisted for only a time before facing financial challenges; some dissolved and others merged to form larger coalitions. By 1976, ACM activists were moving to create a more cohesive, centralized countermovement model. That same year, George Slaughter, the head of Citizens Engaged in Freeing Minds (CEFM), an ACM organization in Dallas, engineered an effort to organize a national coalition of groups. Ultimately, the effort was unsuccessful as it faced problems of fundraising, a self-sustaining membership base, and staffing and also failed to obtain a tax-exempt status as an educational trust (Shupe and Darnell, 2006:35).

A second effort was coordinated by the International Foundation for Individual Freedom (IFIF) based in Ardmore, Pennsylvania, the following year. IFIF was the first ACM organization able to secure a 501(c)(3) designation as a tax-exempt educational trust. Leaders at a national conference that year announced that they had formed a new united front in the battle against cults. ACM activists were hopeful that the IFIF would be the national-level organization to carry the mission forward, but within a year "the IFIF collapsed amid bickering in the ranks of headstrong, independent leaders on how to merge, collect, and disburse funds" (Shupe and Darnell, 2006:36).

In 1978, the Citizens Freedom Foundation–Information Services (CFF-IS) was established as a public relations/education arm of CFF. It became one of the most important and effective ACM organizations in the field. The CFF-IS, which would later evolve into the Cult Awareness Network (CAN), obtained tax-exempt status as an educational trust and was located in Los Angeles. This new effort forged a breakthrough for the ACM; it became the ACM's first successful "national coordinating organization" (Bromley and Shupe, 1993:191). CFF-IS established a budget, elected a board of directors, appointed a national chairman, and gave a degree of stability to its operations in a manner that previous ACM groups had been unable to achieve. Shupe and Darnell (2006:37) observe that as "small local ACM groups dried up, largely because of public apathy, the CFF-IS became a more visible, centralized, conduit for donations."

CFF also generated another important ACM organization, the American Family Foundation (AFF). The AFF was originally a local CFF affiliate in Lexington, Massachusetts. It was founded by businessman K. H. Barney in 1979 and it also sought to avoid the financial problems of previous ACM groups. AFF operated largely as a think tank and clearinghouse for information. It has been referred to as the intellectual wing of the ACM because AFF leaders sought out professionals and academics to serve as advisors and consultants. AFF also took a different route than its predecessors by charging fees for their information service in order to keep the organization solvent. AFF created files on controversial religions, obtained copies of transcripts from legislative hearings around the country, collected reports by "experts," and maintained a mail-order bookstore. The foundation published a variety of periodicals and newsletters, including *The Cult Observer, Cultism and the Law* (targeting law enforcement), *Cults on Campus* (targeting high school and college administrators), and *Cult News Highlights* (targeting journalists). AFF eventually created its own journal, the *Cultic Studies Journal*, to promote the brainwashing model and give legitimacy to ACM theories.

AFF and CFF-IS helped to stabilize the anticult movement by providing it with two key movement organizations that could generate resources, produce documents to support claims, identify experts, and pressure government and elected officials for action. Moreover, AFF and CFF collaborated on projects, sought common targets, shared information, attended each other's conferences, and even had interlocking directorates (Shupe and Darnell, 2006:37–38, 111). This cross-fertilization of AFF and CFF-IS gave impetus to a surging national movement in the 1980s. Bromley and Shupe (1993:191) refer to this phase of the ACM as the "consolidation period." In 1986, CFF-IS changed its name officially to the Cult Awareness Network. Shortly afterward, the movement experienced the "white-hot phase" of mobilization (Lofland, 1979), a period from the late 1980s to the end of the millennium, as North American ACM leaders became emboldened by their success and sought to broaden their mission to Europe and beyond. In the late 1980s and throughout the next decade, North American ACM activists worked intensely with their counterparts abroad to export ideology and literature, hold workshops, serve as consultants,

identify strategies to create public awareness and support, develop contacts with media, and reach out to government officials. While many of
these groups were established independently in previous years, research
suggests that they were dependent on North American ACM resources to
survive and thrive, and in many cases, would probably not have come into
existence without the inspiration and materials from CAN and AFF (Introvigne, 1995:37; Shupe and Bromley, 1994; Shupe and Darnell, 2006:196).

Formation and Mobilization of a Transnational ACM

Scholars have tracked the North American ACM missionizing efforts in
order to craft a transnational movement. These efforts accelerated in the
late 1980s during the "white-hot phase" of mobilization as ACM activists engaged in the "European campaign" (Shupe and Darnell, 2006:197),
extending to countries such as Denmark, The Netherlands, France, Belgium, Germany, England, Austria, Spain, Greece, Scotland, Switzerland,
and Italy, as well as to some Eastern European countries and to South
America (Brazil, Argentina), South Africa, Israel, and Australia. According to Shupe and Darnel:

> By the late 1980s to early 1990s the popular identity of the CAN
> (and to a similar extent the AFF) as worldwide clearinghouses for
> NRM advice and information was established. Activists worldwide
> were in more than occasional communication. A network was in
> place. (2006:211)

Early North American involvement in international ACM efforts primarily consisted of coalition-building. ACM activists in the United States
traveled to Europe to meet with ACM leaders and attend conferences.
European ACM activists reciprocated. As early as 1978, North American
advocates of the brainwashing/mind control model, Dr. John Clark and
Dr. Robert Lifton, were invited speakers at a conference on NRMs hosted
by the German Union for Child Psychiatry in Hannover. In December
1980, the Association for the Defense of the Family and the Individual
(ADFI) held a conference in Paris on "Extremist Cults" that was attended
by American ACM leaders and approximately 60 persons from 14 different countries (Shupe and Darnell, 2006:210). AFF formed several
international committees to facilitate coalition-building, networking,
and strategic framing among a field of ACM organizations and actors.

The AFF Public Policy-International Committee spearheaded efforts at cross-fertilization reaching out to leaders in various international organizations in England (FAIR or Family Action Information Resource), France (ADFI or Association for the Defense of the Family and the Individual), Germany (Commission of Apologetics, Lutheran Church), and Spain (Pro-Juventad [Pro-Youth] and CROAS).

In 1987, the "First International Congress on Cults and Society" was hosted by Pro-Juventad in Barcelona, featuring prominent American ACM leaders such as Louis Jolly West, Margaret Singer, Michael Langone, Richard Ofshe, and Shirley Landa. In 1988, AFF Director of Research and Education Michael Langone wrote to a member of the AFF's International Subcommittee of the Education Committee, Rev. Freidrich Haack of West Germany, recommending the formation of an "International Family Foundation which could serve as a federation of sorts for the various cult education organizations around the world" (cited in Shupe and Darnell, 2006:211).

The second International Congress on Cults and Society was held in Munich in 1989 and a third in Paris in 1990, the latter hosted jointly by ADFI and AFF. At the 1990 Congress in Paris, the new President of AFF, Herbert Rosedale, called for each attending representative of an ACM organization to provide information about their respective group, saying that the purpose of the meeting was "to initiate a process of cooperative planning" among "cult education" organizations to explore collaboration and pursuit of mutual goals (Shupe and Darnell, 2006:219). Indeed, at the 1990 meeting, North American ACM leaders were a dominating force. Rosedale served as chair of the meeting and also as chair of a "consortium of groups and professions" in which AFF and CAN were offered "as models of how European ACM groups could target professionals for proselytization" (Shupe and Darnell, 2006:220).

The internationally expanded version of AFF would later be renamed the International Cultic Studies Association (ICSA) in 2004, but in the interim it was clear that a formidable transnational ACM was already mobilizing. AFF and CAN increasingly served as a catalyst in promoting an international response to NRMs by grassroots organizations. The international efforts at framing, threat attribution, and "brokerage"[9] by American ACM activists contributed significantly to the growth of new anticult organizations in Europe that emerged during the white-hot mobilization phase: Sweden's FRI (Association to Rescue the Individual), Finland's FINYAR (Association for Research and Information of New Religious Movements),

Hungary's VIK (Information Center on Religion), Italy's ARIS (Association for Research and Information on Cults), Belgium's CIAOSN (Information and Advice Center Concerning Harmful Sectarian Organizations), Germany's REMID (Religious Studies and Media Information Service), Luxembourg's CDIF (Circle of Defense of the Individual and the Family), Austria's GGS (Society Against Sects), France's CCMM (*Le Centre Contre la Manipulation Mentale* or Center Against Mental Manipulation) and ADFI, Lithuania's NRTIC (New Religious Research and Information Center), and the Roman Catholic Church's GRIS (Group of Research and Information on Sects), among others (Shupe and Darnell, 2006:216–217).

At the 1993 International Congress on Cults and Society, convened again in Barcelona, a new International Confederation was formed consisting of over 20 North American and European ACM organizations. Jacques Richard of ADFI was appointed provisional secretary and immediately set about applying to various national authorities and private foundations for subsidies.

French Anticultism and the State

In the following year, 1994, the Confederation was officially named the European Federation of Centers for Research and Information on Sectarianism (FECRIS), based in Marseilles. Through FECRIS, ADFI, and UNADFI (*Union nationale des associations de défense des Familles et de l'Individu*), ACM activists in France began to make significant inroads into the national government. FECRIS would eventually become the largest of the European ACM organizations, composed of around 50 anticult groups. By 2009 it had gained consultative status at the United Nations as a nongovernmental organization (NGO) (Palmer, 2011b:12). The French case poses a unique situation which we will visit only briefly here since we discuss France in depth later in the book. The epicenter of government raids on NRMs is France and the explanation for this can be found in the relationship between French ACM organizations and the state.

The tradition of church-state separation in the United States has proven to be a strong impediment to government intrusions into religious liberty. As such, American ACM organizations have had little success moving legislation to restrict the liberties of minority faiths. But in France, while it has a constitutional separation of church and state, there is no "wall of separation" as in the United States, and both the residual influence of the

Catholic Church and the entrenched tradition of *laïcité* (secularism) tied to French nationalism (*la Republique*) have worked hand-in-hand to cast *les sectes*[10] as a genuine threat to society. French ACM organizations have drawn into their ranks devout Catholics and especially Catholic priests. ADFI, for example, which consists of local chapters across France, has historically "networked with local parish priests combating heresy" (Palmer, 2011b:13). From the early days of ADFI, a Catholic priest, Pere Pierre Le Cabellec from Brittany, joined the founders Claire and Guy Champollion and "launched a crusade in Ouest-France against the heresies of 'l'Empire Moon'" (Palmer, 2011b:12). With regard to the Catholic influence in UNADFI, Palmer states:

> The Catholic influences in UNADFI are emphasized by Alain Garay, who cites a Vatican document from May 1986 instructing French Bishops to regard new religions as "challenge to stimulate our own pastoral effectiveness." Two outstanding Catholic clerics have worked closely with UNADFI: Jean Vernette and Jacques Trouslard. The late Monsignor Jean Vernette (1929–2002) was the leading expert on *sectes* for the French National Conference of Catholic Bishops and was the acting chair on their committee on sects and new religious consciousness. . . . Pere Trouslard (b. 1924) has been described in the media as a "one-man crusade" and a "Saint George armed with a telephone in an office the size of a chambermaid's." Since 1982, when he first became aware of a heretical group in his parish in Lyon, he has been an intrepid *secte* hound. . . . (p.14)

The close relationship between private ACM organizations and the French government coalesced following the tragic mass suicides-murders by The Order of the Solar Temple (OTS) in France, Switzerland, and Quebec in three separate episodes between 1994 and 1997 (Lewis, 2006; Mayer, 1996). The OTS was founded by Luc Jouret in 1984 as a blend of Christianity, Freemasonry, and New Age beliefs. In October 1994, 48 people died as part of a ritual in which bodies were found in two villages, Chiery and Granges-sur-Galvan, in western Switzerland. In Cheiry, the bodies were discovered in a secret underground chapel dressed in robes, lying in a circle, feet together and most with plastic bags over their heads. Altogether, 15 members committed suicide by ingesting poison, 30 members were either smothered to death or shot, and eight other members

were killed by other causes. The chalets were set on fire and the discovery
of the bodies was made by firefighters and police on the scene. On the
same day, five members of the OTS died in Morin Heights, Quebec, in
a coordinated suicide/murder and fire. Three of the victims were murdered, including a three-month-old baby who was stabbed to death with
a wooden stake. Evidently, one of the OTS leaders, Joseph Di Mambro,
ordered the murder because he believed the child was the Antichrist. The
child's parents were also murdered. On December 23, 1995, 16 bodies of
OTS members were discovered in another ritual suicide/murder and fire
in the Vercors region of France. And in March 1997, five more OTS members committed suicide accompanied by a fire in Saint-Casmir, Quebec.
The total number of deaths attributed to the OTS was 74.

The OTS murder-suicides horrified government officials, religious
leaders, and the public and set into motion a series of draconian reactions.
After the initial OTS deaths, the French National Assembly voted to establish a commission to investigate the sect phenomenon. Deputy Jacques
Guyard was president of the parliamentary commission and Alain Gest
was appointed chair. In December 1995, the commission released the
Guyard list of 173 sects (cults) and then issued the final Guyard report
on sects in France in 1996. A similar parliamentary commission was established in Belgium, resulting in a report placing 189 sects on a list.
The Guyard report in France recommended the creation of a government
monitoring agency to study the problem and warn the public of potential
dangers. According to Palmer, the Guyard report

> also advocated setting up structures for the governmental admin-
> istrative repression of *sectes*. Before 1995, the cultural opposition
> to *sectes* had been confined (largely) to private, grassroots parents'
> associations and the counter cult activities of Catholic priests, but
> the Guyard report stimulated a growth spurt in France's *antisecte*
> movement. Soon the cause was taken up by politicians, and the
> imperative to "fight *sectes*" moved up into the highest circles of the
> *pouvoirs publiques* until the "*secte* problem" became an urgent item
> on the government's agenda. (2011b:10)

The Guyard list was widely circulated by electronic and print media
and promoted by government officials. Any NRMs appearing on the list
were labeled "subversive" or "dangerous." NRMs were targeted by police
who searched their offices, seized computers and files, interrogated

religious staff, and arrested leaders. Many NRMs received new tax bills, were audited by government accountants, and were put on notice by landlords. Groups that previously had congenial relations with their neighbors and communities found themselves disenfranchised and barred from participation in customary public activities. Rental contracts with hotels for conferences were cancelled, NRM-owned businesses were boycotted, service contracts were dropped. Professionals and laborers alike lost their jobs or were denied promotions. Local chapters of ADFI sought to expose "cult leaders" as depraved and diabolical. Many religious groups protested that they were on the *"liste noir"* and rejected the labeling efforts by government and ACM organizations. But all attempts to obtain evidence or even determine a precise definition of *secte* were futile since neither existed. NRMs were not allowed to see the evidence on which the Guyard list was created because the police (*Renseignements Generaux*) files were secret (Palmer, 2011b:10–11).

Most importantly, for our purposes, private ACM organizations were strategically incorporated into the structure of government. UNADFI was recognized as a "public service" organization by the national government and became eligible for public funding and support. UNADFI leaders "began to work closely with the deputies from the National Assembly who were lobbying for more social control over *les sectes*" (Palmer, 2011b:12). FECRIS was also recognized by the French government and gained advisory status. In 1996, the prime minister of France, Alain Juppe, created the Interministerial Observatory on Sects to begin state monitoring of suspect religious groups. The Observatory was given the mandate to find more effective tools to "combat" dangerous sects. Training and awareness programs were established for police, prosecutors, judges, and teachers in a collaborative effort to crack down on such groups.

A key appointment to the new Observatory was psychiatrist Jean-Marie Abgrall. Abgrall was active in testifying before commissions and preparing official reports in both France and Belgium (Anthony, 1999). Shupe and Darnell (2006:225) note that Abgrall was a "key actor in French official investigations and an illustration of North American-European ACM intellectual cross-fertilization." They go on to state that "Abgrall appropriated wholesale the North American ACM's 'mind control' paradigm in such books as *La Mecanique des Sectes*" (see also Anthony and Robbins, 2004). In this book, Abgrall quoted liberally from American advocates of the brainwashing/mind control model such as Michael Langone and psychiatrist John Clark. Abgrall also was involved in the Belgian commission report that culminated in the blacklisting of 189 groups.

In 1997, the French Minister of Interior appealed to UNADFI and CCMM (Center Against Mental Manipulation) to assist him in raising public awareness of harmful sects. In 1998, the Observatory was replaced by the Interministerial Mission in the Fight against Cults (MILS). Alain Vivien, who was previously the president of CCMM, was appointed the new director of MILS and housed in the prime minister's office (Palmer, 2011b:17). In December 1998, the Ministry of Justice distributed a memorandum to the prosecutor's office calling on prosecutors and judges to support ACM organizations such as UNADFI and CCMM in the state's effort to protect persons and private property from sects.

In the face of international criticism from the United Nations, the U.S. State Department, and various human rights and religious liberties organizations, the French government in 2002 disbanded MILS and created a new organization, *La Mission Interministerielle de vigilance de lute contre les derives sectaires* (MIVILUDES, or the Interministerial Monitoring Mission to Fight against Sectarian Drift/Deviancy). Under the new administration, the focus allegedly shifted from sects to *sect-derived* crimes and not the persecution of religious minorities. But this shift was made meaningless by the passage of the About-Picard Law in May 2001. The law created a new criminal category, "abuse of weakness" (*abus de faiblesse*), which was used to penalize practices or actions by charismatic leaders toward vulnerable followers. It also introduced into French law the concept of brainwashing.

> Built into the new law was the assumption that ... myriad forms of social deviance derived from the ineluctable force of a charismatic cult leader's *manipulation mentale* (mind control) that emanated from the id. Under this new law, any *secte* leaders found guilty of *l'abus frauduleux de l'etat d'ignorance ou de faiblesse* would be liable to five years in prison and a fine of up to 750,000 euros in damages. In this way, the concept of brainwashing was first introduced into French national law. (Palmer, 2011b:22)

Under the French penal code, the state created a concept (mental manipulation) with no objective criteria by which to define it and so vaguely crafted that the law could be used by prosecutors to harass or target any religion classified as a sect (Duvert, 2004). As Shupe and Darnell have observed, it was American ACM organizations CAN and AFF that "literally exported this fundamental premise of anticultism (brainwashing/mind control) to Europe" (2006:195). Specifically, "visits to European anticultists by North American ACM representatives . . . provided opportunities for the latter to expose the former to the panoply of terms and concepts for NRM involvement, such as 'brainwashing,' 'mental servitude,' 'mentacide,' 'thought reform,' and 'psychological incapacitation.'. . . (T)here were a number of key individual visits, or literal tours," they state, ". . . which were intended in part to spread the 'mind control' ideology" (Shupe and Darnell, 2006:212).

It is in this cultural and political context that we locate the largest concentration of government raids on NRMs. The disproportionate number of government raids in France can be explained by a convergence of factors: 1) the exportation of North American ACM ideology to Europe and especially France, 2) the white-hot mobilization of a transnational anticult movement corresponding the OTS murder-suicides (and other violent NRM episodes in the 1990s—the 1993 Branch Davidian siege and fire, the 1995 sarin gas attack by Aum Shinrikyo in Tokyo, the 1997 Heaven's Gate mass suicides in California),[11] 3) the absence of a church-state "wall of separation" in France such as is found in the United States, and 4) the entrenched tradition of laïcité (radical secularism) tied to French nationalism (la Republique).

Summary

In summarizing our thesis for the book, we argue that "missionizing" efforts by North American ACM organizations and actors to frame conflicts surrounding NRMs in Europe and elsewhere as "brainwashing/mind control," to construct and inflate threat attributions fueling public fears about "cults," and to build international coalitions of ACM activist networks paid dividends in the late 1980s and early 1990s, leading to a "white-hot" phase of mobilization. This molten phase of transnational mobilization among ACM organizations took hold particularly in France, for reasons already discussed, but widened to other Western countries as movement ideology, collective action frames, and organizational strategies congealed. ACM networks facilitated diffusion across existing lines of communication and activists brokered new organizational ties. National organizations spawned local chapters and spread across different sectors (governmental, clerical) or ideological divides (liberal, conservative),[12] enlisting allies and sympathizers in a coordinated campaign against allegedly harmful sects and cults. The white-hot mobilization phase of the ACM coincides with the upward trajectory of NRM-state conflict and helps to explain the dramatic rise in government raids on these religious communities in the course of this social movement cycle.

2

Countermovement Mobilization and Government Raids

THE PATTERN OF state mobilization against NRMs in the form of raids can best be understood by employing a social movement analysis. Drawing on the evolving analytical framework of "contentious politics" in social movements (McAdam, Tarrow, and Tilly, 2001), we can identify the social processes and mechanisms by which disputes, conflict, or contention between groups becomes broadened, issues are strategically framed, perceived threats are attributed, and political opportunities are seized by challengers, opponents, state actors, and third parties.

In addition to this analytical framework, we make an effort to incorporate intermediate or "meso-level" dynamics (McAdam, 2003:284) into the analysis, the most significant of which concerns "trajectories of contention" (McAdam, Tarrow, and Tilly, 2001:34). Trajectories of contention between or among groups may take many paths. They are difficult to predict because the driving force in their progression involves the *interaction* of the parties in contention. One must take into account patterns of moves and countermoves among groups over contested terrain. In order to explain the trajectory of contention leading to increased government raids on NRMs we offer a model that focuses on countermovement organization and mobilization. We examine the formation of oppositional networks, the coalition-building efforts of organized opponents with state agents and media, and the framing or branding of targeted religious groups as "cults," affecting public opinion.

Social movements also benefit from favorable social and cultural factors or conditions. We intend to show that as ACM efforts to spread fears about "cults" converged with broader social issues of concern involving child abuse; the strategic linking of a putative cult threat to child victimization created a perfect storm of reactionary forces. The heightened level of public alarm was seized upon by organized opponents leading to broad-based moral campaigns and a sharp rise in government raids on NRMs.

In the first chapter we described the early formation of the American ACM and its development into a transnational movement through missionizing efforts and cultivation of critical networks in Western Europe and elsewhere. The initial thrust of this movement relied heavily on the strategic framing of NRM conversion and commitment as "brainwashing." The ACM remedy for so-called cult brainwashing involved a controversial method of forcible extraction and systematic, coercive deconversion called "deprogramming." However, in the United States deprogramming began to face legal challenges by the 1980s and proved to be problematic for opponents.

Our research shows that key ACM leaders realized this problem and set about to identify a new line of attack on NRMs. The development of the new strategy originated in 1983 by deprogrammer Galen Kelly who was commissioned by Priscilla Coates, Executive Director of the Citizens Freedom Foundation (CFF), to formulate a plan to assail the Northeast Kingdom Community Church in Island Pond, Vermont (also known as the Twelve Tribes). Kelly devised a written plan that relied primarily on child abuse claims. He also outlined a strategy to recruit disgruntled ex-members and local officials while generating unfounded and exaggerated claims about child abuse and neglect. The implementation of the Kelly Plan will be taken up in our case study on the Northeast Kingdom Community Church/Twelve Tribes in chapter 3. But first we want to outline the major features of the Kelly Plan to establish it as a key turning point for opponents in the development of a new and more effective social control paradigm.

The Kelly Plan: A Pivotal Experiment in Social Control of NRMs

As Swantko (2004, 2009) has shown, in the months leading up to the 1984 state raid on the Northeast Kingdom Community Church/Twelve Tribes, the Vermont attorney general's staff and state child protection workers collaborated with anticult leaders in carrying out a written plan conceived by deprogrammer and ACM activist Galen Kelly. Kelly's strategic plan, innocuously titled *Investigative Proposal Regarding Island Pond*, was developed for Priscilla Coates, director of the ACM organization

Citizens Freedom Foundation (which later became the Cult Awareness Network) in 1983, a year before the raid. The plan was designed to discredit the religious group they disparaged as a "cult." The Vermont social services commissioner acknowledged that at "strategy meetings" in the fall before the Island Pond raid that he and other government officials discussed options, including the state action to raid the Church and seize the sect's children. Coates and Kelly met with the attorney general's staff in August 1983. Shortly afterward, state investigators were sent around the country to track down ex-members in order to collect stories of abuse.

The Vermont state raid on the Northeast Kingdom Community Church (NKCC) was significant because it was the result of an ACM "experiment," according to Galen Kelly, not simply to prevent the growth of the NKCC, but "to assist in the dissolution of it" (*Investigative Proposal*, n.d., p.1). The experiment was distinct in that it employed innovative methods of organizing and mobilizing opposition. Kelly states that the plan was "designed not only to develop and document facts about the activities of the group, but *to be used as a vehicle to coordinate law enforcement, media, and grassroots opposition to the organization*" (*Investigative Proposal*, n.d., p.1, emphasis ours).

Kelly goes on to suggest ways in which this may be accomplished, including developing and documenting allegations of child abuse, child neglect, and other legal violations (e.g., failure to report births and deaths, failure to enroll children in school because they practiced homeschooling, violations of zoning and housing regulations, etc.).

In the plan, Kelly formulates a strategy to build a broad-based coalition of opponents to more effectively attack the group. This strategy explicitly involves collaboration with other ACM actors to identify allies within key government agencies (local law enforcement, family and child protection services, state's attorney general staff), persuading them to investigate the accused group; locating, recruiting, and interviewing disgruntled ex-members in order to gather damaging information; and fomenting exaggerated media accounts, inflaming fears of local residents, and essentially creating sufficient public pressure to impel authorities to act.

Kelly's motive for cultivating relationships with law enforcement and family services agencies was to pressure them to adopt the opponents' partisan agenda, as is made clear in his document. He urged opponents to "work closely" with state officials to gain access to detrimental insider information and to build credibility in order to *force* reticent state agencies to take action against the group (*Investigative Proposal*, n.d., p.5).

With regard to influencing news media he recommended using the NKCC case as a platform to expand on the larger "cult issue" by linking it to broader problems of child abuse, while steering clear of "the more clouded issues" of mind control and deprogramming. He also suggests not allowing reporters to frame the dispute as a legitimate religious controversy. Kelly states:

Coordination with appropriate and legitimate news media will allow not only scrutiny to be brought to bear on the Island Pond situation [sic], but to use the Island Pond situation to focus attention on the cult issue—on such clear issues as child abuse and anti-social behavior rather than on the more clouded and controversial issues of mind control, deprogramming and religious controversies. (*Investigative Proposal*, n.d., p.6)

Even as he acknowledged the increasingly problematic tactic of deprogramming, Kelly marked a path forward for ACM activists. Kelly offered three rationales for the NKCC project and explained why it would be important in the future. First, the Island Pond community was "small enough and localized enough to be studied, investigated, and researched as a microcosm," offering lessons *"applicable to other similar groups, presently and in the future"*; second, it would find utility as a "research project to experiment in developing ways to teach communities how to cope with the incursion of a cult"; and third, having the participation of CFF [Citizens Freedom Foundation] "will be a great step forward in taking aggressive action, since the only aggressive anti-cult action has been deprogramming, which of course, entails various controversial problems" (*Investigative Proposal*, n.d., p.2, emphasis ours).

Kelly articulated the lineaments of a plan that the ACM would adopt in future campaigns against new or minority religions. It was not simply developed to attack this one community in a single application, but rather as a kind of crude prototype for countermovement actions against other groups. While the Island Pond experiment was not altogether successful in that the judge in this case ruled the state's action illegal and ordered the children returned to their parents (Swantko, 2004), it was clearly successful in other ways. The experiment was productive in recruiting ex-members and local community leaders, mobilizing a coalition of opponents, inciting public opinion against the group, and effectively compelling state action. Coates, Kelly, and other ACM activists immediately recognized the potential of the Kelly Plan for future use. As Wiseman (2011:206) observes in her comparative analysis of raided NRMs, the "recurring pattern of attacking new or nontraditional religions strategically outlined in the Kelly Plan appears to have become institutionalized and embedded in the ACM organizational culture" (see also Bromley, 1998a, 1998b, 1998c; Hall, 1995; Hall and Schuyler, 1998; Richardson, 1999, 2004b; Wright, 1995b, 1998, 2011; Wright and Richardson, 2011a).

The Kelly experiment leading to the Vermont state raid on the Northeast Kingdom Community Church was particularly significant to ACM countermobilization for two reasons. First, the NKCC raid signaled the beginning of a new strategy that, in a few years, would help produce a surge of coordinated government raids on NRMs. As we shall see, in these raids state agents regularly took action in response to claims by organized opponents and/or became part of an organized coalition, targeting a religious community *collectively* rather than focusing on individual members who were the specific subjects of allegations, as the law requires (see Richardson, 1999, 2004b; Schreinert and Richardson, 2011; Wiseman, 2011). Using overly broad claims, conveniently supplied by ACM activists, state officials extrapolated risks to an entire community as justification for these raids. This is the pattern we have seen repeatedly in government raids in the years following the Island Pond case. It comports with the dynamic of contention aptly described by Bromley (1998c:24) as a "dispute broadening process," where even a single ex-member's claim, amplified by ACM actors and allied opponents, is sufficient to unleash the state's considerable resources against a "cult." In the wake of the NKCC project, ACM leaders realized that the Kelly Plan could be an effective weapon in mobilizing state action against disfavored religions in other settings and places.

The second reason the Vermont raid was significant is that it marked a shift in the ACM social control enterprise based primarily on *child abuse* accusations. The NKCC venture signaled the start of a move away from the failed efforts of deprogramming based on "brainwashing" allegations to the more opportunistic and culturally resonant claims of child abuse. To be sure, this shift was not immediate. Brainwashing and mind control allegations continued to be made against NRMs and deprogrammers continued to practice their craft. But in the late 1980s and early 1990s, courts were beginning to reject legal pleas by families and friends to detain and deprogram NRM members (Anthony, 1990; Anthony and Robbins, 1992; Richardson, 1999, 2004b; Swantko, 2004; Wiseman, 2011). Kidnapping members to coerce disaffiliation using methods akin to brainwashing did not withstand legal scrutiny. It would be only a matter of time before U.S. courts disallowed "brainwashing" or "mind control" theories to be introduced as evidence or in expert testimony (Anthony, 1990; Anthony and Robbins, 1992). Consequently, ACM leaders began to revise and reformulate their methods regarding strategic challenges to NRMs.

ACM leaders recognized and took advantage of critical changes in social and cultural understandings of child protection that peaked in the 1980s. The emergence of a growing concern and rhetoric about child victims or "threatened children" (Best, 1990) provided new and significant opportunities for opponents. In the next section we explain how ACM organizations and actors seized political opportunities and exploited perceived threats arising from what Philip Jenkins (1998) called the "Child Abuse Revolution." The revolutionary change in the social construction of child victimization produced a dramatic transformation in public attitudes, child protection and reporting laws, and media attention, first in the United States, and then in Western Europe.

Political Opportunities, Perceived Threats, and the Child Abuse Revolution

With the increasing challenges and obstacles facing ACM organizations regarding the use of deprogramming as a remedy to NRM expansion in the 1980s, the strategic focus turned to allegations of child abuse. Schreinert and Richardson (2011:245) make this point succinctly: "A major shift in the social control paradigm occurred as the 'brainwashing/mind control' narrative diminished in importance and the 'child abuse' motif emerged as the principal rhetorical weapon to combat 'cults.'"

Child abuse allegations or claims proved to be effective because of heightened political pressure from child advocacy organizations and key changes in child abuse reporting, aggressive new legislation, media attention, and public opinion. By the 1980s, core members of many NRMs were marrying and having children. The movements were expanding largely through the emergence of a second generation (Chancellor, 2000; Palmer and Hardman, 1999a; van Eck Duymaer van Twist, 2015). Some movements experienced high birth rates because they refused to practice birth control, promoted plural marriage, and/or permitted nonmarital relationships that produced children. Not surprisingly, researchers found that in some groups "the children even outnumbered their parents" (Palmer and Hardman, 1999b:1). Thus generational changes and high birth rates in NRMs occurred alongside emerging changes in culture with regard to child victimization.

A brief look at these broader changes reveals the extent of their significance to ACM countermobilization and success. Jenkins (1998) refers to a period between 1976 and 1986 as the "Child Abuse Revolution" in which the intense efforts among child protection advocates, including feminist groups and conservative Christian evangelical organizations, produced a "moral panic." Jenkins carefully documents the explosion of new child abuse laws, a wave of new reports and publications within the therapeutic profession, heightened media interest, the institutionalization of specialized clinics dealing with child abuse, and the creation of numerous local, state, and national organizations combating the perceived threats against children, backed by generous new federal funding.

Jenkins contends that the claims-making and lobbying efforts by special interest groups exaggerated threats of child abuse in society. The new ideas, or "new sensibility" with respect to child abuse, followed the activism of a coalition of disparate pressure groups, not any real rise in child maltreatment. He states:

> Child protection became a national social orthodoxy, a package of basic beliefs and assumptions that weighted discourse on a variety of seemingly unrelated issues.
>
> Shifting attitudes toward child abuse constituted a revolutionary and perhaps irrevocable change in American culture. . . . But these claims were embellished by statistics suggesting an incredible frequency not just of molestation but of the most extreme forms of rape and incest, a process of inflation accomplished by the familiar midcentury device of expansive definition and of assimilating all minor forms of deviancy with the most threatening acts of sexual predation. (Jenkins, 1998:119)

In fact, some of the emerging statistics on child sexual abuse cited by studies, and heralded by child advocates, were shocking. Between 1976 and 1986, annual reports of child abuse and neglect in the United States increased from 669,000 to more than 2 million; and by 1993 they had increased further to almost 3 million. Reports of sexual abuse of children rose 18-fold between 1976 and 1985. The Child Welfare League declared the problem an "epidemic," claiming that child sexual abuse rose 277 percent between 1981 and 1990 (Jenkins, 1998:129).

Jenkins offered several reasons why the "new sensibility" regarding rampant child abuse occurred at this time. First, he points to the definition, or redefinition, that greatly expanded behavior that was included in the classification of child abuse. The new approach made abuse a matter of subjective definition and eroded distinctions between violent or incestuous assaults and interpreted acts. For example, in the best-selling book *Courage to Heal* (Bass and Davis, 1988), forms of sexual abuse included not only rape and forced oral sex but also being "forced to listen to sexual talk," being "fondled, kissed or held in a way that made you uncomfortable," and being "bathed in a way that felt intrusive." If these acts took place within families, they were defined as "incest" (Jenkins, 1998:130). Readers of *Vogue* magazine were told by one expert that "violation is determined by your experience as a child—your body, your feelings, your spirit; some abuse is not even physical" (Tavris, 1986:186).

Second, the official figures likely ignored the vast number of unrecorded cases of abuse from previous years (see also Best, 1990). The increase in statistics was most likely a product of better or more intensive recordkeeping. New federal legislation created state and local agencies solely devoted to investigating child maltreatment. Thus new laws imposed *mandatory reporting* which swelled abuse statistics while the practice of conducting investigations based on confidential and anonymous reports opened the door to a much higher rate of groundless or malicious charges (Jenkins, 1998:120). False child abuse charges skyrocketed, as did the new phenomenon of "false memories" or "recovered memories" of child abuse in suspect therapies using hypnosis (Coleman, 1989; Coleman and Clancy, 1990; Jenkins, 1992; Richardson, Best, and Bromley, 1991; Wright, 2005).

Third, for some interest groups, the child protection issue offered a politically popular and opportunistic rationale for mobilizing against vice. Claims-makers and moral entrepreneurs tied child sexual abuse to pornography, drugs, prostitution, the decline of traditional morality, secularization, the removal of prayer from schools, liberalism, cults, and Satanism, among other things (Best, 1990; Jenkins, 1992; Richardson, Best, and Bromley, 1991). Not surprisingly, the moral panic involving "ritual child abuse" allegedly occurring in daycare centers and carried out by underground Satanic cults arose during this same period (Jenkins,

1992; Nathan and Snedeker, 1995; Richardson, Bromley, and Best, 1991). The McMartin case stands out as the best-known and most tragic example (Nathan and Snedeker, 1995), but dozens of innocent daycare workers and staff were charged and convicted on hysterical allegations with no supporting medical evidence, only the coached testimonies of children.

One of the most disturbing aspects of the child abuse revolution, according to Jenkins, was the legal impact. Child advocates believed that children's testimony was almost invariably truthful. As Jenkins and others have pointed out, it became an article of faith among child abuse experts that a child's account of abuse was to be believed. Since children's testimony was pivotal to many abuse cases, and the state was given expanded responsibilities to protect children, often the mere accusation of child abuse was sufficient to condemn the accused, frequently a parent (most often in a custody case) or family member. In effect, the revolutionary shift in child abuse attitudes and laws *inverted the constitutional presumption of innocence*. The belief that abuse charges were never made falsely and that accusations were justified had the effect of demanding the presumption of the defendant's guilt where a sex crime was concerned. The new "laws reflected the view that a war on child abuse necessitated extreme measures and perhaps the sacrifice of liberties, especially in the courtroom" (Jenkins, 1998:141). For example, in the 1980s, new state legislation removed the obligation that child witnesses must confront the individuals accused. Some children were allowed to give testimony behind screens or on closed-circuit television, reducing the ability of counsel in some cases to conduct cross-examination or interrogation. The result of the new laws to protect child victims assumed that the victimization really had occurred.

Numerous studies on the reliability of child testimony have shown this assumption to be questionable at best. This is particularly true in the context of highly contested child custody cases where one parent stands accused of abuse and the other parent is seeking sole custody (Shreinert and Richardson, 2011:245). Research shows that bitter custody battles may lead to the use of child abuse accusations by one spouse to punish the ex-spouse (Chancellor, 2000; Homer, 1999; Palmer, 1999; Richardson, 1999). Children are often caught in the middle of these disputes and may be prodded by a parent to make an allegation. In some infamous child abuse cases, such as the McMartin daycare case, the involvement of aggressive social workers or child protection investigators to find abuse reveals undue influence and "witness contamination"

through leading questions, inappropriate cues, and the use of "anatomi-
cally correct dolls" to shape the testimony of children to a desired end
(Coleman, 1989; Coleman and Clancy, 1990; Nathan and Snedeker,
1995; Richardson, 2000).

The far-reaching changes in American society regarding child abuse
opened up new opportunities for opponents of NRMs. NRMs became
"soft targets" in new child-saving campaigns. Opponents recognized that
these movements were vulnerable to child abuse claims since they often
practiced unconventional marriage and family arrangements. According
to Richardson (1999:175), "the new situation has led to a dramatic increase
in accusations of child abuse leveled against minority religions. . . . The
very presence of children in many of these groups makes them a target."

The ability of NRMs to defend themselves against such claims became
increasingly difficult in the face of elevated fears about child victimization
and aggressive new laws and regulatory mandates. The communal and
sectarian nature of some groups also made it more difficult to investigate
or verify complaints about the treatment of children through unintrusive
methods (i.e., interviewing neighbors, schoolteachers, or local doctors).
The new laws assumed routine interaction with third parties who could
detect and report possible abuse, but insulated or separatist religious
groups were not organized to incorporate these third-party monitors.

Collective Child Abuse Allegations

Richardson (1999) argues that the new federal and state reporting and investigation laws concerning child abuse made it easier for opponents to make
claims of "collective child abuse." The collective child abuse claim refers
to the allegation that "all children in certain groups are being harmed just
by being in a group that adheres to certain beliefs and practices thought by
some to be harmful to children" (Richardson, 1999:175–176). As opponents
labored to make "cults" synonymous with child abuse, public concerns
about children in new or nontraditional religious communities intensified.

Richardson identifies four types of "collective" or "mass child abuse"
claims. The first involves *religious homeschooling*, which some critics
regard as a form of indoctrination that inculcates intolerance and prejudice in children. Many new religions practice homeschooling, as do large
portions of conservative Christians. There was an estimated 2 million
homeschooled children in the United States in 2012, and according to one
study, they are "overwhelmingly Christian"; 78 percent of homeschooling

parents attend church frequently ("Keep It in the Family," *The Economist*, Dec. 22, 2012). The beliefs underlying religious homeschooling among both new/nontraditional religions and conservative/fundamentalist Christian groups are virtually the same, as are the concerns of detractors. The second type of collective child abuse claim focuses on *corporal punishment* of children practiced in some communities, many emerging out of Christian fundamentalism. "These traditional punitive measures," he states, "are perceived as physical abuse by many in our society" (Richardson, 1999:176). A few isolated cases of child deaths resulting from corporal punishment have fueled public outrage and encouraged social control agents to take actions when allegations of collective child abuse are made. A third collective child abuse accusation involves a *low living standard* (real or imagined) among some communal or sectarian movements. This claim is problematic since many children in secular families live in poverty. According to the U.S. Census Bureau, in 2010 approximately one in five children lived in poverty, that is, roughly 16 million children (DeNavas-Walt, Proctor, and Smith, 2013). Richardson says the courts have avoided addressing this allegation because it raises more troubling issues generally about social inequality. Finally, a fourth type of mass child abuse claim is *sexual abuse*. This is the most provocative type of allegation and often elicits a forceful response from authorities.

Richardson (1999) points out that distinctions between types of collective child abuse claims are often not clear, and that it may be implied from one type (corporal punishment) that another type is taking place (sexual abuse). In their analysis of the child abuse claims against David Koresh and the Branch Davidians, Ellison and Bartkowski (1995) found that opponents used sweeping generalizations about "cult child abuse" to leverage public opinion against the group and push for a more forceful response from federal agents. Palmer (2011a) has suggested that allegations by opponents are often interlocking so as to conflate and amplify the alleged threat of abuse. This tactic had the added effect of creating a barrage of intertwined charges so that the group's ability to defend itself was severely impeded.

Schreinert and Richardson (2011) discuss the definitional problems of child abuse claims against NRMs in relation to government raids, suggesting that the subjective and interpretive elements of the new laws that arose in the 1980s encouraged overreach by officials. They argue that issue of collective or mass child abuse "entails deeply flawed assumptions and strained interpretations of the law" (2011:246). The idea that "child abuse" might be inferred simply by virtue of growing up in a religious community, they contend, was never contemplated when the laws of the United States and other countries were designed. Such laws were developed with the assumption that violations were a matter of *individual* actions and accountability. They point out that laws require a great deal of *specificity* when child abuse accusations are made. The accused has to be named, the alleged victim has to be identified, and the information provided must stipulate the date, time, and location of the suspected abuse. But through effective reframing and claims-making efforts of opponents, expanded interpretations of abuse have come to mean that all members of a "cult" are abuse victims even if only one or two individual members are accused. As will be made evident in case studies we examine in later chapters, this was precisely the assumption made by state officials in launching raids on the Northeast Kingdom Community Church, The Family International, the Fundamentalist Latter Day Saints, and others.

A Model of Countermovement Organization and Mobilization

Originating with the Kelly Plan, ACM leaders recalibrated their strategic assault on NRMs to take advantage of a heightened climate of fear regarding child abuse while seizing new opportunities opened up through a growing transnational network. The basic plan called for the creation of a core alliance of ACM organizations/actors and apostates, with the possible inclusion of concerned relatives and family friends, to press claims and pressure authorities to act.

In the following pages we identify both the *dynamic processes* that impel or hasten the extreme action of the government raids on targeted religious communities and the *structural components* of our raid model (ACM organizations/actors, apostates, media, state agents, claims). Figure 2.1 illustrates how components of the model interact to effect the goal of a government raid. The core opponents, ACM organizations/actors and apostates, and concerned relatives and friends of NRM members, form an alliance to lodge claims and recruit sympathetic or opportunistic media and state agents (law enforcement, family and child protection services, elected officials) to their cause. When news reporters and state agents are persuaded by the ACM framing and inflated perception of a "cult" threat—frequently predicated on claims of child abuse—it engenders a loose coalition of opponents, setting into motion the forces that drive urgent state action. We include in this model the presence, but not involvement, of

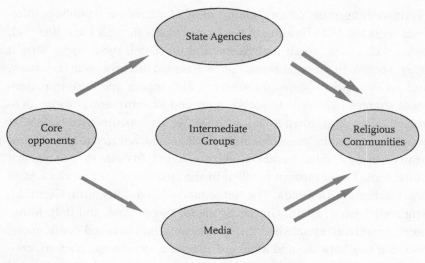

FIGURE 2.1. Dynamics of Countermovement Campaign to Impel Government Raids

"intermediate groups." Intermediate groups are defined as independent and impartial entities (human rights organizations, civil liberties groups, ecumenical organizations, scholars of religion) whose policy or research challenges intolerance toward minorities, and which would tend to mitigate ACM campaigns (Wright, 2002b). Intermediate groups are intentionally circumvented by core opponents since they would likely provide tempered information or data that do not support sweeping ACM claims and broad stereotypes of NRMs, and thus quell raid actions.

Structural Components

The structural components of our model comprise ACM organizations/actors, apostates, media, state agents, and claims. We want to examine each of these structural components briefly to show how they function to galvanize and promote countermobilization.

ACM Organizations/Actors

ACM organizations and actors serve as the essential vanguard of countermobilization. In chapter 1, we discussed the history and background of the anticult movement in its efforts to discredit and destroy NRMs. These efforts reveal some successes early on as the popular media adopted the "brainwashing/mind control" claims of ACM activists and public opinion polls reflected ACM framing in the United States (Bromley and Breschel, 1992; Richardson, 1992; Richardson and van Driel, 1984, 1997; Wright 1997, 2007a). In the legal arena, courts accepted brainwashing testimony, and juries acquitted deprogrammers of kidnapping and false imprisonment charges (Anthony, 1990; Anthony and Robbins, 1992, 1995; Richardson, 1985, 1991, 1995; Robbins, 1988). We also documented how ACM activists engaged in "missionizing" efforts abroad, referred to as its "European campaign" (Shupe and Darnell, 2006:197), in order to craft a global movement. The campaign resulted in the creation of a network of ACM organizations in Denmark, The Netherlands, France, Belgium, Germany, England, Austria, Spain, Greece, Scotland, Switzerland, and Italy. Movement organizers established European contacts, convened conferences, brokered ties between and among disparate anticult organizations, constructed and refined a uniform framing of the "cult" problem, and forged a consolidation of interests and goals to build an effective transnational network. This same transnational network also expanded to some countries outside Europe, including Israel, Australia, Argentina, and Japan.[1] With the shift in strategic attacks on NRMs focusing on child abuse, following the crude prototype of the Kelly Plan, ACM organizations and actors have functioned as the organizational base for countermobilization campaigns leading to government raids.

Apostates

We use the term "apostates" here as defined by Bromley (1998b). Apostates are distinguished from ordinary defectors or ex-members in that they embrace a posture of confrontation through public claims-making activities. In effect, the apostate is not simply one who is pursuing a different belief, but rather is involved in a struggle against the old faith seeking its negation (Coser, 1954:250). The newly constructed role places the apostate in a position that is diametrically opposed to one's former beliefs and commitment.

Contrary to popular beliefs, research indicates that most defectors from NRMs have favorable, sympathetic, or at the very least, mixed responses toward their former groups (Barker, 1984, 1988; Beckford, 1985; Galanter, 1989; Goldman, 1995; Levine, 1984; Lewis, 1986; Skonovd, 1983; Taslimi, Hood, and Watson, 1991; Wright, 1984, 1987, 1988, 1991). The vast majority of leavers do not engage in public campaigns to denounce the group or proclaim grievances; they quietly transition to new roles and social networks. Apostates, on the other hand, seek to sustain and broaden disputes and align themselves with an oppositional coalition to achieve that goal (Bromley, 1998b:5).

With the aid of ACM allies, apostates are able to amplify disputes by adopting a *victimization* narrative (Wright, 1998:100–102). Paul Martin, director of the Wellspring "cult rehabilitation" center in Ohio, epitomizes this facilitator role for the apostate: "In coming to grips with what has happened to the ex-cultist, it is quite helpful to employ the victim of trauma model. . . . The former cult member has been traumatized, deceived, conned, used, and often emotionally and mentally abused" (Martin, 1996:3). Prominent ACM figure Michael Langone (1993a) in his book *Recovery from Cults* compares "ex-cultists" to other "victims" of abuse: "When they leave, for whatever reason, they will tend, as do victims of other forms of abuse, to believe that they have left because something was wrong with *them*" (Langone, 1993b:11). "Ex-cultists are not merely misguided or troubled seekers," Langone contends, "they are victims" (Langone, 1993b:12). [Apostates may indeed have experienced some real abuse or mistreatment, but their alliance with ACM actors enables them to *turn personal grievances into public campaigns* that effectively serve the interests of ACM political objectives. It is this dynamic that forms what Bromley (1998b) calls "the politics of religious apostasy." The coupling of the apostate narrative with the broader anticult narrative functions to "fortify" the denunciation of the targeted group (Johnson, 1998:121) and influence public opinion about "cults" more generally.

Even conceding that some apostate accounts are true, research suggests that they are more often unreliable, given to exaggeration, embellishment, "artificial contextualization," selective description, defensive posturing, distortions, and even outright fabrication (Beckford, 1985; Bromley, 1998a, 1998b; Foster, 1981:50–54, 1984; Johnson, 1998; Lewis, 1986, 1992; Mauss, 1998; Miller, 1983; Palmer, 1998, 1999; Wright, 1995b, 1998; Wright and Ebaugh, 1993). The historical case of Maria Monk (1836) brings to mind the most egregious example of a fabricated apostate account. Maria Monk claimed to have been a nun in the Hotel Dieu Nunnery in Montreal in the 1830s where she allegedly witnessed fellow nuns giving birth to, baptizing, and then suffocating the progeny of their priestly trysts (Frink, 2009; Johnson, 1998; Pagliarini, 1999). Other notable examples of fabricated apostate accounts in the past include the ex-Catholic Rebecca Reed and the ex-Shaker Mary Dyer (Johnson, 1998). The faux ex-Satanist account circulated for years by Christian evangelist Michael Warnke is a more recent example. Warnke (1991) claimed to have been a high priest in the Satanic Brotherhood, a network of underground Satanists numbering 1,500 members spanning three cities until he was exposed (Trott and Hertenstein, 1992). These, of course, are extreme examples, but they do point up the central problem of apostate accounts; they require some independent corroboration and should not be taken at face value. Research indicates that there are an array of motives for construction and dissemination of apostate accounts and "atrocity tales" (Bromley, Shupe, and Ventimiglia, 1979).

According to Mauss (1998), apostates may need to justify their departures by finding fault with, or attributing blame to, their former groups. Presentation of the emergent self after NRM disengagement often requires a defense against a "spoiled identity" in the face of stigmatizing efforts by significant others. To save face, the apostate is compelled to negotiate a new identity that plays to a "new audience" and is calculated to explain the old self. The new associates in an oppositional group may encourage the defector to participate in appropriate *rituals of denunciation* (testimonials, confessions). Beckford found that ex-members of one NRM were "persuaded to take part in carefully arranged public testimonies" of their apostasy while privately confiding "that their participation had been largely an inauthentic attempt to conform with parental wishes" (1985:175). "When social actors deal in apostate narrative," Johnson (1998:119) reminds us, "they are dealing in powerful shapers of past and present identities. For it is the stories that these people tell that confirm them in the role of apostate, and this is the role that defines them for who they are—sometimes for the rest of their lives."

Indeed, ongoing conflict between oppositional coalitions and NRMs provides opportunities for what Bromley calls *apostate careers* (1998c:37–38). Career apostates are a more passionate subset of apostates whose credentials, status, and income are dependent on being a "professional ex" (Brown, 1996). The moral and experiential qualifications of the career apostate allow the individual to make "legitimate claims to the entitlements of their stigma" (Brown, 1996:444). Lawrence Foster provides a detailed analysis of career apostates Jerald and Sandra Tanner, ex-Mormons who "devoted their lives to exposing and trying to destroy Mormonism" (1984:35). Wright and Fagen (2011) have examined the impacts of career apostates Marc Breault and Flora Jessop on the planning of the Branch Davidian and Fundamentalist Latter Day Saints raids, respectively. Both Breault and Jessop documented their achievements as career apostates in autobiographies in which they describe considerable efforts to discredit their former groups (Breault and King, 1993; Jessop and Brown, 2009). According to Bromley (1998c:38):

> Apostates may pursue a variety of strategies to solidify their careers: consolidating their experience and acquiring credentials that support a more permanent social niche; reconstructing their position and experience with the [ACM] organization, particularly status inflation, so that their testimony becomes more valuable in sanctioning the organization; modifying the narrative content so that it appeals to the specific interest of one or more elements of the oppositional coalition; and embellishing the narrative so as to maintain niche viability, particularly when the existence of a cohort of apostates creates role competition.

Ironically, it is often *only* the accounts of apostates that are publicly aired and widely disseminated. These accounts tend to shape the public perception of NRMs, giving the impression that the apostate's experience is normative and obscuring the experiences of the ordinary leave-taker. We cannot overstate the critical importance of this powerful core alliance between ACM activists and apostates. ACM organizations provide apostates with valuable resources; venues from which to express grievances, lodge claims, locate contacts and networks; and appropriate effective anticult frames or narratives. Apostates, in turn, give credibility to the most serious ACM depictions of "cults" since these individuals offer firsthand accounts as former members. Apostate accounts are often given uncritical acceptance by journalists and news reporters, as well as state agents such as law enforcement and child protective services.

As such, the successful mobilization of NRM opponents has been rooted firmly in this core alliance of ACM actors and apostates: "Apostates have been an integral element of countermovement organization and strategy . . .; countermovements arguably could not have successfully mobilized opposition and imposition of sanctions without this role-resource" (Bromley, 1998c:20).

Media

As the Kelly Plan outlined, a vital part of a successful oppositional campaign involves coordination with news media to bring allegations against the targeted group, arouse suspicions, and attribute threat. Such efforts do not necessarily require mass news coverage or a flock of reporters; at least not in the initial phase of the campaign. The cultivation of contacts with a local reporter in the community where the NRM resides is often sufficient to generate a story. Sympathetic journalists, responsive to the victimization narrative of an apostate, alongside charges of child abuse, sexual abuse, or other sensational tropes that play to the cult stereotype, will likely be drawn to the story as it will make "good copy" and appeal to the prurient interest of readers or television viewers (Beckford, 1985; Richardson and Introvigne, 2007; Shupe and Hadden, 1995).

In our research, we found it to be almost universally true that the "source" of news stories about a perceived "cult" threat in the wake of a government raid was an apostate coupled with, or backed up by, anticult organizations or activists. When confronted about the questionable veracity of information, we found the journalists who wrote the news stories tended to treat their sources uncritically and offered little in the way of balance. They defended their stories as fair or objective by pointing to "cult experts" who supported these apostate accounts, not recognizing that the "cult experts" were ACM operatives who were part of the oppositional alliance, not impartial observers.

Media are a critical component in oppositional campaigns because they shape public opinion. Inflammatory news stories can incite outrage against a religious community. Religious leaders are often castigated as "cult leaders" who pose a danger to members. As Richardson (1995) has shown, media reporting can "manufacture consent" about alleged threats attributed to a religious leader or group. The influence of media in shaping public opinion is greater when there is very little known publicly about the group, which is often the case. In this instance, media reports and images provide primary information that serves as a baseline to define the target (Beckford, 1985:231). Shupe and Hadden observe that when there is a dearth of information about a subject such as a secluded religious group, media tend to draw on a general cultural stock of knowledge. This stock of knowledge relies on a set of presuppositions that are not necessarily true, but fall back on widely accepted narratives or tropes about "cults." Thus Beckford observes a "narrowness" of media coverage about NRMs that is characterized by the "sheer repetition of the same images and arguments." "Stories about 'cults,'" he states, "are remarkably standardized" (1985:240).

The shaping of public opinion about NRMs by media can be seen in some public opinion polls. In examining a series of Gallup polls in 1981, 1987, and 1989, Bromley and Breschel (1992) found an increase in negative sentiments and attitudes toward NRMs. A national Gallup poll in 1981 found that 30 percent of respondents "would not like to have as neighbors" members of religious sects or cults. In 1987, the percent of respondents expressing the same view climbed to 44 percent, and by 1989, the percent rejecting sect or cult members as neighbors rose to 62 percent (Bromley and Breschel, 1992:42–43). Not coincidentally, these data correlate with the growing climate of perceived threat of child abuse in "cults" as propagated by opponents.

There have been a number of studies examining media coverage of NRMs (Beckford, 1985; Beckford and Coles, 1988; Richardson, 1995, 1997; Richardson and Introvigne, 2007; Richardson and van Driel, 1997; Selway, 1992; Shupe and Hadden, 1995; Wright, 1997). The findings of this research indicate that most of the coverage has been negative in tone and content. Scholars of religion are notably absent in the reporting, while "cult experts" (ACM operatives) are regularly consulted (Richardson and Introvigne, 2007:99). In-depth reporting is seldom employed; instead, a "stream of controversies" approach (Beckford, 1985) tends to define media coverage in place of serious investigative reporting. Elsewhere, Beckford has noted that "the most elementary observation about print and broadcast media's portrayal of NRMs is that the movement's activities are newsworthy *only* when conflicts are involved" (1994:20, emphasis ours). Audiences rarely have the opportunity to evaluate other kinds of information about such groups that is not related to conflict. According to Beckford (1994:20), "Conflict is the *Leitmotiv* which connects journalistic portrayals of NRMs together."

Richardson and van Driel (1997) obtained the mailing list of the Religion Newswriters Association (RNA) and mailed questionnaires to members inquiring about journalists' attitudes toward NRMs. They found that religion newswriters knew very little about the scholarly research on NRMs and tended to regard these groups as "deviant" and in need of government control. The researchers also found that religion newswriters were likely to accept the "brainwashing" explanation of conversion or involvement.

A second feature of this research is the identification of the importance of media in oppositional campaigns. For example, Beckford found that reporters helped to fuel ACM campaigns and operated as networks to bring together components of the oppositional coalition.

Indeed, journalists have played a major part in helping to fuel anticult campaigns and to keep them "in the news," if not in the headlines. In many cases journalists have functioned as an unofficial channel of communication among ex-members or anguished parents who would not have otherwise have known of each other's plight. And the extensive preparations for some television programmes have brought together many far-flung components of the anti-cult movement. (Beckford,1985:232)

Richardson and Introvigne (2007:98) state that "arguably, the mass media are the most important resource available to the ACM industry." The mass dissemination of stories about "cults" does irreparable damage because the promotion of ACM framing, or "victim" narratives, is published or broadcast under the guise of objective news reporting. Beckford (1994:21) contends that the wholesale adoption of ACM framing "turns many investigative journalists into allies of the ACM" and "helps to set the scene for the official agents of control." Indeed, Richardson and van Driel (1997) found in their survey of religion newswriters that approximately one-third said they would, if contacted, refer people to ACM organizations, essentially functioning as accomplices or advocates for the opposition.

State Agents

As discussed previously, the reframing of the cult threat primarily in terms of child abuse inevitably drew into the conflict state family and child protective services. The wave of new and more aggressive legislation regarding child abuse, including mandatory reporting, placed state social workers and mental health professionals in a more proactive role. Since some child abuse cases involved NRMs, there was an effort on the part of state agencies to better understand these problems if and when they arose. It should not come as a surprise that ACM-affiliated psychologists and mental health specialists were recruited and hired to assist state agencies in cases to evaluate "child abuse in cults," to conduct seminars and workshops, or to offer expert testimony in hearings and trials (Perry, 1994; Perry and Szalavitz, 2007; Wright, 2011; Wright and Richardson, 2011a). ACM-affiliated psychologists and social workers have also sought to cultivate ties to state agencies in an effort to shape practice and policy.

Law enforcement has often been persuaded by core opponents' exaggerated threats aimed at NRMs, ranging from child abuse and brainwashing to stockpiling weapons, mass suicide, and even terrorism. Responding to inflated claims, including threats of violence, law enforcement officials are likely to take more extreme actions such as surprise raids, rapid insertions, or "dynamic entries" (Wright, 1995a, 1999, 2005). This helps to explain why, in the aftermath of a raid, questions often arise about the overreach of authorities. In many of the cases we have examined, the actual problem posed by the religious community is grossly disproportional to the official reaction. The state response frequently amounts to swatting a gnat with a sledgehammer.

There is also research to suggest that some law enforcement agents hold personal religious beliefs that rigidly define nontraditional groups as "cults," thus making them allies (intentional or not) with ACM actors. Nancy Ammerman, who was asked by the U.S. Department of Justice to review the actions of federal agents at Waco in 1993, found that "some agents fell victim to the images inherent in the label 'cult'" (Ammerman, 1995:285). She observed that "the depth of their own [federal agents'] faith sometimes made it difficult for them to identify with someone whose faith was so different" (p.285). Moreover, Ammerman (1995:289) reports that the most important outside consultant to the FBI and ATF before and during the Branch Davidian standoff was a deprogrammer and ACM activist, Rick Ross. Ammerman cites an FBI interview report that states "Ross has a personal hatred for all religious cults" and would willingly aid law enforcement in any attempt to "destroy a cult" (Ammerman, 1995:289). Other scholars have noted the disturbing religious intolerance in statements made by federal officials during the Branch Davidian standoff. FBI officials Bob Ricks and Jeff Jamar ridiculed David Koresh's beliefs as "bible-babble" and called him a "phony messiah," "fanatic," "con-man," and a "cheap thug who interprets the Bible through the barrel of a gun" ("FBI Heaps Ridicule on Koresh," *Houston Chronicle*, April 17, 1993, p.1A). In 2013, the authors had an opportunity to discuss the events at Waco with one of the FBI negotiators on the scene, Gary Noesner. In response to questions about these belittling statements by Ricks and Jamar, Noesner described the special agent in charge of the ground operation, Jeff Jamar, as "very religious." In Noesner's own book, *Stalling for Time*, he also expressed concern over his fellow negotiator Cliff Van Zandt because he was a fervent "born-again Christian." "I worried that Van Zandt would attempt to convince Koresh to surrender by presenting his own interpretation of biblical prophecy," Noesner states (2010:127). Noesner notes that after handing over the negotiations to Van Zandt in early April, "the situation in Waco deteriorated" (p.128).

Claims

Exaggerated or embellished claims made against NRMs have followed a predictable pattern, based largely on cult stereotypes promoted by organized opponents. The most common claims include child abuse, sexual abuse, brainwashing or mind control, forced servitude/slavery, stockpiling weapons, mass suicide, and terrorism. Some of these claims may be credible when focusing on a single case, or perhaps in a few cases. But as we shall see, the tactic of opponents has been to make sweeping generalizations about all such groups based on anecdotal evidence in a few cases. ACM activists and allied opponents rely on a type of "definitional reductionism" in which the above claims are intrinsically part of the definition of "cult" (Wright and Fagen, 2011:168). This rhetorical tactic has been effective in projecting a false and overly simplistic uniformity in the public arena but it is clearly a logical fallacy and even more importantly, it lacks any empirical support. The vast majority of NRMs have no history of abuse or violence. Those that have come under public scrutiny for such violations represent only a small percentage of the total population of NRMs, which even conservatively estimated is in the tens of thousands globally and has "a following that has to be counted in the millions" (Clarke, 2006:xiii).

Six Case Studies

In the following chapters we offer six in-depth case studies of raided NRM communities. Ideally, we would like to examine each of the 38 raided groups listed in chapter 1 (Table 1.1). But space does not permit such an endeavor. Instead, we have selected six cases based on the following criteria: scale, severity, and recurrence. We define *scale* as the size of the raid force and the amount of state resources expended in the enforcement action. *Severity* is defined as the extent of real or threatened use of lethal force, particularly the deployment of paramilitary police units. *Recurrence* refers to the circumstance of multiple raids on the same group. We determined that raid cases best meeting these criteria include the Twelve Tribes, The Family International, the Branch Davidians, Scientology, the Fundamentalist Latter Day Saints, and the Nuwaubians. The Branch Davidian, FLDS, and Nuwaubian cases involved the most massive enforcement actions, ranking highest on the scale criterion. The Branch Davidian and Nuwaubian cases also ranked highest on the severity criterion; each involved extensive paramilitary operations. In terms of recurrence, Scientology and the Family International were distinguished as the groups most often raided. The Church of Scientology has been raided 31 times in seven different countries. The Family International has been the target of 12 government raids in seven countries.

3

The Twelve Tribes

THE TWELVE TRIBES bears a close resemblance to other Christian-based NRMs and revitalization movements that emerged out of the Jesus People Revolution of the early 1970s. Yet it is unique, for it will stand out in the history of church-state relations as one of the first new religions in the United States to be accused of collective child abuse. Over the years, this communal, millenarian movement has expanded internationally and has adopted various names: the Vine Community Church, the Apostolic Order, the Northeast Kingdom Community Church, the Messianic Communities, and most recently the Twelve Tribes. Each local Tribe has its own Hebrew name. In France, it is called the Tribe of Reuben. At the time of the first raid in Island Pond, Vermont, the group was called the Northeast Kingdom Community Church.

Overview of the 1984 Raid

On June 22, 1984, 90 Vermont state troopers arrived at dawn in their cruisers at the homes of the Northeast Kingdom Community Church in Island Pond, Vermont, armed with a court order and accompanied by 50 Social Rehabilitation Services workers (Palmer, 2010a). The state police searched the households and took 112 children into protective custody. The children, accompanied by their parents, were bussed 20 miles to the courthouse in Newport. District Judge Frank Mahady, after holding 40 individual detention hearings in one day, ruled that the search warrant issued by the state was invalid and that the raid had been "unconstitutional," since there was no a priori evidence of abuse of the children. All 112 children were released to their parents without submitting to a search for bruises, or medical examinations (as had been the intentions of the state authorities), and the legal process ended abruptly.

In spite of this resounding legal victory, the Twelve Tribes has continued to be a target of raids involving law enforcement officers and social workers, in Canada, in Germany, and in France. In every instance, the rationale for these raids has been to rescue the community's children. Since the 1984 Island Pond raid was the largest in scale, the most widely publicized, and the most significant of the various raids (in terms of its legal/judicial outcome), we will focus mainly on this NRM's epic confrontation with the state over the custody of children that cast Vermont into the national spotlight.[1] We will also provide brief sketches of other raids in Canada, France, and Germany.

History and Background of Twelve Tribes

The history of this NRM began in 1973 in Chattanooga, Tennessee, where Elbert Eugene Spriggs and his wife, Marsha Ann Duvall, founded the Vine Christian Community Church. They started a biweekly Bible class, then opened their house to young people "who didn't go to church" and taught them the ethic of selflessness, brotherly love, and in accordance with the New Testament Book of Acts (2:37–47), sharing all things in common.

In 1975 an important incident triggered their break with conventional Christianity. The Spriggs and their followers had been regularly attending Sunday services at the First Presbyterian Church, but in 1975 their local church cancelled their Sunday morning service for Super Bowl weekend. In response to this worldly affront to spiritual priorities, the Spriggs and their friends decided to hold their own service called "Critical Mass" outdoors in Warner Park every Sunday (see Palmer, 2010a). Soon they began to perform their own baptisms in Chickamauga Lake. Since Eugene Spriggs was not an ordained minister, this practice elicited criticism from local church leaders (Murray, 1978a).

The Vine Church bought and renovated three run-down Victorian houses in Chattanooga and set up a restaurant called the Yellow Deli, open 24 hours a day, which became a refuge for runaways, hitchhikers, and lonely teens. The menu offered the following item to customers: "We serve the fruit of the Spirit. Why not ask?" Six more Yellow Delis opened in the Chattanooga area, and the downtown Areopagus Café invited local Christians for dialogue in the city's center. The Vine Church also developed small craft industries like candle-making, a leather shop, and a bakery. They set up a separate corporate entity for tax purposes called T.H.E. Community Apostolic Order, which functioned as a nonprofit religious organization according to section 501(d) of the Internal Revenue Code. This permitted the Vine Church—as an "apostolic order"—to have a common treasury and engage in for-profit businesses "for the common good of the members" (Murray, 1978b).

Today, the Twelve Tribes communities continue to "hive" and thrive in the United States, Canada, Europe, Australia, and South America, with between 2,500 and 3,000 members worldwide (Swantko, 2004). Its members span four generations, since many elderly parents of the first disciples have been taken in by the community. The group's membership remains stable with a high birthrate cancelling out a high turnover rate.

The Tribes adopt the names of their local towns, and members are given Hebrew names, to identify them with the "lost and scattered tribes" of the Jews (Bozeman and Palmer, 1997). They embrace a radical Christian Perfectionism and believe that by renouncing the sinful world and private property and striving to overcome selfishness, they will become part of the "Body of the Messiah" and overcome physical death. They believe their church is the "Pure and Spotless Bride" depicted in the Book of Revelation awaiting the advent of Her Bridegroom, whom they call by His Hebrew name, Yahshua. Through multiplying their ranks, founding global communities, and "raising up a people," they are preparing the way for the Jubilee horn that will herald Yahshua's return (Palmer, 2001).

In the early phases of the Vine Christian Community Church in Chattanooga, its success in converting young people to a radical, communal (and hardworking) way of life provoked criticism and negative reactions from the local religious leaders, businessmen, and members' parents. Ex-members and parents were quoted in the *Chattanooga Times* complaining that the Vine Church "lured in" susceptible youth, isolated them from their parents, indoctrinated them, and made them work up to 90 hours a week with no pay (Murray, 1987c). In December 1977, Ted C. Mercer, the president of Dayton's Bryan College, issued a statement advising all members of the college not to patronize the Yellow Deli, due to its "brainwashing techniques" and the "cult of the personality of Gene Spriggs." Jesse Warwick, a Methodist church minister in Chickamauga, formed a local opposition network and posted signs bearing anticult slogans on the grounds of his church. In March 1978, the Yellow Deli was formally declared off-limits to Bryan College students, and the Tennessee Temple and Covenant College followed suit, claiming the Vine Church had "exceeded its ministerial function, and was taking on magisterial power" (Murray, 1978a).

Elbert Eugene Spriggs was labeled a "cult leader." He was condemned as a self-proclaimed "Apostle" who exerted "total control" over his followers and molded them into religious fanatics who held themselves above the law. He was said to employ "mind control" techniques to enlist his followers in communal and voluntary labor that undercut local businesses (Beverly, n.d.). He has often been described in anticult literature and news reports as a former "carnival barker"—a colorful term that conjures up images of the American frontier snake-oil salesman, the charming charlatan with a fast patter. In fact, Eugene Spriggs was by profession a high school teacher and fairly successful travel agent and tour guide who did work for one day in a carnival, but not as a barker (Palmer, 1998:194).

The first serious conflicts began when worried parents of converts, rival restaurant owners, and ministers of local congregations consulted, or were approached by FREECOG (Free the Children of God), an early anticult movement association founded in 1972 by deprogrammer Ted Patrick as a response to his son's attraction to the Children of God (COG). The Vine Community Church bore a cursory resemblance to COG, since both movements were communal, millenarian, and evangelistic and had emerged from the Jesus People movement. Patrick began kidnapping and deprogramming members of COG and soon turned his efforts to the Vine Church, abducting eight of the Chattanooga members between 1978 and 1980.[2]

In March 1979, the Vine Church decided to sell almost all of its properties and businesses in Chattanooga and to relocate its congregation in Island Pond, in northern Vermont. After settling in Island Pond, the Vine Church became known as the Northeast Kingdom Community Church (NEKCC). Journalists labeled the group after the corner of Vermont known as "the Northeast Kingdom." Church members were highly conspicuous in a small, conservative village of dairy farmers. They started new businesses and trade markets in an effort to tie into local community networks. They purchased an old building on the main street in Island Pond and opened up the Common Sense Restaurant (Hertic, 1978), among other ventures. But soon, the church community was targeted by drive-by shooters and vandals who trashed their wholesome food store and restaurant.

Allegations of abuse first came to the attention of the authorities in 1982 in connection with custody battles involving three families: the

Gregoires, the Alexanders, and the Mattatalls (*Gregoire v. Gregoire*, 1983). In May 1983 the court awarded custody of the 11 children to the three fathers residing outside the community rather than allow the children to be "subjected to frequent and methodical physical abuse by adult members of the community, in the form of hours-long whippings with balloon sticks" (*Gregoire v. Gregoire*, 1983). Judge Mahady, who presided over the Gregoire case, expressed his opinion that the children were trapped in "some sort of holy war" between the parents. Out of this single case, the career of a formidable "arch-apostate" Juan Mattatall was launched (Palmer, 1998:194–198).

Organized Opposition

In the aftermath of the Island Pond raid, one might analyze the trajectory of this NRM's escalating conflict by identifying the interested parties in the oppositional coalition that formed a network in their common mission to rescue the putatively abused children from the "cult."[3] This network depended heavily upon ex-members' testimonials to provide the rationale for the moral campaign against the Community.

As in other cases we discuss throughout the book, we can trace the influence of different interest groups that formed alliances in order to lay grievance claims against the targeted religious community. A recognizable process began to take shape during Mattatall's court case when various interest groups responded to a key apostate's initiative and began to form a network dedicated to the common cause of "saving the children." Integral participants in the network included anticult organizations and actors, social services officials, journalists, state law enforcement, and local business leaders. This network gradually formulated and nurtured a portrait of the Northeast Kingdom Community as a dangerous, child-abusing "cult."

Apostates

Juan Mattatall was a Chilean hippie "head"[4] and successful soft dope dealer in the 1970s counterculture. He led a band of hippies called the Lighthouse Family that fashioned jewelry to sell at crafts fairs across the country. He met the community in 1976. He and his pregnant girlfriend, Cindy, joined the Vine Church, where they were married in 1976.

Initially, the elders found Juan an asset to community life, but the trouble started when two young girls complained to their parents that he had made sexual advances toward them as they were sleeping. After the elders made some effort to rehabilitate him and his wife refused to take him back, he blamed the community for breaking up his family. He reportedly told Spriggs just before he left, "I will destroy the community!" (Palmer, 1998:194–198).

Mattatall filed for divorce and subsequently sought out Suzanne Cloutier, a nurse working for Social Rehabilitation Services (SRS), in Island Pond. Mattatall alleged that members of the Northeast Kingdom Community were abusing children. Upon hearing his claims of abused children, Cloutier quickly became a formidable opponent of the Church.

Mattatall also contacted Galen Kelly and Priscilla Coates of the Citizens Freedom Foundation (CFF), which was established in Orleans, Vermont, in 1982, and was the most powerful anticult organization in the United States at that time.[5] A November 28, 1982 news report states that CCF Director Priscilla Coates and a "private investigator," Galen Kelly (a well-known deprogrammer), arranged to meet with the citizens of Orleans and Island Pond but refused to allow members of the Northeast Kingdom Community Church to attend because he claimed their mission was "educational," not confrontational (Swantko, 1998). With their aid and support, Mattatall won custody of the five children in 1982, despite three sworn affidavits of alleged victims of Mattatall that were available to the court but not considered (Swantko, 2004:183).[6] His wife, Cindy, fled with the youngest but was eventually tracked down in Nova Scotia, where the daughter Lydia was seized by the authorities and given to her father (Palmer, 1998:195).

As a result of early oppositional activity, media stories began to appear on the methods of childrearing and discipline with the Church. Mattatall sought out journalists to strengthen his case, and his own account appeared in various media outlets, including the Canadian Broadcasting Corporation network, United Press International, and the anticult publication *The Cult Observer*. The front page of the *Burlington Free Press* featured a photo of Mattatall as the triumphant father reunited with his five blonde, mop-haired kids (Palmer, 1998:196) in a story that played to the "rescue motif" (Wright, 1998).

Mattatall also appealed to counter-cult activists from mainline Christian churches. After he settled in Burlington, he began attending a local church. Speaking from the pulpit on one Sunday he regaled the congregation with a story of the dramatic rescue of his children from the "cult" and declared that his next step would be to save his wife. But Mattatall's relationship with his wife was strained in the wake of the battle over child custody. In fact, only after a court order did Mattatall agree to take the children to Island Pond to visit their mother. However, he made the visits more difficult than they had to be. On one occasion he arrived in a camper with CFF workers and parked outside the Island Pond Maples household for the night. Mattatall handed out whistles to each of the children and told them to blow the whistles when the abuse started so that they could be "rescued" (Palmer, 1998:196).

Mattatall's troubles with regard to child sexual abuse allegations soon resurfaced; this time from another source. The nanny he hired in Burlington became disturbed about his apparent sexual advances toward a young girl next door. The woman complained to the authorities who then launched an investigation. Mattatall evaded the Burlington authorities by moving to Orlando, Florida. In Florida he placed his children in the Baptist Christian Home where they resided from 1982 to 1990. During this time he was reported to the Adam Walsh Center (which later became the National Center for Missing and Exploited Children) for sexually abusing a local prepubescent girl. Mattatall arranged a plea bargain for a lesser offense and was placed on probation. Despite his previous criminal charges, the director of the Baptist Home, who had been warned that the mother was in a "dangerous cult," cooperated with Juan in blocking Cynthia Mattatall's access to the children. The mother had obtained a court order granting her permission to see her children, but every time she traveled to Orlando to see them, she was turned away. Eventually, she gave up her visitation attempts and remarried (Palmer, 1998:196).

In 1990 she learned that Juan had been shot dead by his own mother. This event was reported in the Clark's Harbour, Nova Scotia, *Guardian*:

> A well-known defector from the Northeast Kingdom Community Church, Juan Mattatall, 47, and his 74-year-old mother, Maria Palmer, were found May 7 . . . by his step-father, Bernard Palmer. Juan Mattatall . . . [had] faced two charges of child sexual assault. . . . [His father, Bernard] Palmer . . . said . . . his stepson's life had been a non-stop series of problems with children and the law. He speculated that his wife foresaw that Juan's problems would continue and so she shot him to save him from the grief that seemed destined to continue. (Blades, 1990:1)

Mattatall's death was also reported in the *Orlando Sentinel*, as follows:

> Orlando police Tuesday identified the mother-and-son victims of
> what is believed to have been a murder-suicide shooting as Maria
> Palmer, 74, and Juan Mattatall, 47. The bodies were found by the
> woman's husband at 6:45 p.m. Monday when he returned to their
> home at 2240 E. Gore St. Investigators said the mother shot her
> son in the head twice with a.38-caliber handgun and herself in the
> head once. The motive remained uncertain. ("Shooting Deaths,"
> *Orlando Sentinel*, May 9, 1990)

ACM Organizations and Actors

The most influential ACM organization in the oppositional alliance was
the Citizens Freedom Foundation, whose officials first visited Burlington
in response to Mattatall's invitation in 1982. The CFF established a chapter in Orleans in November, 1982, collected funds, contacted the local
media, and recruited deprogrammer Galen Kelly to aid and facilitate the
"escape" of members from the "cult." CFF launched a campaign heralding
the dangers posed by the Island Pond Community and warned residents
that their children were in peril. Posters appeared on the streets of Island
Pond warning residents: "The Northeast Kingdom Community Church
Abducts Children." CFF meetings were held in Barton where townspeople were urged to boycott all products made by the Northeast Kingdom
Church. Townspeople were persuaded to stop buying the Community's fresh-baked breads and store owners were pressured to stop stock-
ing other Community products. The subversion narrative propagated by
ACM actors had an immediate impact. The night of the first meeting in
Barton someone drove through Island Pond and shot bullets through the
windows of the Common Sense Restaurant, the Maples household, and
a gas station owned by the Community. It is perhaps significant that this
event was not reported in the newspapers nor was it investigated by the
police (Bozeman and Palmer, 1997).

ACM activists went to great lengths to damage the Northeast Kingdom Church. Kelly formulated an investigative strategy to identify
potential allies within key government agencies, persuade them to
investigate the Church, find and interview disgruntled ex-members,
foment exaggerated media accounts, gather damaging evidence, and

build a case for child abuse with the intent to force state action (Wiseman, 2011:201–202). In the document, Kelly proposed conducting a "well-structured investigation designed to develop and document facts about the activities" of the Northeast Kingdom church "as a vehicle to coordinate law enforcement, media and grass roots opposition to the group." The goal of the plan, as envisioned by Kelly, was not simply to prevent the Church's growth but to "assist in the dissolution of it" (*Investigative Proposal*, n.d., p.1).

In an effort to implement the plan, Kelly organized local public meetings and met with residents to broaden the campaign and to spread alarm about alleged abuse at Island Pond. One of the first such meetings was in Barton in November 1982; Suzanne Cloutier was asked to coordinate this meeting as well as to cultivate press contacts. Cloutier was also encouraged to coax members to defect and write affidavits lodging claims against the group (Palmer, 1998:199). As a result of this countermovement activism, Kelly obtained affidavits from a handful of defectors calling for criminal charges and in some cases the affidavits were used in custody battles. The ex-members, some of whom were deprogrammed, were put in touch with media and state authorities to press publicly for legal action. In a matter of months, Kelly's strategy to build a broad-based coalition of opponents—defectors, reporters, ACM activists, and state officials—was effectively achieved.

The state raid, based on charges of child abuse, was a remarkably successful effort to pillage public resources in order to carry out a partisan campaign. The alleged "problem" at Island Pond was framed by public officials strictly in ACM terms and rationalized as a necessary action taken in the public interest. According to Wiseman (2011:202):

> The ill-conceived and ultimately illegal state incursion would not have occurred apart from the actions of Kelly and the coalition of opponents that served as the mobilizing force behind the raid. In preparation to lobby the state to act on behalf of opponents, Kelly was quite specific about the strategy: ACM actors should "work closely during an investigation with law enforcement and regulatory agencies to gain access to information that they (have) developed themselves" with the goal of "establishing credibility with them" so as to "subtly or not so subtly force any reluctant enforcement or regulatory agency to take appropriate action." (*Investigative Proposal*, n.d., p.5)

Wiseman observes that the Kelly Plan outlined a stepwise strategy that would later serve as a prototype for assailing other new or minority religions by ACM organizations and actors. In the document, Kelly provides reasons for why the plan should succeed: 1) the group is "small enough and localized enough to be studied, investigated and researched as a microcosm," providing lessons "applicable to other similar groups presently and in the future"; 2) the plan could serve as a "research project to experiment in developing ways to teach communities how to cope with the incursion of a cult"; and 3) having the participation of CFF "will be a great step forward in taking aggressive action, since the only aggressive anticult action has been deprogramming which entails various controversial problems" (*Investigative Proposal*, n.d., p.2). The Kelly Plan makes explicit that the "experiment" to disrupt the Northeast Kingdom Church would provide a model applicable to other new or nontraditional religious groups in the future. The significance of the model is underscored by Kelly in noting that it would propel the ACM past the dilemma of the movement's increasingly problematic reliance on deprogramming (Wiseman, 2011:202–203).

As mentioned above, Kelly and Cloutier worked with state investigators to recruit ex-members, soliciting testimonies, and tailoring the stories to win public support for their campaign to rescue the children. New defectors were encouraged to emulate Mattatall's model, to echo the themes he had originally laid out. Some ex-members who were not particularly disgruntled were coaxed to appear in public as ad hoc apostates. Examples of these were Michael Taylor and Roland Church, who complained of child beatings (spankings) in the NEKCC (see Palmer, 1998:199).

When these two apostate accounts proved to be less than spectacular, opponents launched a search for more corroborating evidence of physical abuse of children. Coates met with the Vermont attorney general's staff and provided names of more defectors. Social services official Conrad Grimms and Vermont state police officer Peter Johnson traveled around the country between 1982 and 1983, tracking down ex-members in seven different states to interview them for child abuse information. Statements from these interviews were then collected from the 18 affidavits that became the basis for the Vermont state raid (see Palmer, 1998). One of these, the *Moran Affidavit*, featured the stories of 14 defectors. Six of these individuals, all of whom had been deprogrammed by Galen Kelly, recounted stories that were curiously and suspiciously similar. This collection of atrocity tales was used to convince authorities that the group was engaged in criminal activity and a legitimate target for state action.

Coates and Galen Kelly also told the state attorney general's staff about two cases of child beating fatalities that had occurred in other "cults"; the Stonegate community in West Virginia and the House of Judah in Michigan. Evidently, they hoped that their meeting would provide justification for emergency measures taken against the NEKCC (Malcarne and Burchard, 1992).[7]

State Agents

Suzanne Cloutier of Vermont Social Services worked passionately to pressure authorities to intervene on behalf of the children, but she was also frustrated due to lack of evidence that abuse was taking place. From her perspective, and shared by other ACM activists, the inaccessibility of the Northeast Kingdom community was due to "cultic secrecy"; the collective nature of the abuse impeded their progress to get information. State laws regulating child abuse were based on the assumption that claims could be readily investigated through talking to teachers, neighbors, family doctors—a situation that does not apply to religious communes ("Officials Tell Why They Pulled Island Pond Raid," *Caledonian Record*, June 22, 1985:12).

Cloutier embarked on a personal crusade to save the children. She referred to her own home as a "safe house" and sought out defectors and invited them to stay with her. She taped their stories, kept files, and organized and dated everything she heard about the alleged abuse; she even invested around $5,000 of her own money in "fighting the cult" (Harrison, 1984).

Three days before the raid, Attorney General John Easton summoned seven Elders from the Northeast Kingdom Community into court, and took them before a family court judge one at a time and asked them to name the children they lived with (Summons, June 19, 1984, *In re C.C.*, Vermont District Court, Unit III). Each man offered the same response, "My conscience will not allow me to give this information," and was promptly jailed for contempt of court. Hours later, the 85-year-old Judge F. Ray Keyser released them, saying the court lacked authority to act unless the state produced specific names of people and specific evidence (Swantko, 1998).

Frustrated by the failure of court actions and thwarted by the Elders' unwillingness to cooperate, the opponents met with Governor Richard A. Snelling and Attorney General John Easton in Montpelier and convinced them to approve their plan to take all the children into custody simultaneously so that they could be examined for bruises and other signs of abuse. Suzanne Cloutier's files and the police investigators' reports were turned over to Phil White, the Orleans' County state attorney who was sworn in as a special assistant attorney general. Judge Wolchik issued a search warrant that was brought to Governor Snelling, and the raid was launched (Palmer, 1998:201–202).

Media

During Mattatall's custody suit, journalists from the Canadian Broadcasting Corporation and United Press International appeared in Island Pond and interviewed him for stories employing a condensed anticult framing of the story. Some reporters went on to solicit more defectors, taping angry testimonials and exchanging notes and allegations with Suzanne Cloutier. The *Cult Observer* was frequently quoted in news reports warning worried relatives of "some 200 pages of affidavits [that] tell us of systematic, frequent, and lengthy beatings of children by parents and church elders with wooden and iron rods and paddles, often drawing blood . . . stripped naked and beaten for several hours" (Braithwaite, 1984).

In one of the most lurid portraits of the Church, journalist Barbara Grizutti Harrison (1984:58) claimed in an article entitled "Children of the Cult," that "the cult is robbing children of their childhood," and compared the youth of Island Pond to the telekinetic extraterrestrial children of the science fiction film *Village of the Damned* (see also Harrison, 1993).

Several Vermont journalists assumed activist roles and were instrumental in bringing about the raid (Bilodeau, 1994:36). Sam Hemingway of the *Burlington Free Press* admitted that he "advocated for action in his columns and hoped the coverage would bring results." John Donnaly, also of the *Burlington Free Press,* claimed he had covered stories where he had "up to 18 subpoenas from lawyers for his notes."

The most active and outspoken opponent of the Island Pond Community among the news media was Chris Braithwaite, editor of the Vermont *Chronicle.* Braithwaite was approached by the Orleans County state's attorney, Phil White, and asked to look at Cloutier's files. He worked closely with state officials and resolved to "get involved as a citizen." He covered the Mattatall custody case, interviewed ex-members and outside relatives, and later admitted that he "contributed information that aided in getting a warrant to seize the children." A lawyer involved in a NEKCC custody battle phoned Braithwaite and asked for his files, which the reporter readily shared. Despite his partisan and activist role in discrediting the Church, Braithwaite (1983:1) claimed he was "objective enough to do the news analysis," even in the midst of the raid. Later, in 2000, interviewed by the *Burlington Free Press*, Braithwaite admitted that "I crossed the [journalistic] line . . . having covered it so extensively as a reporter, I had come to believe that the state bureaucracy was totally hamstrung. . . . There were terribly affecting stories about very young children who were being beaten way beyond the standards of the norm" (Bazilchuk, 2000).

Results of the Island Pond Raid

The Island Pond raid proved to be a mystifying disappointment for opponents' intent on rescuing the children. Some blamed Thomas L. Hayes, chief administrative judge for the Vermont courts, for its failure. On the evening before the raid, Judge Hayes pulled Judge Wolchik (who had issued the search warrant) off the case and assigned Judge Frank Mahady to preside over the emergency hearings, with himself and another judge as backup. Once the search warrant was served, state officials had to return to the court to show they had acted within their authority and to request permission to detain the children for another 72 hours. Deputy Attorney General Bristow and others complained that it was "unprecedented" to prevent Wolchik from reviewing the search warrant after it had been executed. White also argued that Hayes wanted a judge who would reject the state's action and deliberately chose Mahady, who had a reputation for being a strong civil libertarian.

But the search warrant was perplexingly vague, failing to list the names of the children the state sought to take into custody. The warrant identified the children only as "*In re: C.C.*" ("C.C." meaning "certain children"). The warrant provided only the addresses of the 19 buildings owned by the Northeast Kingdom Church and authorized the seizure of "any and all children under the age of 18 found herein." The sweeping nature of the warrant to authorize mass custodial detention by the state would prove to be problematic.

District Court Judge Mahady conducted some 40 detention hearings on the afternoon of the raid, and by 9:00 that evening he determined that the state had overreached and released all the children from state custody. He also offered the parents the opportunity to speak in court. After hearing descriptions of their day and profuse expressions of gratitude, the judge expressed regret at the state's action and told the parents, "I'm just doing my job."

In reviewing the evidence for the search warrant and the raid, Judge Mahady chided prosecutors and law enforcement for conducting a mass raid with little specific evidence and overly broad claims. The state was attempting to employ a "collective child abuse" theory to justify mass custodial detention (see Schreinert and Richardson, 2011).[8] Prosecutors had a simple assault case pending against one person but reasoned that all the children in the community were at risk because they lived in the same community. The judge roundly rejected the logic of the state's argument, calling the raid "pretextual" for the purpose of "investigative detention":

> Indeed, it is all too clear that the State's request for protective detention permitted by the statute upon appropriate showing was entirely pretextual. What the State really sought was investigative detention. In effect, each of the children was viewed as a piece of evidence. It was the State's admitted purpose to transport each of the 112 children to a special clinic where they were to be examined. . . Not only were the children to be treated as mere pieces of evidence; they were also to be held hostage to the ransom demand of information from the parents. (*In re Certain Children*, 1984, p.5)

Judge Mahady also warned in his written decision that the state's attempt to take such an extreme action such as mass custodial detention of children based on the accusation that the group was a "cult" would set a disturbing legal precedent:

> No person who cares the least about individual dignity would claim that such evidence would allow the State to round up all such children to be inspected for evidence of abuse. To select an unpopular neighborhood labelled a "cult" compounds the threat. If the Court were to allow the State action here, a Pandora's Box would be opened which would prove difficult, if not impossible, ever to close again. (*In re Certain Children*, 1984, p.26, n.1)

Judge Mahady further reprimanded Judge Wolchik for signing the search warrant. Wolchik later stated at a 1986 confirmation hearing, "I now believe that I relied on false or unreliable information" (Hoffman, 1984:4).

Wolchik also acknowledged that he had been "pressured by bad information" and conceded that he had made "a terrible mistake" ("Judge Who Ordered Raid Questions Info He Had," *Caledonian Record*, Feb. 11, 1987).

In the end, Judge Mahady pronounced the raid "a grossly unlawful scheme" and declared that the state's motive was not the issue: ". . . for even when the state acts in a noble cause, it must act lawfully" (Hoffman, 1984:3). He criticized the language of the original search warrant as follows: "(It is) more general in scope than any this court can find after careful research in the recorded literature. It may, indeed, set a modern record for generality" (Hoffman, 1984:3). In the weeks that followed the June 22, 1984 raid, Judge Frank Mahady issued five separate opinions that addressed the various legal issues raised by the state's action. He explained the legal reasons why social workers were not permitted to detain the children for examination; he rebuked the state for taking illegal photographs; he said belonging to a religious association was an unlawful basis to allege danger or harm; he pointed out the absence of specific facts in the allegations of harm which gave the state no jurisdiction in the matter; and he deemed the general warrant unlawful and without probable cause (*In re Certain Children*, 1984).

The Raids in Canada and California

A father in the Nova Scotia branch of the Twelve Tribes, Edward Dawson, was the primary target of several smaller-scale raids involving his son only three years after the Island Pond event. This situation resulted from a custody battle in which the estranged spouse contacted the Canadian anticult organization, Infosecte. Together they approached authorities riding the wave of negative publicity from the 1984 Island Pond raid to influence state officials to take similar actions.[9]

Edward Dawson was living in the 25-member community at Myrtle Tree Farm with his four-year-old son, Michael, when in 1987 five police cruisers filled with Royal Canadian Mounted Police (RCMP) arrived at the property accompanied by social workers who said they had a report of child abuse. They insisted they take Michael to the local hospital for an examination and seized the boy by force. Dawson was later served with a notice to appear in family court in Kentville, Nova Scotia. A signed affidavit by a doctor who examined Michael was produced in court but the court transcript revealed, under cross-examination, that the doctor had not written the affidavit substantiating Michael's need for protection. The doctor had "just trusted the social worker and signed it" after reading a negative news report (court transcript in *Family and Children Services of Kings County v. Dawson*, Sept. 1987, quoted in Swantko, 2004:187). After 44 days in which Edward Dawson was not allowed to see his son, the boy was returned to his father as a result of an appeals court decision. The Nova Scotia Court of Appeal admonished the social services agency for overreach. The state's action derived from inflated claims by a visitor to the Myrtle Tree Farm who had been influenced by ACM reports of alleged childrearing practices. The Nova Scotia social services attempted to build a case based on a file containing inflammatory news accounts culled from the Vermont raid and from opponents.

Although Michael's mother, Judy Seymour, had executed a written agreement giving Edward sole custody in 1986, she later came into contact with anticult activists associated with Infosecte in Montreal. According to Swantko, in the years between 1988 and 1992, "Michael's mother took advice from anticultist Michael Kropveld, head of *Infosecte Montreal*, a major Canadian ACM organization, who reinforced her fears about the Community and influenced her to seek custody" (2004:187). In 1992, the mother went to court without giving Edward Dawson notice of the hearing. She used an anticult witness who had never visited the Myrtle Tree Farm Community to testify that the group was a "cult" and presented a threat of abuse to her son. The judge in the hearing gave custody to the mother without the father having a chance to appear or present evidence. Upon learning of the court's ruling, Edward Dawson fled the Community with his son to avoid giving him over to the mother (Dawson, 1994).

On February 4, 1994, 15 FBI agents launched a raid on the communal house where Dawson and his son were living in California. They put Dawson in handcuffs, separated him from his son, who was handed over to his waiting mother, who immediately boarded a plane and took him to Canada. Dawson was given to the U.S. Marshals, who escorted him with chains around his waist and ankles. He appeared before a U.S. magistrate and was extradited to Canada. There he spent two months in jail and then was released on bond.

In September 1994 Dawson went to trial in Nova Scotia for abduction. However, Dawson was acquitted of the charge as the judge determined that he had lawful custody of his son during that time. The Crown appealed to the Supreme Court of Nova Scotia, winning a new trial. But again the state failed to prevail. In a two-week court trial in 1997 in which Edward Dawson represented himself, the court found that the mother,

her lawyer, and an anticult "expert" had plotted to exclude Edward from the 1992 hearing because of his religious association. Judge John Davidson ruled that Edward Dawson had been denied his rights because of his faith and that the court's exclusion of him on this basis was improper. The son, now 15 years old, testified in his father's defense. The Supreme Court acquitted Dawson of kidnapping his son, ending years of legal entanglements (Swantko, 2004:186–188).

Dawson (1994) writes of the involvement of Stephen North, whom he referred to as "Nova Scotia's one-man anticult movement" in his custody battle. Dawson's ex-partner, Judy Seymour, applied through her lawyer for an emergency ex parte hearing that took place between Seymour, the judge, and Stephen North, on March 10, 1994.[10] Seymour feared her son would disappear if the court order was delivered openly. North, the so-called cult expert, was a 38-year-old real estate appraiser whose younger brother had joined the Hare Krishnas in 1974. With the assistance of Professor Colin Macpherson at the University of Ottawa, he hired Ted Patrick to kidnap and deprogram his brother. Subsequently, North began to work for Patrick and assisted him in 30 deprogrammings (Dawson, 1994). North was seen by members "spying" on Myrtle Farm with binoculars. In the transcription of the hearing it became evident that North possessed no academic credentials, displayed poor grammar ("Sleep deprivation is very involved with these groups"), and offered a thoroughly discredited pop version of the theory of brainwashing (Palmer, 1999:164). North's role in the hearing was to convince the judge, as an expert on cults, that the NEKCC was dangerous and harmful to children.

Dawson also attributes much of his troubles to Nova Scotia's television and newsprint media, which recycled stories of child abuse in Vermont's Island Pond Community—charges that had been dropped for lack of evidence years ago. Dawson made the following observation in a written statement:

It is only in the last year that our community has come to understand that a network of so-called "cult" experts are committed to destroying groups who choose to live outside the mainstream. It has become abundantly clear that there is a deliberate plan at work to incite government agencies, police authorities, and courts into actions that are neither based on truth nor founded in law. Often the actions which we have been accused of are the very actions which have been used against us – kidnapping . . . separating families, and outright child abuse. (Dawson, 1994:81)

The Raids in France

The Twelve Tribes community in Sus, France, near the southern border with Spain, was targeted in three separate raids by the state. The first raid was in response to the reported death of a baby in their community. The second was an investigation spurred by complaints of ex-members who wanted the money they donated to the commune returned to them. The third was an unannounced foray by a group of deputies from the National Assembly who were writing a report on the well-being of children in France's *sectes*.

The History of the Tribe of Reuben

The Tribes first came to Europe from the United States in the early 1980s. Twenty-four German youth, friends since high school, set up a small community. After being evicted from their home, and encountering strict regulations concerning homeschooling, they left Germany and traveled around France, Spain, and Portugal in 1982. In 1983 they were invited by a woman named Teresa to come and live in the stately 18th-century chateau she had inherited in the foothills of the Pyrenees. They dubbed it "Tabitha's Place" after the first Frenchwoman who joined their company. They renovated the chateau, preserving its 18th-century style, and reside there today (Interview, Elder Ephraim, 2009). By 1995 the community at Sus had attracted around 200 members from all over Europe. Their daily meetings were conducted with assistance from simultaneous translators in French, Spanish, German, and English. At this time they were a thriving community, supported by hard work in several cottage industries. The men fashioned furniture and leather shoes and sandals. The women sewed cotton and linen clothing and baked whole-grain bread and croissants. These goods were sold at local marketplaces, at fairs, and in boutiques in Paris. Cordial relations with their neighbors and local authorities were cultivated. But their troubles first started once the French anticult organization ADFI (Association of the Defense of the Family and the Individual) became aware of the presence of this new *secte* in France (see Palmer, 2011b:111–127).

As the Twelve Tribes' leaders make clear in a short documentary film produced for outsiders, most if not all their problems arose out of ADFI's anticult agenda:

ADFI, with the CCMM (Center Against Mental Manipulation) are the principal and certainly the most active of the anti-*secte* associations in France. These two associations work to discover, de-nounce, and fight against all groups that appear to be *sects;* that is to say, all groups or movements that could be a menace to individuals or to society. Certainly, it is a noble cause to want to fight against criminals. But there is a problem, because if you read the litera-ture of associations like ADFI, and especially their criteria used to distinguish a *secte,* you will find that any movement tending to diverge from society's mainstream is considered to be a *secte,* there-fore dangerous and requiring strong opposition. Our community has suffered greatly from attacks by ADFI.[11]

The first ADFI-generated conflict began in 1985. Two sets of parents, worried about their adult children who had joined the Sus community, contacted ADFI for information on the *secte*. Mr. and Mrs. Topfer, from Berlin, eventually came to terms with their son's choice and soon began to visit their son and his family regularly (Swantko, 2004:193). But the other parents of adult members, such as the Neilsens from Los Angeles, went so far as to hire an American deprogrammer to kidnap their daughter, Kirsten. Indeed, Kirsten was twice the target of deprogrammings.

Ten years after her first abduction, Kirsten was living in Sus with the Tribe of Reuben, married to a German member, with two children. Her twin sister wrote to her asking for reconciliation, and flew to Sus to visit her. The two sisters walked down to the river that borders the property and sat down to talk. Kirsten's sister had begun to brush Kirsten's long blonde hair, when suddenly a deprogrammer jumped out of the brush, grabbed Kirsten, and with the assistance of Kirsten's brothers, forced her into the back seat of a car where her mother was waiting. The team of deprogrammers then drove off hurriedly (Neilsen, 2007). This event was witnessed by a leader, Johan Abraham, who jumped into a car with another member and gave chase down the winding wooded lanes—in vain.[12] But Kirsten proved again not to be dissuaded by the deprogram-mers and soon rejoined the Tribes. She currently resides with the Tribes in Germany with her husband and children.

In 1988 the first news article on the Twelve Tribes in France appeared and recounted the story of the 1984 raid on the Island Pond Community (Chaintrier, 1988). What the news report did *not* mention was the out-come of the raid; that the judge had in fact dismissed the case, deemed the raid "a grossly unconstitutional scheme," and ordered the state to return the children to their parents without submitting to inspections.

The Twelve Tribes' leaders wrote to ADFI and to the newspapers, send-ing relevant documents in an effort to correct the misinformation, but they received no response. The leaders also invited ADFI officials to visit the Community, but "they never responded . . . for that is part of their policy never to have any direct contact with the groups they are fighting against."[13] Following a period of silence from the media and ACM activ-ists, ADFI issued a bulletin in 1991 referring to Tabitha's Place as *"une secte inquiète,"* where children were "forbidden to play" and forced to work "six hours every morning." Again an invitation was extended to the media and to ADFI to visit the Community but their overtures were ignored.

After the 1994 Solar Temple mass suicides dominated the headlines in France, ADFI began to distribute flyers in the marketplaces where the community sold its products. ADFI also mailed letters to the mayors of the nearby villages, and soon the Tribe of Reuben was banned from selling its products. This resulted in a severe financial loss. In 1996 the National As-sembly published the official Guyard Report on *sectes* in France and Tabitha's Place was on the new blacklist. That same year, the police began to pay regu-lar visits to observe the children and examine their papers. According to the *Renseignements Généraux,* Tabitha's Place was a potentially suicidal *secte,* like the Solar Temple. A concurrent report in *Sud Ouest,* however, reported that the substitute of the *procureur de la République de Pau* in charge of minors, Frederique Loubet, had issued a positive report on the community, and said it was not necessary for the state to intervene (Aristiqui, 1996). Nonetheless, state officials working with ADFI utilized an array of measures to harass the group. Tabitha's Place found it necessary to hire a lawyer, Me Pierre Pe-castaing, after they received an inexplicable bill sent by the government for 585,000 FF in unpaid social taxes (Palmer, 2011b:118).[14]

By May 1996 ADFI officials began to organize meetings and press conferences in nearby towns to warn the local citizens about the danger-ous *secte* in their midst. An article titled *"Les élus sont inquiets"* described one of these meetings. Two representatives of the canton and the mayor of Sus told the news journalists that since the Guyard Report described Tabitha's Place as a "dangerous *secte,"* local citizens should be vigilant.[15]

In April, 1997, an infant died at Tabitha's Place. The parents, Michel and Dagmar Ginhoux, had joined the Tribe of Reuben less than a year earlier, bringing with them their four children. The youngest, ten-month-old Raphael, was afflicted with a congenital malformation—a hole in his heart that caused him to be undernourished. Dagmar was breastfeeding her baby constantly and giving him almond milk; her doctor had advised them to wait for the operation until Raphael gained weight, because he was still too weak to withstand it. The baby continued to lose weight, however, and became very weak. Then he caught a cold and died in his sleep.

The Ginhoux family was charged with "non-assistance to a person in danger"—a serious crime in France, where socialized medicine is considered one of their greatest triumphs. The same morning the chateau was visited by the *procureur* Jean-Pierre Dreno, 40 *gendarmes*, 12 doctors, and an interpreter. The prosecutor spoke to the press, saying "there are no signs of child abuse," but he also noted that "we have found with the death certificate . . . documents concerning commune-sanctioned bodily punishment. We suspect there was foul play, and this is why we are here today." The members of the commune were questioned by Judge Thierry Pons, and all the 80 children in the group were inspected by the doctors.[16] The parents were arrested and the three other children were removed from their custody and sent to live with relatives.

When the Ginhoux parents went to trial, they were found guilty of the deprivation of medical care and food, which led to the death of their infant. In his closing statement, the judge proclaimed, "Let this be a warning to *all* parents in *sectes*!"[17]

A second raid on Tabitha's Place took place in March 2008, when 30 police came early one morning and surrounded the chateau. They blocked the exits and arrested several of the leaders and held them for two days of questioning. This action was a response to complaints from a couple who had left the community and wanted the money they donated to the community returned. They claimed they had had to "escape" in the middle of the night; the media featured the ex-members' account without criticism or offering the Twelve Tribes leaders a chance to respond to the allegations. Community members complained of an ongoing police investigation, with helicopters flying overhead, hovering low, with the side doors open and cameras poking out.

A different kind of "raid" occurred on the morning of November 21, 2006. No policemen or social workers were present, just four deputies from the National Assembly who made a surprise visit to the chateau.[18] They were accompanied by an academic inspector, a national education inspector, a doctor, and a nurse.[19] These deputies were well-established figures in France's anticult movement and newly appointed commissioners involved in a special project.

In June 2006 the National Assembly had created a third parliamentary commission to investigate France's *secte* "problem." It was called the

Commission d'enquête parlementaire sur les sectes et les mineurs.[20] Its mission was to investigate the role of children in "sectarian movements," as well as their physical and psychological well-being. Msr. Brard, the secretary of this new commission, had already informed the media that children in *sectes* "are condemned to live in a closed vase [and] there exists in this case a veritable psychological threat due to an intellectual closing off" (Chaffanjon, 2008).

France's interministerial anticult mission, MIVILUDES, had published a report in April 27, 2006 that set the stage for this new initiative by claiming that "60,000 children grow up in the jungle of *sectes* and around 600 of these are victims of grave abuse, physical, psychological and often sexual."[21]

On November 11, 2006, *Le Parisien*'s headline ran: "*60,000 enfants victimes des sectes.*" Exactly ten days later, the four deputies staged a surprise visit to Tabitha's Place. These deputies had spent several days auditing ex-members and consulting anticult experts in the National Assembly, and this visit was a final effort to gather supporting data as the Commission neared its December 18, 2006 deadline. According to Shomer, an administrator in Tabitha's Place, "We welcomed them with smiles. They wanted to go to see the [18] children in school. . . . Later on, they had a private interview with one of our youth. . . . We asked them what their conclusions were. The deputy Georges Fenech said, "I must admit, I am pleasantly surprised. You greet us with a smile, you open your doors, we find the place clean; it is a nice environment. We must say the children look happy, they play. . . . But you cut them off from the world. They live in a bubble, with no TV, no internet access" (Interview, Elder Shomer, 2009).

The members found out later from journalists that the deputies had a press conference scheduled in Paris that evening at 6 p.m. to announce their findings. The morning papers announced the next day that the 18 children were "*coupés du monde à Tabitha's Place*" (cut off from the world in Tabitha's Place). Commission President Georges Fenech was quoted saying, "they don't go to school, don't go out, they don't play—and they have never even heard of Zinadine Zidane!" *Nice Matin* headlines blared, "18 children in the psychological hell of the *secte*" (*Nice Matin*, November 22, 2006). *Le Figaro* reported the deputies' discovery of 18 children "cut off from the world, forced to work and to adhere to the ideology of their parents" (Atchouel, 2006). Reuters warned, "children are easy prey for sects" ("Les enfants proies de plus et plus faciles pour les sectes," Reuters, December 19, 2006).

Jean-Pierre Brard was quoted as saying, "I found the children very sad. There is no echo of life outside. They are forced to work, their birthdays are not celebrated. There are no vaccinations despite legal obligations. They are taught a diabolical vision of outside society. These youth cannot be open to the outside world" ("Les enfants proies . . .," Reuters, December 19, 2006). The commissioners also noted, sadly, that Tabitha's children had never even heard of the Beatles . . . or any other "real singer" ("Les enfants proies . . . ," Reuters, December 19, 2006).

In the end, nothing came of this surprise inspection. There were no government initiatives launched to rescue children from the Twelve Tribes, despite an aggressive campaign by state officials and ACM actors in France.

The 2002 Raid in Germany

On October 7, 2002, a raid was launched against the Twelve Tribes community in Klosterzimmern in the state of Bavaria, where the group had settled in 2000.[22] The local county chief arrived at dawn with dozens of police and seized the Tribes' children and loaded them onto a waiting bus that drove them to the local high school in Deiningen, accompanied by their parents. The state's apparent intent was to force the parents to send their children to public school (homeschooling was illegal in Germany) after a long legal struggle with the Ministry of Education, and the parents had refused to pay the $60,000 in fines. The children sat in the bus for several hours while their parents conferred with the principal and teachers of the high school, and then returned home again. The media responded in a sympathetic manner and compared the raid to the deportation of Jewish families during the Nazi regime (Interview, Elder Ephraim, 2009).[23]

Seven Community men were taken to jail and served 14 days for refusal to pay the fines. One of the brothers drew a Star of David on his arm to protest the incarceration. However, according to one member we interviewed, Ephraim, "they (the guards) treated us well." The men were allowed to be paired in cells together and not mixed with the other inmates. They were also allowed time in the courtyard together.

The origins of this conflict can be traced to both "countercult" and anticult influences. Pastor Gert Glaser, who was an official Commissioner of Worldviews appointed by the Lutheran Church, sent inflammatory reports on the "Sekt" to government officials. In 1995 a few families moved to Oberbronnen, and the same pastor wrote letters to local officials. Michael Kropveldt of *Infosecte Montreal* was interviewed by the same journalist who initially had written, "All You Can See Is Happy Children," but then wrote a series on negative articles on the Community. Officials from ADFI, France's powerful anti-*secte* organization, were also quoted by journalists. These reports alerted social services, who sent a letter to family court, which began an investigation into the Community.

In 2003, the minister of education, who had refused to speak to Community leaders, suddenly resigned. The new minister of education exhibited a greater willingness to work with the Twelve Tribes and approached the Community about resolving the issue. Leaders met with the minister in Augsburg and the regional governor. Subsequently, Church leaders met regularly with the school board and developed a solution for the Community homeschool effort to be designated as a private school. However, in 2013, German police again raided the sect and seized 40 children based on "fresh allegations" of child abuse linked to the practice of corporal punishment, initiating a new round of hearings and litigation. As of this writing, many of the children still remain in foster homes, and the family courts' decisions are still pending or under appeal.[24]

Conclusion

These international raids targeting the children of the Twelve Tribes clearly show the influence of an oppositional network much like we have described and delineated in our model. Apostates and ex-members allied with anticult activists were primarily the catalysts that set into motion the mechanisms that led to the government raids. In each of the cases examined, a network of opponents and interest groups shared information, constructed a threatening portrait of the Tribes, and pressured authorities to "save the children" from alleged beatings, medical neglect, a separatist culture, and/or a sectarian education.

The first raid in Vermont was organized around a basic template, the Kelly Plan, that identified specific tasks and goals that comport with our model. In Kelly's own words, the plan was intended "to prevent its (the Church's) growth" and "assist in the dissolution of it" (*Investigative Proposal*, n.d., p.1). The Kelly Plan acknowledged the increasingly problematic strategy of deprogramming and marked a path forward for ACM activists. The new strategy shifted the focus to children and exploited state-mandated child protection laws. Combined with the stigma already associated with "cults," this strategy signaled a change in the social control paradigm and the dynamic of state control machinery to "combat cults"; first targeting the Twelve Tribes, and ultimately expanding to assail NRMs more generally.

It is not a coincidence that in each of the succeeding cases involving the Twelve Tribes, we find a similar pattern. In Nova Scotia, the raid developed from a custody battle in which the estranged spouse and ex-member contacted the Canadian anticult organization *Infosecte*. Together they approached authorities riding the wave of negative publicity from the 1984 Island Pond raid to influence state officials to take action. Indeed, social workers in Nova Scotia utilized a file provided by social services in Vermont that contained inflammatory and disparaging news articles (Swantko, 2004:187). The Canadian cult "expert," Stephen North, worked closely with American deprogrammer Ted Patrick and also relied on anticult literature supplied by CFF.

In France, the opposition came mainly from the anti-*secte* group ADFI. Provocative media reports from Island Pond were also recycled by opponents and used to inflate threats that the group allegedly posed to its members and others. The second raid was launched in response to complaints from a couple who had left the community and wanted the money they donated to the community returned. They claimed they had had to "escape" in the middle of the night; news reports featured the ex-members' account uncritically and neglected to obtain a response from Church leaders.

In Germany a Lutheran pastor and a Canadian cult expert from *Infosecte* were active in mounting a concerted oppositional campaign against the Twelve Tribes. Opponents distributed, and German news media printed, stories about the early, but unproven, allegations of child abuse at Island Pond. These were clearly efforts to inflame public fears and apprehensions about the suspect religious group among local residents. Though there was no evidence of child abuse in the Klosterzimmern community, authorities launched a government raid based on the group's homeschooling practices. Comments to the media by government officials seemed to infer that homeschooling was a form of child abuse by virtue of depriving the children of exposure to aspects of secular society. But the state's reaction—a raid—was grossly disproportionate to the violation or charge. Here we see yet another government overreach driven by an exaggerated perception of a threat.

The first raid on the Twelve Tribes is significant not only because it was the first to be predicated on collective child abuse but also because it marked a shift in the social control paradigm by organized opponents. Countermovement activists recognized and seized the opportunities opened up by the evolving structures of state-mandated child protection laws in advanced societies. As we previously argued, the expansion of child protection policies and laws (Best, 1990; Jenkins, 1998) made possible a unique and opportunistic means to assail unpopular religions; or at least those with families and young children (Carney, 1993; Palmer and Hardman, 1999a; Richardson, 1999; 2004a, 2004b). The communal groups such as the Twelve Tribes were particularly vulnerable to these attacks. As the Kelly Plan was developed, disseminated, and adopted by the larger ACM network, both here and abroad, we can see how this critical paradigm shift contributed to the dramatic increase in government raids in the following years.

4

The Family International/Children of God

Overview of Raids

THE FAMILY INTERNATIONAL, formerly the Children of God, has been a frequent target of government raids. We have documented at least twelve government raids on The Family International in seven different countries since 1978. The patterns in these raids are remarkably consistent. Indeed, we could have selected state raids from any of these countries, but here we focus on the Argentina raids. The government raids on The Family International in Australia (Palmer, 2011a; Richardson, 1999), France (Bainbridge, 2002:11–12; Melton, 1997; Report on Discrimination Against Spiritual and Therapeutical Minorities in France, 2000), Mexico, and Spain (Bainbridge, 2002:6–12; Melton, 1997) have been analyzed elsewhere.

The Family International (hereafter "The Family") was the target of two large raids in Argentina, in 1989 and 1993.[1] On October 27, 1989, a Family home in Buenos Aires was raided by a SWAT team consisting of more than 40 paramilitary police from three different units, dressed in black, armed with automatic weapons, and accompanied by a police helicopter. The raid team descended on the home and burst through the front door at 7 a.m. in a predawn operation (Bainbridge, 2002:9–10). Fifteen adults were arrested for corruption of minors and drug abuse[2] and 18 children were placed into state custody. The adults were held for approximately two weeks as the children were medically examined for evidence of child sexual and physical abuse. The children remained in their own homes with state social workers who moved in with them to conduct their investigation. The state raid was particularly disturbing to Family members because Argentina had only a few years earlier emerged from its infamous "Dirty War" in which the government, a military dictatorship, carried out a violent seven-year campaign against suspected political dissidents and subversives. Thousands of people were "disappeared" by police and the military, usually abducted in the middle of the night and taken to secret government detention centers where they were tortured and murdered (Donnelly, 1998:38–45).

The 1989 Argentinean raid on The Family was triggered by a custody dispute. A 41-year-old woman named Rosa Elena Noriega, who was estranged from her husband, decided to join The Family with her two children in early 1989. Her husband, Michael Hyland, did not object initially. According to eyewitnesses, he visited the home regularly and the children visited him as well. But Mr. Hyland was unemployed and did not have a stable livelihood for the children. Eventually, Mr. Hyland changed his mind and decided he wanted custody of his two children, a difficult challenge because the courts in Argentina usually favor the mother as custodial parent unless she is proven unfit. Mr. Hyland sought out a journalist, Alfredo Silleta, an outspoken anticult movement activist who was known for making lurid and sensationalist claims on television, warning viewers of the "dangers" and "proliferation of cults" in Argentina. According to Bainbridge (2002:10), Mr. Hyland "saw an advantage in allying himself with an anticult movement that had been trying to stir up public hostility toward The Family. The authorities were already suspicious of any form of unconventional religion, so they were quite ready to believe wild claims about child abuse." Silleta and Hyland approached authorities, alleging that the latter had witnessed abuse and neglect of minors at the Family's Buenos Aires home. The complaints prompted an investigation by police and led to the 1989 raid. 15 adults were arrested and held for 14 days; the women were placed in prison and held in solitary confinement for the first 7 days because there was insufficient room in the jail. Afterward, the women were taken back to their home and placed under house arrest. At the end of the 14 days, the court determined there was insufficient evidence to support the charges of child abuse and neglect. The adults were released and the children were returned to the custody of their parents.

The second state raid on The Family in Argentina occurred in 1993. At the time, it was the largest state action taken against The Family in any country. On September 1, approximately 200 heavily armed police stormed five Family homes simultaneously in Buenos Aires. Thirty adults were detained and 137 children were seized and placed into state custody (Honore, 1993; Nash, 1993). The children were sent to Garrigos, the children's juvenile institution in Argentina. Though the state was putatively "rescuing" the children from abuse, they were placed in a large warehouse not unlike a prison, with moldy, unpainted walls and poor bathroom facilities. According to members we interviewed, the facility was dark and dirty and some of the children contracted lice. The treatment of the adults was no better. The adults were sent to a maximum security prison where they were placed with violent criminals and HIV-positive inmates. The prison housing the adults, it was later learned, was the same facility used by the Argentinean government during the Dirty War. Authorities brought charges of racketeering, violating children's rights, and kidnapping against 21 adults.

In this second raid, the state's action was prompted by the activities of a former member, Abigail Berry, working with José María Baamonde, the founder and director of the Catholic anticult organization SPES (Servicio para el Esclarecimiento de las Sectas). Berry and Baamonde approached authorities with claims that the children in the sect were being sexually abused. Allegations were also made that Family leaders were holding children as "prisoners," and against the will of their parents (Honore, 1993). The 137 children seized in the raid were handed over the same day to court-appointed doctors for medical and psychological examinations. The morning after the raid, on September 2, Argentinean media broadcast "findings" of sexual abuse, child prostitution, and illegal drug trafficking. Newspapers quoted Roberto Marquevich, the federal judge in charge of the investigation and raid, saying that the raid had uncovered 268 children living in cramped quarters where many were underfed and poorly clothed. "We found these children in the virtual state of servitude" he said. "The evidence of abuse is very strong" (Nash, 1993). Judge Marquevich's statements about child abuse to the press proved to be premature and unsupported. There were only 137 children taken by the state (not 268), and doctors had not yet completed the examination of the children or reported their findings.

All 137 children were forced to undergo multiple psychological as well as painful and degrading medical/gynecological examinations. This time around, however, The Family launched a public campaign to condemn the government's actions, protesting in front of government buildings, holding press conferences, requesting letters of support from scholars and human rights activists, and visiting the courts. In the end, no forensic or medical evidence of abuse, sexual or otherwise, was found in any of the mandated tests. On December 13, 1993, the Federal Court of Appeals, San Martin, ruled in favor of The Family, declaring that the federal judge who ordered the raids, Judge Marquevich, did not have legal or jurisdictional authority in the case. The appellate court ordered the immediate release of all the adults, who by that time had been imprisoned for more than three months. The court also ordered that all the children be released from state custody and returned to their parents.

History and Background of The Family International

The Family International began in 1968 as a coffeehouse ministry in Huntington Beach, California, run by a former Christian and Missionary Alliance (CMA) minister and itinerant evangelist, David Brandt Berg. Berg and his wife and four teenage children set out to evangelize countercultural youth on the West Coast. His ministry was known as Teens for Christ and Berg encouraged his own children to take the lead in reaching out to hippies in the drug culture. As the Berg teens discarded their church clothes and dressed more in the style of the restive youth they were attempting to reach, they achieved surprising and dramatic success. The Light Club coffeehouse began to draw a packed crowd every night and became a central place for prayer, singing, and spiritual exploration. Berg framed the successful conversion of these hippie youth as the beginning of the "Jesus revolution." He drew principally from themes of the counterculture, modifying the antiestablishment narrative and condemning the corruption of the "System" (Chancellor, 2000:2). This message resonated with countercultural youth and by the spring of 1969 Berg had 50 committed disciples. Using the energy of these newly converted "rebels for Christ," Berg engineered a growing antisystem activism and rhetoric employing disruptive "church visitations" to protest and confront the lazy monopoly of established churches. In April of 1969, Berg took his band of disciples on the road, traveling in repainted old school buses to spread the message and recruit new converts. In the latter part of 1969, the group traveled the eastern seaboard of the United States, demonstrating in sackcloth and ashes warning society of impending doom and God's judgment on a corrupt America. The Children became known for this kind of performance ritual as they toured the country. A New Jersey newspaper gave the group their name, the "Children of God," which they heartily embraced, enjoying for at least a brief time some favorable attention and publicity.

By February 1970, the Children of God (COG) numbered nearly 200 as they settled on Fred Jordan's Soul Clinic Ranch in west Texas. In March, a second colony was established at Jordan's mission house in Los Angeles. During this period, Berg's vision for the movement began to emerge. He left the daily tasks of leadership to a small group of second-tier leaders, mostly his own children and their spouses, while he withdrew to pray and receive revelation. Berg's contact with and instruction to his disciples were now occurring exclusively through letters (Mo letters) and written in a form emulating the Apostle Paul's letters to the Christian churches in the New Testament. With Berg's revelations came a personal religious transformation in which he identified as a prophet and took on the name of Moses David. His disciples began calling him Father David, "Mo," or Dad. Another reason for Berg's withdrawal was that he began an intimate relationship with his secretary, Maria, whose real name was Karen Zerby. Berg announced to his most trusted leaders that he was taking Maria as his new wife. Berg claimed to be acting in response to a new revelation; God had instructed him that Maria was a symbol of the "New Church." But Berg's first wife found this arrangement unacceptable and terminated their marriage. Berg's unconventional views and beliefs about sex would be a trademark of the group as it moved forward.

In early 1971, Jordan had a falling out with Berg and the Children of God were evicted from both properties. Chancellor (2000:3) observes that this event actually "facilitated the spread of the movement." By forcing the Children to return to the road, they were more actively engaged in recruiting and outreach. By the end of the year, 69 colonies had been formed in the United States and Canada with almost 1,500 disciples (Chancellor, 2000:3). The expansion of the movement was facilitated further when in 1972 Moses David claimed he received a vision that America would suffer mass destruction in the near future and urged his followers to flee the country as soon as possible. He combined the doomsday message with one of hope declaring that the mass destruction was an opportunity to fulfill the missionary task of reaching the world for Jesus. By the end of 1972, COG colonies had been created in Western Europe, Central America, Australia, New Zealand, Japan, and India. The antiestablishment element of the group's message sparked less controversy in these countries "where denunciation of American society as corrupt was hardly revolutionary" (Chancellor, 2000:5).

Initially, the Children of God were met with little animosity in these other countries. By December 1973, the movement had grown to 180 colonies and over 2,200 members in 23 countries on six continents. At the same time, the movement had less than 300 members left in the United States. In Western Europe, Moses David shifted the emphasis to distributing their literature ("litnessing"), music and performing, and establishing discos or "Poor Boy Clubs" to reach new converts. Thereafter, Wallis (1982:80) observes, "a movement which had seen its purpose as proselytizing among the alienated of society, the hippies and drop-outs, would begin to direct itself more to the respectable and influential." During this time, the prophet also began a radical experiment using female disciples to attract and convert males through sexual encounters. The experiment was called Flirty Fishing or "FFing." It was carried out in Tenerife in the Canary Islands for more than two years and was made known only to a few trusted disciples. In 1976, Moses David revealed the Flirty Fishing principles in a series of Mo letters and encouraged members to embrace the "new ministry." The revelation of Flirty Fishing combined with the shift to target older and more established members of society for recruitment created some discontent among both leaders and members.

In 1975, Moses David reorganized the leadership structure, taking control away from some top leaders, including some members of his own family. The new structure was referred to as the "Chain of Cooperation" and instituted to decentralize much of the intermediate level of control while enhancing the authority of the prophet. But the new structure continued to inhibit his plans and "the extensive administrative apparatus was becoming both a substantial expense and a potential alternative base of power" (Wallis, 1982:91). Serious problems were becoming apparent by 1977 as a number of leaders in the Chain of Cooperation openly questioned Father David's prophetic claims and some high-level leaders were accused of abusive and authoritarian behavior.

In January 1978, Moses David instituted the "Re-organization Nationalization Revolution" (RNR), abolishing the Children of God as an organization and renaming the movement "The Family of Love." Colonies were downsized and now called "homes." The Family homes were instructed to elect leaders who would be directly responsible to the prophet. According to The Family's own documents, over a hundred leaders were dismissed and approximately 1,800 full-time members left, a third of the total membership at that time (Worldwide Services, 1995:25). Key figures were among the COG leaders dismissed, including David's oldest daughter, Deborah; her husband, Jethro; Timothy Concerned, a highly trusted disciple; and Rachel, a prominent officer and executor of his policy and one of his spiritual wives. Wallis and others suggest that Berg felt compelled to institute the RNR not only to fend off a power struggle, but also to liberate the group from conservative Christian beliefs about sexuality in order to facilitate FFing. In the years just before the RNR and for a period of time ending in 1983, the movement underwent an exploration of sexual freedom, sometimes referred to among members as the "love bomb." In one publication ("Happy Rebirthday!—RNR Rules, ML #663, 2/78), Father David wrote "No permission needed for sex!—If legal and with mutual consent. No Servants need to be consulted. Fire away!" His teachings and writings about the Law of Love (against love there is no law) encouraged freedom from traditional practices and mores. Sexual liaisons between members of the homes and in cross-home fellowships became common practices (Chancellor, 2000:11). The sexual liberation extended to experiments in childrearing. While there were no specific instructions or guidelines regarding contact between adults and children by Father David, the Mo letters could be interpreted to expand in this direction and some leaders were aware of its occurrence. This period of sexual experimentation would brand the group for years to come and give ample ammunition to opponents and detractors.

November 1978 marked the year of the Jonestown mass suicides in Guyana, where over 900 people took their lives. Between December 1978 and January 1979, Father David published a series of Mo letters instructing The Family to go underground in anticipation of a hostile wave of anticult activity. He further decentralized homes and encouraged smaller and more mobile units. Wallis states that "from 1979, they were encouraged to adopt a life of constant movement, in caravans and campers, traveling virtually the whole time, even though this might mean leaving behind 'fish,' friends and peripheral members" (1982:102).

By the end of 1980, the movement had grown to over 7,800 members. Because of the decentralization effort, the number of homes increased to 1,973 from approximately 600 just two years earlier. Father David also began to stress the use of technology during this period, including radio programming and videos. The Family launched an international radio ministry, Music with Meaning (MWM), which became quite successful; it was carried by nearly 100 stations worldwide by December. Within three years, the radio programs were produced in five languages and broadcast on over 1,300 radio stations (Worldwide Services, 1995). The Family was also experimenting with videotaping. In 1981, the first "dance videos" were produced. David encouraged women in the MWM ministry to send him videos of female members dancing topless or draped in sheer veils ("Nudes Can Be Beautiful," ML#1006, 3/81), as well as romantic/erotic scenes of couples. Some of the dance videos included underage girls, and were seized by opponents as child pornography. The practice was soon abandoned as some of these videos found their way into the possession of the anticult movement, fueling claims against The Family. The videos would play an important role in future government raids as these state actions were premised largely on child abuse allegations.

Beginning in the early 1980s, the spread of AIDS and the discovery that some Family members had contracted sexually transmitted diseases (STDs) halted the open sexuality of The Family. In March 1983, Father David instructed members to cease sexual sharing between homes and at area fellowships; sexual relationships were limited strictly to persons residing in the same homes and FFing was severely curtailed ("Ban the Bomb," ML#1434, 3/83). This marked a significant shift in Family practices regarding sexuality. By 1987, sexual contact with outsiders was banned in all cases except "close and well-known friends," effectively abolishing the practice of Flirty Fishing (Chancellor, 2000:22).

The unconventional sexual practices of The Family were also exacerbated by the aging of the membership, the growth of families with children, and the expanding second generation. By late 1985, The Family already had 600 preteens and teens (Worldwide Services, 1995:62). Teen Training Camps (TTCs) were established to educate and prepare young people for missions. But results from a questionnaire distributed at a TTC in Mexico revealed some troubling sexual relations between teens and adults. A memo by Maria was issued prohibiting sexual contact between adults and minors ("Liberty or Stumbling Block?" 8/86). Subsequent Mo letters, however, suggest that the problem was not vanquished. As late as 1989, the issue continued to be addressed with strong warnings: "Just because we promote sex and we believe God made it and that it's his wonderful creation doesn't mean that it's always good under every circumstance. . . . it's definitely not good when it involves a minor!" ("Flirty Little Teens, Beware!" ML#2590, 10/89).

At the close of the decade of the eighties, the transnational anticult movement began to catch up with The Family in foreign countries. Shifting its rhetorical strategy from brainwashing claims to allegations of child abuse gave anticult activists and ex-members added legal tools to pressure state officials in foreign countries to act. A key incident occurred in 1988 when ex-member Vivian Shillander, accompanied by a television crew from ABC's 20/20 program and two private detectives, traveled to Thailand to reclaim custody of her four older children. Ms. Shillander voluntarily left The Family and her husband, Richard, a few years earlier, taking her youngest child with her. At the time of her departure she signed a power of attorney at the U.S. embassy in Bangkok authorizing her husband to retain custody of their other four children. But after coming into contact with anticult movement actors in the United States in 1988, Ms. Shillander changed her mind. Allied with cultural opponents and a complicit media, she made a surprise visit to Thailand and forcefully abducted her children, delivering custody papers to her husband signed by a judge in South Dakota. The custody papers had no legal authority in Thailand. But in the glare of the cameras and the chaos, the bewildered husband was blindsided and at a loss to know how to respond. It was later learned that the U.S. State Department aided Vivian and her accomplices, issuing special passports for the children and helping to spirit them out of the country before the husband could alert Thai authorities (Worldwide Services, 1995:72).

The Shillander incident in Thailand was a portent of things to come. Over the next several years, international ACM activists allied with ex-members to level charges of child abuse and sexual molestation against The Family in France, Spain, Australia, and Argentina. Moses David recognized the threat, issuing a warning to Family homes to prepare for a wave of legal battles and encouraging them to obtain attorneys (It's Time to Fight!" #2464, 8/88).

Organized Opposition

In the late 1980s, public pressure on government authorities in Argentina to take action against new religions began to mount. Alfredo Silleta, a journalist for the newspaper *Faustino*, was a vocal advocate and active campaigner against *las sectas*.[3] Silleta engaged in a highly public crusade warning the public of the "dangers of cults" in Argentina. He was seen on television frequently as well. In 1984 he wrote and published a book inveighing against the Unification Church, entitled *La Secta Moon: Como Destruir la Democracia* (*The Moon Cult: How It Is Destroying Democracy*). In 1986 Silleta published a second book entitled *Las Sectas Invaden la Argentina* (*The Cults Invade Argentina*), calling for an urgent response to the incursion of fundamentalist sects and cults. In 1990 he established the Foundation for the Study of Sects (FAPES [La Fundacion Argentina para el Estudio des las Sectas]), an anticult organization. And in 1992 he published a third book entitled *Sectas: Cuando el Paraiso es un Inferno* (*Cults: When Paradise Is an Inferno*). Silletta's crusade was a reaction to an influx of new religious groups after the arrival of democracy in Argentina in 1983. According to one news report, nearly 3,000 new religious groups had registered with the National Register of Religion by 1990 (Rosas, 1994). Some of these included charismatic and Pentecostal sects, "electronic churches" from North America, evangelical/fundamentalist churches, Jehovah's Witnesses, Brazilian spiritualist groups, and others which were becoming "a growing source of competition for traditional Catholicism" (Rosas, 1994; see also Baamonde, 1994). As such, Silletta's campaign reflected the increased concerns of a historically Catholic population and entrenched Church authorities. The perceived threat of invading Protestant sects and cults was not received well by the dominant religious powers. Fears of a religious siege were fanned by reports estimating that "up to 6 of every 10 people adhere to 'charismatic' Christian sects in certain districts of the Greater Buenos metropolitan area" (Rosas, 1994).

According to one scholar (Frigerio, 1993), there were two stages of development in the sect controversy in Argentina. The first stage (1985–1988) was marked by reactions focused on sects funded from outside the country that were believed to be taking advantage of the needs and the ignorance of the people. Its ultimate purpose was to collect money. Much of the criticism was driven by religious professionals. In the second stage (1989–1992), there was a change in the idea of "sect"; there suddenly appeared anticult groups who were comprised not merely of detached specialists but activists in the debate. Almost all of the incidents were due to allegations of anticultists. In this stage the idea of "brainwashing" appears, based on the North American anticult model. The latter stage corresponds with the period in which the two government raids on The Family occurred.

Silleta's influence was also acknowledged by legislators in the Argentine Parliament who drafted a bill in 1991 designed to limit the registration of new religions. Legislators Alberto Piotti and Antonio Cafiero introduced a bill highlighting the dangers of *las sectas*, stating that they "utilize techniques of mind control and coercive persuasion so that all their members lose their identity and become dependent on the group, abandoning their family and social surroundings" (Blanco, 1994a:45). Cafiero requested that a special parliamentary commission be established to monitor "the growing expansion of these movements (which) obliges the State to take precautions and develop the preventative mechanisms within our power, as other nations of the world have already done, to protect the juridical and moral tenets that constitute our very foundation" (Blanco, 1994a:45).

In this political climate, The Family was an easy target for reactionary forces. The Children of God had been banned previously in Argentina in 1978 under the previous regime for being a "promiscuous group." Members of The Family argued that ban did not apply because the COG had been disbanded years earlier, along with their more libertine sexual practices. But Silletta and pro-Catholic forces easily revived fears of sexual deviance in attacks on The Family. When Silletta was approached by the estranged husband of Rosa Elena Noriega, Michael Hyland, the crusading journalist recognized an opportunity to press state agents for action. Silletta and Hyland collaborated to devise a strategy that would compel the state to act on behalf of opponents' interests. Hyland supplied the claims; he said had witnessed abuse and neglect of minors during visits to The Family home where his children resided. Silletta marshaled apostate accounts and tropes about the Children of God from previous years in Argentina. Silletta and Hyland then confronted legal authorities in Buenos Aires to report these claims and demand enforcement of child protection laws. As a result of their efforts, an investigation was conducted and a raid plan was developed by police.

The state raid on The Family home was launched on October 27, just before dawn. More than 40 paramilitary police, accompanied by a helicopter, stormed the residence in a surprise attack. Members we interviewed reported being terrified, shocked, and confused by the bellicose show of force. The raid team brandished automatic weapons against unarmed members and children. Police stormed through the house tossing tables, chairs, and furniture aside, pulling out drawers, and dumping the contents on the floor. One member we spoke with said the police took their literature and outreach products and threw them on the front lawn. The raid team also was also trailed by a group of reporters. It was not clear if Silletta was one of the reporters on the scene. One police officer apparently attempted to plant cocaine in a kitchen drawer but the effort was foiled because the presence of the reporters compromised the crime scene (Bainbridge, 2002:10). The contrived drug charge was later thrown out by the court.

Fifteen adults were arrested and charged with child abuse. Eighteen children were placed in state custody but remained in the home for interrogation by social workers and medical examinations. One of the young adolescent girls examined was Abigail Berry. Berry told investigators she had never been abused and the examinations failed to turn up any such evidence regarding Berry or any of the children. But Berry would later leave The Family and become a key apostate assisting anticult movement activists and other opponents in efforts that propelled the second raid on the group in Argentina in 1993.

The adult women were arrested and placed in solitary confinement and not allowed to make phone calls to attorneys or to their families. One of the women arrested, Claire Borowick (1994), later described the abysmal conditions of the lockup; they were housed in narrow concrete cells, roughly three feet by six feet, completely dark, with no window or light. The women were offered no blankets and no food for three days; the water was contaminated and undrinkable, causing Claire to become sick. Untreated and ignored, she was forced to vomit into a cardboard box. Claire and the other women arrested were sometimes forced to scream for hours before a guard would come and take them to the toilet. After a period of a week, the women were released from solitary confinement and allowed to return home under house arrest. The men were held for two weeks before the court determined there was insufficient evidence to support the charges and released them.

The federal court hearing the case in Buenos Aires declared it did not have proper jurisdiction and transferred the case to a criminal tribune. The following year the case was officially closed, but the court did so provisionally stating that if new evidence was filed it could be reopened.

Apostates

The role of apostates in the first raid appears to be indirect, through testimonies or recorded statements made and reproduced in anticult literature and passed on to opponents and Argentine authorities. But there was a direct link between the two raids with regard to one ex-member, Abigail Berry. Between the time of the first and second raids, Abigail turned 18 and left The Family. She apparently ran away with a lawyer whom she met while out witnessing with her mother. The lawyer took her to meet José María Baamonde, the founder and director of SPES.[4] Baamonde was a psychology professor who also taught courses in Catholic culture at Pontificia Universidad Católica Argentina. Baamonde had developed a program for cult members similar to deprogramming, but he called it "reinsertion" (back into society). After a year, Ms. Berry's relationship with the lawyer dissolved but her association with Baamonde became stronger. She fled to the United States with the help of Baamonde and during that time made contact with American ACM organizations. The following year, in 1993, Abigail returned to Argentina prepared to lodge claims against her former group. Baamonde accompanied Abigail to see Judge Roberto Marquevich's First Secretary in Buenos Aires with the intent to make allegations of sexual abuse by members of The Family. Ms. Berry also recruited another former member, Cherish Lloyd, and together they paid a visit to the U.S. embassy in Buenos Aires. Apparently, the embassy had already been contacted by anticult activists in the United States and had in its possession documents about three American children purportedly held by The Family against the wishes of the parents. It was later learned that the embassy collaborated with Argentinean authorities in the 1993 raid. U.S. Ambassador James Cheek refused to comment on the incident at the time, citing the privacy rights of the Americans involved.

In conjunction with these efforts, another ex-member, Edward Priebe, was flown to Argentina by American anticult activists to deliver stolen "dance videos" from a storage facility in the Philippines that was leased by The Family. Preibe and another ex-member, Daniel Welsh, broke into the storage facility in 1992 and stole numerous video and audio master recordings and sent them to fellow anticultists in the United States. Although the practice of making dance videos had been abandoned a decade earlier, it was used to bolster child abuse allegations against the group and provide additional rationale for the government raid. After the raid, Argentine authorities released copies of a dance video to the media and portions were shown on television networks all across North and South America and Europe (Chancellor, 2000:28–29).

The clearest picture of the role of apostates is provided by court documents, particularly the final decision of the federal court of San Martin, handed down in December 1993. The court's ruling refers to the statements of five ex-members—Berry, Priebe, Richard Dupuy, Miriam Faith Padilla, and Oscar Lauce—on multiple occasions throughout the document. The allegations brought by these ex-members include rape, child abuse, corruption and concealment of minors, promotion and facilitation of prostitution, fraud, servitude, illegal deprivation of liberty, and forgery of documents (Federal Appeals Court of San Martin, 1993:13). None of these charges were supported by evidence and were roundly rejected by the federal court.

The testimonies of Dupuy, Padilla, and Priebe were rejected by the court on evidentiary matters because their statements of wrongdoing by The

Family 1) occurred 10 to 15 years earlier or 2) because the former members said they were not witness to any crimes committed *in Argentina*. Essentially, the apostates delivered stories of years past and in different countries. Members of The Family conceded past mistakes and argued that they had abandoned the sexual practices upon which the most serious charges were based.

The charges made by Abigail Berry, on the other hand, were leveled by someone who lived in the country, so the court gave substantial consideration and space to her claims. Ms. Berry offered a litany of charges; she claimed that the children in the group were sexually indoctrinated, had access to explicit sexual material, could observe with other children how female members practiced FFing, and were expected to turn over any money obtained in the process (Federal Appeals Court of San Martin, 1993:14). She also claimed she was raped twice, once by a leader on the orders of another home leader. Ms. Berry said she suffered a serious infection due to the lack of prevention on the part of members of the sect and had to go in the hospital to have a fallopian tube removed. She alleged that the home leader, Claire Borowick, used a power of attorney to have Ms. Berry removed from the hospital prematurely, causing the stitches of an incision to become infected, which resulted in her readmission to the same hospital. Ms. Berry complained that sect members were told not to consult a physician when they became sick, just to pray. Finally, Ms. Berry claimed that the group maintained a kind of prisoner-like security system in which "dogs, alarms, light reflectors and guards with rubber bullets and sticks" prevented people from escaping (p.15).

It is hard to overstate the court's repudiation and criticism of Ms. Berry's testimony, so we quote extensively from the verdict in order to convey the manner and tone of the court's ruling.

The testimony of Abigail Julia Berry is especially full of . . . flaws. In this same case, she previously made statements which were totally contrary to what she affirms today. Her declarations were also discredited by specific references made in regard to her psychopathic misconduct and proclivity to lie which are contained in sworn affidavits made by her brother and her mother. Berry's testimony was refuted by Sara Bechard Salem, whom Berry had named as a passive victim of a rape, as when Salem was questioned on this point, she replied "I have never been sexually abused." Lastly, parts of Berry's very declarations totally contradict what one can accurately deduce from reality. . . .

We also studied her account of the neglect which she suffered due to a serious infection she contracted because of the alleged opposition on the part of the sect to seek medical treatment and administer medicine—the request of such assistance by members was considered to be a lack of faith in God—a policy which resulted in the deaths of many members. However, without regard as to what purpose it would serve to totally clarify this subject, the timely request of Miss Berry's medical records from Cetrangolo Hospital, where she was attended, revealed her sinister story did not concur with the absence of sickness that all of the medical examinations recorded on pages 1378/1575 indicate; also the accusation of multiple deaths caused by a lack of medical care is absurd when placed next to the specific recommendation made to the "Home Shepherding Teamwork" in a document retained with the file of materials provided by the Intelligence Department of the Buenos Aires Police: "Pray and look for private clinics and good doctors who can attend us, especially our pregnant mothers and children."

And finally, nothing remotely resembling the affirmed presence of armed guards and dogs guarding the properties of the group—to prevent members from escaping—was found by the officials who conducted the raids on the group's houses. Nor were any basements or underground passages found, through which—according to Berry—group members would escape should they notice the police had arrived. (Federal Appeals Court of San Martin, 1993:40–41)

The Federal Court's assessment of the credibility of the apostates' declarations was revealing. The court found that "the testimonies given by the ex-members of the sect" offered "very little evidence" of the charges. The judges concluded that "this could be due to the fact that they were brought by people who have never had direct contact with the communities," as in the cases of Dupuy, Padilla, and Priebe. Or that because their accounts covered past incidents but not contemporary cases, and the medical reports showed no evidence of sexual abuse. "Or lastly, because their own declarations reveal an apparent eagerness to exaggerate vague memories of past events, to the point of having resorted to accounts which have been proven beyond doubt to be false and have therefore significantly weakened their declarations in terms of their credibility" (Federal Appeals Court of San Martin, 1993:40).

ACM Organizations and Actors

The most significant ACM figures in the two Argentine raids were unques-
tionably Alfredo Silletta and José María Baamonde. Silletta enjoyed multiple venues from which to assail the sect. He was a journalist at a major
newspaper, he founded the anticult organization FAPES, and he authored
three anticult books: *The Moon Cult* (Silletta, 1984), *The Cults Invade Argentina* (Siletta, 1988), and *Cults: When Paradise Is an Inferno* (Silletta, 1992).
Accordingly, he was widely treated by the media as an expert on *las sectas*
(Frigerio, 1993). Silletta played a role in both state raids on The Family. We
have already described Siletta's activities in the 1989 raid. But our research
reveals that Silletta was also involved in the second raid as well. According
to Claire Borowick, a leader in one of the Family homes raided:

> A police officer mentioned . . . that all the policemen, psychologists,
> and others involved in the operation had been required to attend
> seminars by anticult activists José María Baamonde and Alfredo
> Silletta, where they were propagandized with wild and untrue tales
> about The Family. Because of this, the police were so paranoid that
> we might hypnotize them that they wouldn't look us in the eyes!
> (Borowick, 1994:1)

Borowick suggests that Silletta and Baamonde worked as a tandem of "cult
experts" for Argentine authorities, presenting a unified anticult model in
the training of police in preparation for the raid. Silletta and Baamonde
had direct involvement in and collaboration with apostates in pressuring
state authorities. As such, legal officials should have seen this as a conflict of interest with regard to their state-sponsored training seminars for
police in preparation for the second raid in 1993. Silletta and Baamonde
were hardly objective, dispassionate experts or scholars on the subject
("Myth of Dangerous Sects," *La Maga*, 1994).

The 1993 raid clearly features Baamonde as the key ACM catalyst. Baa-
mondo was aligned with Abigail Berry and the other ex-members (Lloyd,
Priebe, Dupuy, Padilla, Lauce) involved in the case. Baamonde, through
SPES, also collaborated with the U.S.-based Cult Awareness Network to
press for legal actions against The Family in Argentina and to gather information for a book (Spina, 1994). Indeed, only a month after the raid, Baamonde published a sensational paperback, *The Family: The True Story of the
Children of God*. The book was dedicated to Abigail Berry and one chapter

in the book described Berry's own experiences growing up in The Family, including alleged abuse and medical neglect. Baamonde also had contacts with state officials that proved vital. It was Baamonde who arranged a meeting between Ms. Berry and Judge Roberto Marquevich's staff. It is likely that Baamonde's contacts with high-ranking state officials paved the way for the mandated anticult seminars to police prior to the raid.

Social workers and psychologists involved in the raid also attended anticult training seminars conducted by SPES or were linked to SPES in other ways. According to members we interviewed, the state's social workers on the case "had all been through a course on 'cults' offered by SPES. So they saw us as brainwashed, dehumanized cultists".[5] According to one news report, a source of evidence used by Judge Marquevich to order the group's temporary imprisonment was a report filed by Dr. Maria Lourdes Molina, of the National Council of Minors and Family. The choice of Dr. Molina was noteworthy because "by soliciting the services of this professional, the judge rejected the forensic medical corps which is normally used by the Judicial Branch" (Spina, 1994:46). The news report further observed that Dr. Molina was "a member and financial supporter of the SPES Foundation" (Spina, 1994:46). Not surprisingly, in Dr. Molina's report submitted to Judge Marquevich, she found all the members of the sect to be "paranoid fanatics with restrained aggression tendencies." Judge Marquevich relied on this assessment to justify holding the adults in pre-trial detention.

Baamonde also had links to the international anticult network which proved to be important. He acknowledged to Argentine news reporters only months after the raid that he maintained ties with the American-based Cult Awareness Network, attended their conventions, and "exchanged information about sects" (Spina, 1994:46). His connections to the international anticult movement first became apparent with the publication a 1991 book entitled *Cults and Brainwashing*. Baamonde also held a teaching position at the Universidad San Pablo-CEU, a private Catholic university in Madrid from which he often espoused his views on "destructive cults." His views served to support the work of the Spanish anticult organizations Pro-Juventud and CROAS (Center di Recuperatcion, Orientacion, Y Asistancia Afectados por las Sectas). Pro-Juventud and CROAS teamed with the Barcelona Catholic Bishops Conference to play a critical role in pressuring authorities in Spain to launch a raid on The Family in Barcelona in 1990 (Chancellor, 2000:28). It is no coincidence that Baamonde and SPES were deeply linked to both the Catholic Church and the two Spanish anticult organizations (Frigerio, 1993; Soneira, 1993). As an advisor to the Argentine Catholic bishops, Baamonde likely served a similar role for the Barcelona bishops. The 1992 raid in Barcelona produced Family literature and documents that later surfaced in the Argentine raids, connecting ACM activists in the two countries (Shupe and Darnell, 2006). Apparently, materials seized in the Barcelona raid were passed to Argentine police officials and studied before the latter's raid operations in Buenos Aires.

By the time of the second Argentine raid in 1993, The Family had some idea of what to expect. Government raids on The Family were occurring in a wave of orchestrated attacks in France, Spain, and Australia. Reports from these raided communities revealed carefully coordinated, joint actions by an expanding international network of anticult organizations as they followed similar patterns and charges. The Cult Awareness Network (CAN) and the American Family Foundation (AFF) in the United States, the Association for the Defense of the Family and the Individual (ADFI) and the Center Against Mental Manipulation (CCMM) in France, Pro-Juventud and CROAS in Spain, Infosect in Canada, Family Action Information Resource (FAIR) in England, and other organizations were coordinating activities, sharing resources, constructing unified rationales and concepts, and building international coalitions and alliances in a transnational mobilization against NRMs (Shupe and Darnell, 2006:195–233).

State Agents

On December 13, 1993, the federal appeals court ruled in favor of The Family. The court ordered the immediate release of all 21 adults and ordered that the children be released back into the custody of their parents. In the ruling, the federal court rejected the charges of child abuse brought against The Family and reproved Judge Marquevich for his actions in the case. In one part of the ruling, Judge Marquevich was reprimanded by the court for using "state coercion" on children to determine paternity.

> The Judge used compulsory means to determine whether or not the five children of the spouses (of the Robb-Rambur family) were in fact children of this father, or rather the fruit of adulterous relations of the wife. This intermission into the private life of persons, to the point of using state coercion in order to investigate action

which, at the most, constitutes merely criticizable moral behavior, borders on abuse of authority not to mention ignorance of clear legal regulations. (Federal Appeals Court of San Martin, 1993:7)

In another part of the court's ruling, the raid operation itself was criticized for being authorized under the pretext of finding missing minors presumably being held against the will of their parents. The court found this elaborate operation, which did not produce the minors, "ostentatious" and "disturbing." The court noted lack of proper procedure in the raid, allowing journalists to accompany police into the homes and compromising evidence. It also expressed concern about the "ideological" comments of the Judge and District Attorney.

It is also disturbing to note the absolute lack of discretion employed during the police operation, as it was carried out without the indispensable reserve which should govern the entrance into private property where there is a large number of children (Law 20,056), taking into account the wide journalistic coverage from the moment of entrance into the homes, which irreparably affected the legally protected environment[Also disturbing is the distortion of information detected in the comments of undeniable ideological content, or pre-judgements regarding the procedural destiny of the prosecuted attributed to the Judge and the District Attorney of the case] (Federal Appeals Court of San Martin, 1993:22)

In another part of the transcript, the court castigated Marquevich for "secret proceedings" and not allowing the defense to have their own experts examine the children.

Paradoxically, the defense was faced with the insurmountable barrier of unnecessary secret proceedings and the participation of experts for the defense was not facilitated when the minors lodged at official institutes were examined. Furthermore, any other psychodiagnotistc evaluation not carried out by an expert and his/her team belonging to the Board of Minors and Families was excluded. (Federal Appeals Court of San Martin, 1993:22)

Judge Torres concluded this section of the ruling as follows: "This manner of proceeding represents an arbitrary use of penal power, by removing the case from the framework of rationality inherent in the fundamental right of the defense to a proper trial, which is precisely the guarantee which enables all the others to operate" (p.23). He then proceeded to compare the raid ordered by Judge Marquevich to a witch hunt.

> This panorama, as will be seen, not only weakened the very "corpus probatorium" itself—without benefitting in any way the investigation—but also puts into evidence an anachronistic continuation of the most severe inquisitive system, one in which people were summoned only to confess their sins, being considered "witches" or "heretics." (Federal Appeals Court ofSan Martin, 1993:23)

Marquevich was a devout Catholic and his religious views uniquely informed his own version of anticult ideology. One Family member, whose name was John, described how Judge Marquevich interrogated him by shouting, "Do you believe in the Virgin Mary? Do you recognize the Pope?" John said the interrogation "sounded like the Holy Inquisition" (Borowick, 1994:3).

Other state agents allied with opponents include legislators Alberto Piotti and Antonio Cafiero who introduced at least three bills in the Argentine Parliament in 1991 attempting to severely limit the rights of sects. The bills contained easily identifiable anticult language and framing, asserting that sects "utilize techniques of mind control and coercive persuasion" (Blanco, 1994a), among other things. Cafiero proposed establishing a special Parliamentary Commission "to study the origin, operation and financing of the sects." Piotti and Cafiero worked closely with Silleta and FAPES; one news story reported that the legislative proposal by Cafiero "was drawn up by Aflredo Silleta" (Blanco, 1994b).

State officials at the U.S. Embassy in Buenos Aires also became part of the allied opposition. Two of the young girls we interviewed, who were taken into custody after the raid, spoke of collusion between the U.S. consulate and the Cult Awareness Network.

> The American Consul came to our jail and offered to get us kids out. But the deal was, "forget your parents! They are cultists and child abusers; they'll be in jail for the next twenty years." We would have to renounce our parents and our religion and hook up

with our grandparents. The Brazilian Consulate was much more helpful. They called my mom after I had been sick for four days with strep throat and they sent for a doctor. The Mexican Consulate was also helpful to our Mexican members. But the American Consulate always told us, "Only if you leave the group will you get free!"

We received a copy of the case against us—a huge stack of papers—and we found letters from the American Embassy to the judge with the names and addresses of our parents and plans to remove the kids from the homes. There was a letter from a lawyer with CAN. We could see this was a conspiracy to deprive us of civil rights. (Palmer, 1994)

According to news reports, while Family members were incarcerated, Judge Marquevich received a memo from the Minister of Foreign Relations and Religious Worship. The memo requested the judge advise "the Embassy of the United States, which had been visited by the legal representative of the Cult Awareness Network, lawyer David Barden, in Washington D.C." regarding the possibility of relatives in America taking custody of the detained children (Spina, 1994:46).

Media

Opponents of The Family skillfully used the media to make their cases. Alfredo Silleta, of course, was a journalist and a reporter for *Faustino* who had an influential platform to lodge and press claims. In a special issue of *La Maga* on "dangerous sects," the report confirms Silleta was a major force in the Argentine anticult movement (Riera and Blanco, 1994a). The issue features a full-page interview with Silleta and highlights the work of his Foundation for the Study of Sects. The article also features a photo of Silleta with Michael Langone, the Director of the American Family Foundation, a key anticult organization in the United States. In the same issue of *La Maga*, the country's other leading cult expert, José María Baamonde, is profiled (Blanco, 1994b). Baamonde's newest book, *Questions and Answers about Cults*, is also reviewed. The piece notes that the prologue to the book was written by Cardinal Antonio Quarracino and it observes that the Archbishop of Buenos Aires makes "regular contributions" to Baamonde and his organization, SPES.

It is significant that journalists and news reporters were actually permitted to accompany the SWAT team into Family homes on the morning of the 1993 raid. This type of arrangement is highly unusual, and the police chief who headed the raid, Juan Carlos Rebollo, was later charged with violations regarding the protection of minors by allowing the press to photograph the children. These protections in Argentine law are designed to ensure privacy and avoid the exploitation of minors "for sensationalistic purpose." The photos taken were widely circulated on the news wires and appeared in newspapers all over the world. Photos of confused- and disoriented-looking children being aroused out of bunk beds by police were accompanied by headlines such as "Sex Cult Enslaved 268 Children" (Nash, 1993).

The sensationalism of the "sex cult" story was broadcast internationally without much restraint by new organizations or patience for evidence and fact-finding. Newspapers ran stories of adult-child sexual relations, prostitution, kidnapping, racketeering, and even snippets of drug use, satanic rituals, weapons, and other dicey themes (Honore, 1993; Nash, 1993). But media interest in other stories—legal irregularities, the state's degrading treatment of the children in custody, the prejudicial statements of the judge and prosecutor, the wild and questionable allegations by apostates—was negligible. Only after the case was resolved and the federal appellate court found no evidence to support the criminal charges three months later did mainstream media begin to ask more penetrating questions. Even then, the culmination of this tragic incident did not get anywhere near the same media attention as the initial story, creating what Wright has called the "front-end/back-end disproportionality" problem (1993:107). The front end of the story created a barrage of publicity while the back end was relatively ignored, leaving most people with the impression that the charges at the front end were true. This pattern has had an alarming impact on public opinion and public policy toward new or minority religions.

Claims

We address some of the major claims by opponents here, leaving aside the "dangerous cult" claim which, by now, should be self-evident to the reader. In keeping with our theoretical argument, we contend that claims-making by the oppositional alliance involved exaggeration and deviance amplification in order to gain the attention of authorities and compel them to take action against the targeted religious group. The opponents' claims are weighed against the findings of fact by the federal court.

Child Abuse and Sexual Abuse

The principal claims driving the oppositional coalition centered on child abuse. Both raids involved the state detention of the sect's children, followed by extensive medical and psychological examinations. The claims by Abigail Berry were quite specific, including the claim that she was raped twice by leaders in the home where she resided. She also claimed that her friend Sara Bechard Salem was raped. She made allegations that children were sexually indoctrinated and had access to explicit sexual material, that she observed with other children how female members practiced FFing, and that these female members were expected to turn over any money obtained in the process. These charges in concert with the dance videos turned over to authorities by Edward Priebe and the allegations of other apostates were offered as evidence of child sexual exploitation and the promotion of a promiscuous culture that involved children. But the court determined that the dance videos, the practice of FFing, and other controversial practices had been abandoned years earlier. The court also noted that some alleged incidents described by ex-members did not take place in Argentina. Most importantly, the examinations of the children by medical staff and social workers found no evidence of sexual or physical child abuse (Federal Appeals Court of San Martin, 1993:35–44).

Brainwashing

Key ACM activists Alfredo Silleta and José María Baamonde relied almost exclusively on the North American anticult model of "brainwashing" and "thought reform" in their books, in their training sessions conducted for police, psychologists, and social workers, and in media interviews (Frigerio, 1993; Riera and Blanco, 1994a, 1994b). Silleta helped legislators draft at least three bills in the Argentine Parliament in 1991 attempting to severely limit the rights of sects. Silleta cited legendary ACM activist Margaret Singer in his defense of the brainwashing model (Riera and Blanco, 1994b) and openly talked about his ties to the American Family Foundation and Michael Langone (Riera and Blanco, 1994a). The allegations of brainwashing also appeared in court documents; Judge Marquevich, the district attorney, cult experts including Baamonde, and apostates all promoted "brainwashing" as an explanation for membership in The Family.

But the Federal Court rejected this assertion, stating "this theory is not backed up by the scientific community and nowadays is considered as a metaphor to disqualify religious movements considered deviant" (Federal Appeals Court of San Martin, 1993:52).

Servitude/Illegal Deprivation of Liberty/Kidnapping

Some of the claims involved holding children involuntarily and "against the will of their parents" (Honore, 1993). Abigail Berry and Cherish Lloyd collaborated with CAN to press the U.S. Embassy to take action to protect three American children purportedly held by the sect against the wishes of their parents. Some apostates also provided accounts of extended hours of forced labor and servitude. One day after the 1993 raid, Judge Marquevich held a press conference and announced that "we found these children in the virtual state of servitude" (Nash, 1993). These claims helped to shape the narrative of "captivity" (Wright, 1998) that is common in anticult framing and popular in media coverage. However, the federal court of appeals found no evidence for the charges of servitude and deprivation of liberty. The court declared that "no commission of an act of slavery on the part of any person in any of its forms had been proven" (p.48). The court also found the "deprivation" claim was predicated on a "methodology which has no scientific basis, along with a collection of dubious data" (p.48). The raid also failed to turn up the three American children (Houmans) identified by apostates, CAN, and the U.S. embassy who purportedly were being held against their will by The Family.

Prison-Like Conditions/Torture

According to court documents, Berry claimed that in the Family home where she resided, members were like prisoners trapped in a heavily guarded compound reinforced by "dogs, alarms, light reflectors and guards with rubber bullets and sticks" (Federal Appeals Court of San Martin, 1993:15). She also claimed that in the event of a raid, members were "trained to escape on hearing the signal, with the exception of a small group of persons who know what to say," presumably to authorities (p.15). In addition, Berry alleged that there were tunnels and underground passages in the basements of the homes by which members could escape (pp.40–41). Berry stated that children in the sect were separated from their parents at the age of 12, and "physical punishment and torture were normal." The teenagers who exhibited behavioral problems "were threatened with being sent to reformatory camps" (pp.14–15). But the federal court found "nothing remotely resembling the affirmed presence of armed guards and dogs guarding the properties of the group—preventing members from escaping . . . Nor were there any basements or underground passages" (pp.40–41). The claims of torture and physical punishment were not supported by any material evidence or by the extensive medical examinations on the children by state officials.

Conclusion

The two large raids in Argentina targeting The Family provide support for our model. Oppositional coalitions formed in both cases to lodge claims, embellish facts, proclaim a "threat" to society and traditional values, enjoin selected state actors, and press for action. In the first raid, an alliance was formed between an estranged spouse of a NRM member and an anticult activist. Oppositional alliances usually involve one or more apostates. But we see from this case that the alliance was effective even in the absence of ex-members' direct participation. Mr. Hyland, in anticipation of a custody battle he was not likely to win, became the functional equivalent of the disgruntled apostate. He claimed to be an eyewitness to acts of abuse. Hyland teamed up with Alfredo Silleta, the journalist, author, and outspoken critic of las sectas, and together they approached government authorities. The political climate was inhospitable to new sects or religions by the late 1980s (Rosas, 1994), increasing the likelihood that the complaint would prompt some type of state response.

The 1993 raid features all the aspects of our theoretical model. Apostates were a critical part of the oppositional alliance. Abigail Berry, the chief apostate, allied with José María Baamonde, the most prominent anticult activist in Argentina at the time. Baamonde put her in contact with CAN in the United States and together they helped to organize the campaign against The Family in Argentina. Berry joined with other ex-members—Cherish Lloyd, Edward Priebe, Richard Dupuy, Miriam Faith Padilla, and Oscar Lauce—to supply the charges of child and sexual abuse. Baamonde accompanied Berry to see Judge Marquevich's staff. He augmented the abuse claims of apostates with claims of brainwashing and prostitution. Baamonde also collaborated with Silleta to provide anticult training for police, psychologists, and social workers involved in the raid, evidently with the imprimatur of Judge Marquevich. This coalition of opponents, including officials with the U.S. embassy, served as a catalyst for the state's mobilization against The Family International in Argentina.

5

The Branch Davidians

Overview of Raid

ON FEBRUARY 28, 1993, the U.S. Bureau of Alcohol, Tobacco and Firearms
(ATF) executed a massive raid on a small Seventh Day Adventist sect, the
Branch Davidians, outside Waco, Texas. The federal raid on the Branch
Davidian community was the "largest enforcement effort ever mounted
by ATF and one of the largest in the history of law enforcement" (U.S. Department of Treasury, 1993:134). The raid was undertaken with the intent
to serve search and arrest warrants for its leader, David Koresh. The warrants asserted that Koresh and others had violated federal firearms laws,
possessing illegal weapons and explosives.[1] The raid plan developed by the
ATF was largely fashioned as a paramilitary operation. In preparation for
the raid, an ATF Special Response Team (SRT) comprised of 80 federal
agents trained for three days at the nearby Ft. Hood military base in close-
quarters combat and rapid-response maneuvers. Assistance in planning
and rehearsal of a proposed "takedown" by the U.S. Army's Special Forces
Rapid Support Unit also included company-level tactical C2, medical evac-
uation training (techniques for treating battlefield injuries), and assistance
with Range and MOUT (Military Operation on Urban Terrain) sites. Counterdrug National Guard units conducted surveillance overflights of Mount
Carmel in UC-26 aircraft equipped with infrared cameras (FLIR) in the
days and weeks before the raid. On February 28, the day of the raid, Texas
National Guard supplied ten counterdrug personnel and three helicopters:
two OH-58s and one UH-60 Blackhawk. ATF requested and obtained military support for the raid by laying claim to a drug-exception statute to the
Posse Comitatus law, alleging to the U.S. Department of Defense that the
Branch Davidians were involved in drug manufacturing. Evidence later

showed that ATF agents knowingly made false claims of a "drug nexus" to DOD to secure military assistance (*Investigation into the Activities of Federal Law Enforcement toward the Branch Davidians*, 1996:45–46; Wright, 2005).

The ATF raid plan was named "Operation Trojan Horse." At approximately 9:00 a.m. on February 28, the federal agents arrived at the Davidian property in two cattle cars covered by tarps and pulled by pickup trucks. But the ploy to hide the agents in the cattle cars proved to be futile since the element of surprise had already been lost. A local Waco TV news reporter and cameraman had inadvertently tipped off the Davidians by asking a mail carrier for directions to the sect property. The mail carrier, David Jones, was a Branch Davidian. Jones returned to Mount Carmel a few minutes later and alerted Koresh of the impending raid. An undercover ATF agent, Robert Rodriguez, was present with Koresh at the time. Rodriguez quickly withdrew to inform the ATF raid commanders at the surveillance house across the road from Mount Carmel that the raid had been compromised. However, ATF raid commanders Phil Chojnacki and Charles Sarabyn, knowing that the element of surprise was lost, decided to accelerate rather than abandon the raid. The decision proved to be disastrous.

As soon as the SRT arrived at Mount Carmel, two ATF agents assigned to the "dog team" filed out of the cattle cars and shot four dogs housed in a dog pen in front of the main building. These were the first shots fired and it was likely the catalyst that triggered a shootout between sect members and federal agents. After a lengthy gun battle, four ATF agents and six Branch Davidians were mortally wounded. In the wake of the shootout, the FBI's Hostage Rescue Team (HRT) was called to Waco to take control of the incident which had now become a standoff. The standoff continued for 51 days as negotiators attempted to persuade the barricaded sect members to surrender. On the 51st day, April 19, the FBI launched a dangerous CS assault on the Davidian settlement, which culminated in a deadly fire, killing 76 men, women, and children. The final death toll for the federal siege stood at 86, including the 10 people killed in the initial raid and shootout.

A congressional investigation later condemned the federal raid as an egregious overreach and openly criticized the manner in which the operation was carried out (*Investigation into the Activities of Federal Law Enforcement Agencies toward the Branch Davidians*, 1996). The report first called into question the ATF investigation upon which the raid was predicated. It cited the investigation as "grossly incompetent" and unprofessional, containing "an incredible number of false statements." It also concluded that the raid was unnecessary because Koresh could have been arrested on numerous occasions when he left Mount Carmel.

David Koresh could have been arrested outside the Davidian compound. The ATF chose not to arrest Koresh outside the Davidian residence and instead were determined to use a dynamic entry approach. In making this decision ATF agents exercised extremely poor judgment, made erroneous assumptions, and ignored the foreseeable perils of their course of action. (p.3)

The government report condemned the ATF's planning of a military-style raid fully two months before the surveillance and infiltration operation even began. In other words, the ATF had determined to execute a paramilitary raid long before they had obtained any actionable intelligence from the surveillance and undercover operations. Thus, the strategy of an assault or "dynamic entry" appears to be the only option ever considered by the ATF, or what the Treasury Department report later condemned as "steps taken along what seemed to be a preordained road" (U.S. Department of Treasury, 1993:174).

Among other things the Bureau mismanaged, the ATF's principal investigator on the case, Davy Aguilera, refused an invitation by David Koresh to come to Mount Carmel and inspect the Davidian's weapons a few months before the raid. Instead, the ATF elected to conduct a massive and high-risk paramilitary raid, eschewing a more modest and less dangerous course of action in serving the warrants. A partial explanation for this puzzling series of decisions by ATF was later provided in the Department of Treasury investigation. According to the Treasury report, ATF officials concluded that a request for Koresh to surrender would be pointless because the sect leader would never cooperate. The report noted that these conclusions were based largely on "intelligence obtained . . . from former cult members" (U.S. Department of Treasury, 1993:141). Apparently, ATF officials failed to consider the possibility that the accounts of some disgruntled ex-members might be distorted and unreliable.

History and Background of the Branch Davidians

The Branch Davidians emerged in Los Angeles in 1929 as a movement calling for reform within the Seventh Day Adventist (SDA) Church. The movement was founded by Victor Houteff, a member of the Los Angeles church who claimed to have received a revelation which he referred to as the "Shepherd's Rod," based on a passage from the book of Micah in the Old Testament (Pitts, 1995). Houteff began teaching his revelation in the Sabbath School and asserting that Seventh Day Adventist doctrines and beliefs were deficient. He assumed a prophetic role and inspired a small following of dissidents. Local church leaders were quick to isolate Houteff and charge him with heresy, threatening to disfellowship any church members who listened to his teachings. Houteff eventually left Los Angeles and moved his flock in 1935 to a site a few miles outside Waco, Texas, and established the Davidian Seventh Day Adventists (DSDA). He named the property Mount Carmel and over the next few years the group proceeded to build their own houses, establish their own schools, and create a complex, communal organization with various cottage industries (printing and publishing Davidian literature, food and lumber production farming) and even their own currency. By 1940, the Mount Carmel community had grown to almost 70 members.

Following the war years, the Davidians launched an aggressive evangelistic campaign, sending out missionaries to Adventist churches in Australia, England, India, the West Indies, and Canada. These efforts paid dividends as new converts were brought to Mount Carmel. But the community faced a temporary setback when Houteff died unexpectedly in 1955. Houteff's wife, Florence, subsequently became entangled in a power struggle with a prominent couple, Ben and Lois Roden, for control of the Davidians. In an effort to assert her claim as the next prophet-leader, Florence announced that she had received a revelation that Christ would return on April 22, 1959. Florence Houteff's authority as the Davidian leader hinged on the millennial expectation she created. The Mount Carmel community drew considerable energy from the anticipated event and it helped to solidify her reign for the next four years. However, when the date came and went, the period of expectation turned into great disappointment. Florence was exiled to California and the Rodens assumed leadership of the Davidians.

Ben Roden adopted the name "Branch" to both mark the new era of leadership and establish his own vision based on inspiration from a biblical passage in Isaiah ("and a branch shall grow out of his roots"). Roden claimed the mantle of prophet and wrote numerous tracts calling the Adventist church to reform. But as Pitts (1995:35) observes, "the new Mt. Carmel offered little in the way of structural changes." Moreover, the Davidians struggled in the 1960s and 1970s to overcome the loss of members after the failed prophecy. Roden showed little interest in growing the community through evangelism or recruitment of new members. By 1977, Ben's health was declining rapidly and his wife, Lois, began to ascend to power. That same year Lois claimed to receive a vision that she was visited by an angel who represented the Holy Spirit Mother. Ben died in 1978 and their son George began to insist on his divine appointment as the true prophet. But Lois Roden was able to leverage the apparition to legitimize her prophetic status in the Davidian community, leading to a bitter struggle between mother and son (Bromley and Silver, 1995:52).

In 1981, a young man named Vernon Wayne Howell joined the community and impressed the prophetess with his consuming hunger for the faith. He demonstrated an extraordinary ability to memorize whole passages in the Bible and showed promise as a teacher. Lois Roden groomed young Howell as the next prophet, much to the chagrin of George. As Lois's health deteriorated, George Roden and Vernon Howell became locked in a battle over leadership of the group. In 1985, the control of Mount Carmel passed to George after he used monopolized mailing lists to manipulate the outcome. Roden promptly purged the community of Howell loyalists at gunpoint. Howell's flock settled in Palestine, Texas. The followers of Roden dwindled over the next year even as Howell's popularity and support grew. In 1988, Howell and his flock managed to retake Mount Carmel by paying the $68,000 in back taxes owed to the county that Roden had failed to pay.

Howell began to rebuild the community and restore its financial base. The Davidians started several new businesses, including an automobile repair and renovation enterprise, Mag Bag, and a gun and gun accessory business. The latter was operated through wholesale purchases of guns and hunting-related products (military-style food pouches, camouflage jackets and pants, backpacks, knives, ammunition, hand-grenade casings mounted on plaques) and sold retail at gun shows. Howell also expanded the membership base by converting a new cohort of adherents who were attracted to his teachings. He launched strategic recruitment campaigns in the United States and abroad targeting current and former SDA members and doubling the size of the group within a few years.

In 1990, after receiving a revelation of his own while in Israel, Howell returned to Mount Carmel and changed his name to David Koresh. Koresh is Hebrew for "Cyrus," the Persian king who defeated the Babylonians and freed the Israelites from captivity. Howell took the name of David claiming to be the spiritual descendent of the biblical King David.

As a result of his revelation, Koresh assumed the role of a messianic figure appointed to carry out an Endtime mission. Koresh believed that it was his mission to open the "Seven Seals" cryptically described in the Book of Revelation as the prelude to the final cleansing of the earth and the return of Christ (Tabor, 1995). Part of this vision also entailed the implementation of the "House of David," a divine mandate to beget 24 children by select women in the group who would become spiritual wives. The children were to be raised strictly in the confines of the community and eventually serve as the 24 elders spoken of in the Book of Revelation who would rule during the Millennium. This practice led to the development of a polygamous family headed by Koresh and explains some of the allegations of sexual misconduct (Ellison and Bartkowski, 1995). By the time the ATF laid siege to Mount Carmel in 1993, Koresh had already fathered 17 children by eight different women. At least one of the women, Michelle Jones, was only 13 when she became a spiritual wife and bore three children for Koresh. Though still illegal under Texas law, Michelle (who was also the younger sister of Koresh's legal wife Rachel) had the consent of her parents, Perry and Mary Belle Jones, to spiritually wed the prophet. It was this unconventional sexual and marital practice at Mount Carmel as much as the firearms allegations that provoked the actions of opponents.

Organized Opposition

The Branch Davidian incident offers compelling evidence to support our model linking government raids to organized oppositional networks. Prior to the federal raid in 1993, the Branch Davidian sect was virtually unknown to the larger public outside of the Waco area. Within the immediate region, the separatist community was seen largely as a benign group seeking seclusion and solitude but posing no threat to its members, to its neighbors, or to residents of the city (Pitts, 1995). The Davidians had a longstanding presence in Waco covering more than 50 years. Faculty and graduate students at nearby Baylor University had on occasions studied the group, conducting ethnographic research, collecting interviews with members and leaders, and producing oral memoirs that are archived in the university's renowned Institute for Oral History (Green, 1989; Pitts, 1995; Saether, 1975). But in the early 1990s, a dramatic shift developed in the branding of the Davidians as a "dangerous cult" requiring urgent attention and drastic state intervention. What changed?

In a period of approximately 24 months leading up to the 1993 raid, apostates, concerned relatives, anticult activists, and journalists worked together to press claims, express grievances, lobby government officials, and mobilize resources against the sect. As a result of this concerted moral campaign, organized opponents were able to broaden disputes and successfully persuade key state actors and agents to move on the targeted group. To that end, opponents and countermovement activists effectively co-opted the state into acting on behalf of the special interests groups seeking to dismantle the sect. In the following sections, we identify and describe the roles played by each of these groups and explain how their coordinated claims worked to build momentum for federal actions.

Apostates

Several former Branch Davidians were critical to the claims-making activities that facilitated and helped to mobilize official reaction. None was more important than Marc Breault, a self-described "right-hand man" of Koresh who defected in 1989. Breault became a primary source for the ATF investigation following a 1992 incident in which a UPS package delivered to the Davidians broke open revealing empty pineapple grenade shells. Breault alleged that Koresh and the Davidians were "stockpiling weapons" in preparation for a possible conflict with the government, among other things. Indeed, Breault had been deeply engaged in a crusade against Koresh for more than a year when he was contacted by the ATF investigator assigned to the case, Davy Aguilera. Breault provides a detailed description of these "cultbusting" activities in a highly sensationalized paperback released only a month after the deadly FBI siege and fire (Breault and King, 1993). Coauthor Martin King describes Breault's mission as follows: "Breault became a cultbuster. He committed his life to righting the wrongs of the past and, more importantly, to putting a stop to Vernon Howell before he could destroy many more lives" (Breault and King, 1993:208).

Breault boasts of a number of activities in his campaign to dissolve the group, including 1) flying to Waco to alert police; 2) hiring a private investigator to gather damaging information on the sect; 3) approaching authorities in LaVerne, California, alleging statutory rape of young female adherents; 4) working with TV news reporter (and coauthor) Martin King on an exposé of Koresh; 5) contacting a sect member's estranged husband and alleging sexual abuse of his daughter; 6) serving as a witness in the custody battle over the sect member's daughter; and 7) enlisting a congressman to bring pressure on law enforcement to act against the Davidians (Wright, 1995a:84).

Breault also recruited and organized other ex-members and families of sect members. By his own account, he was actively engaged in persuading Australian Davidians, particularly the Gent family, to defect. He put ex-members and families of sect members in touch with each other and with anticult movement organizations and activists in the United States. Breault adopted an explicit ACM framing of the Davidians to cast them as a "dangerous cult" to news reporters and authorities, constructing a crudely exaggerated narrative. Breault claimed, among other things, that Koresh might kill children, using them in "human sacrifice"; that he employed "brainwashing" to control members; and that he might murder ex-members and even order mass suicide (Hall, 1995:212–213).

These claims were baseless but may be attributed to the frustration that Breault experienced after failing to get authorities to act after an initial round of allegations. By his own admission, Breault's early pleas and claims made to U.S. officials "fell on deaf ears" (Breault and King, 1993:13). Facing the prospect of state inaction, Breault began escalating claims about threats posed by Koresh and the Davidians, engaging in a determined exercise of "deviance amplification." As the work of Stuart Hall et al. (1978) and others has shown, deviance amplification occurs when claims-makers engaged in moral campaigns feel they have to push the putative threat upward across a threshold of legal tolerance in order to force official reaction. The embellished threat is then later rationalized by claimants as "necessary" because authorities "weren't doing anything." In effect, a strategy of *threat escalation* is undertaken by claims-makers with the intent to mobilize the machinery of state control.

In December 1992, only ten weeks before the federal raid on the Branch Davidians, Breault's contacts with ATF and other federal agencies agents intensified. Breault states in his book that he received "almost daily phone calls . . . (from) senior officials of the United States Government, which included the BATF, the FBI, Congress, the State Department, and the Texas Rangers" (Breault and King, 1993:295). Breault was also the source of the false claim by the ATF to the Defense Department that the Davidians were manufacturing drugs.

Breault's book is instructive in chronicling the organization and mobilization of apostates, famiiles of members, journalists, anticultists, and government officials. These facts are corroborated by other sources as well. Davidian survivor David Thibodeau describes Breault's pivotal role in spearheading an organized campaign against Koresh in his own autobiographical account (Thibodeau and Whiteson, 1999:119–122). Other Davidian survivors we interviewed—Catherine Matteson, Rita Riddle, Clive Doyle, Wally Kennett, Sheila Martin—have provided similar observations. These sentiments may be summarized in the words of life-long Davidian Catherine Matteson: "Well, that man (Breault) started it all. He started all our problems. He started them about three years before we had any contact with the government in any way . . . And I personally hold him totally responsible, because without him then we never would have had any problems" (Interview with Catherine Matteson, 1993).

Other key apostates included the Gent and Bunds families. As early as April 1992, Australian Bruce Gent, father of Nicole Gent (one of Koresh's plural wives), complained that government authorities would take notice "only when there's a pile of bodies." "They're going to go in," Gent said, "and find them and then it's all over. It'll be another Jonestown" (Breault and King, 1993:249). In the same month, the U.S. consulate in Australia sent a cable to Washington warning of a possible "mass suicide" at Mount Carmel and citing "local informants" as its source. The consulate also described in the cable how "informants . . . believe that (Koresh) has armed himself with guns and ammunition in order to effect a shoot-out with authorities if they attempt to enter the cult's Waco property" (U.S. Department of Treasury, 1993:D4). The information passed along by the consulate closely mirrored Gent's complaints and indeed, Breault indicates in his book that Gent was one of the "local informants" (p.249). Relying on Breault as a confidant and advisor, King conducted and filmed interviews with the Australian apostates and relatives in December 1991, suggesting that the formation of an organized opposition was well underway.

The Bunds family was an integral part of the organized opposition, especially David and Debby Bunds. David and Debbie Bunds were expelled from Mount Carmel in June 1990 for violating dietary rules. Soon after the expulsion, Breault contacted David Bunds and successfully converted him to "cultbusting" (Breault and King, 1993:218). David Bunds later persuaded his sister Robyn to defect and encouraged her to contact Breault. Robyn was reportedly one of Koresh's wives and bore him a child. Allegations lodged against Koresh by Robyn in LaVerne, California, centered on a custody battle for the child. The claims of child abuse made against Koresh appear to have begun at this juncture. Debbie Bunds was interviewed by the ATF investigator and her testimony appears in the ATF affidavit accompanying the search warrant regarding weapons violations. According to the affidavit, Ms. Bunds "observed Howell shooting a machinegun behind the main structure of the compound" in 1989 (U.S. District Court, 1993:10). But as the congressional report later observed, Ms. Bunds was not qualified to judge the difference between the rapid fire of a legal semiautomatic rifle and that of a fully automatic rifle, thus throwing her testimony into question. Jeannine Bunds, a former member and Robyn's mother, told agent Aguilera that Koresh had mentioned something to her about a "hit list." Aguilera's affidavit also cites David Bunds' recollection of a conversation he had with his father, Donald, who said he was armed and prepared to die for Koresh. Robyn and Marc Bunds (Robyn's half-brother) were quoted extensively in the initial days following the ATF raid in news stories, and the Bunds family is generally credited by Breault as being instrumental in the federal investigation (Breault and King, 1993:297).

In sum, the ill-fated tactical plan developed by the ATF was based in large part on the accounts of apostates and opponents. Incredibly, investigators and planners never seemed to question the integrity or reliability of their sources. As the 1993 Treasury report notes, ATF officials treated these accounts as factual without considering whether the former members had "individual biases, or if they had an ax to grind" (U.S. Department of Treasury, 1993:129–130). Both the warrants and the ATF raid plan drew substantially from information supplied by organized opponents who were engaged in a countermovement campaign against the sect and its leader.

ACM Organizations and Actors

The involvement of anticult movement organizations and actors in the Branch Davidian case can be traced to the deprogramming of a former member, David Block, by ACM activist and deprogrammer Rick Ross in the summer of 1992. According to a sworn affidavit, Block was deprogrammed in the home of Priscilla Coates, who was the national spokesperson for the Cult Awareness Network (CAN) at the time. CAN was the leading anticult organization in the United States by the early nineties and Ross was CAN's most recognized deprogrammer (Shupe and Darnell, 2006). Ross extracted information from Block during the deprogramming about stored weapons at Mount Carmel and passed this to the ATF. According to the 1993 Treasury report on the ATF raid, the information regarding the weapons (which turned out to be inaccurate) "was based almost entirely on the statement of one former cult member, David Block" (U.S. Department of Treasury, 1993:143). In reviewing the actions of the ATF, the Treasury report later criticized the agency's inordinate reliance on a single dubious source and its "failure to consider how Block's relations with Koresh . . . might have affected the reliability of his statements" (p.143).

The link between Ross and the ATF was confirmed on several occasions by the deprogrammer himself in news interviews shortly after the initial raid. The deprogrammer boasted of his ties with the ATF on several occasions to the news media during the standoff. Ross described himself to reporters as a "cult expert" and consultant to the ATF investigation (Ammerman, 1995:286). According to Nancy Ammerman, who was asked by the Department of Justice to review the actions of federal law enforcement at Waco, Ross supplied the ATF with "with all the information he had regarding the Branch Davidian cult" (Ammerman, 1995:286). She also states that the ATF "interviewed the persons (Ross) directed them to and evidently used information from those interviews in planning the February 28 raid" (Ammerman, 1995:289).

This is further corroborated in Marc Breault's autobiographical account leading up to the ATF raid. Breault initially learned about Ross from *Waco Tribune-Herald* reporter Mark England, who co-wrote the scandalous "Sinful Messiah" series that appeared the day before the federal raid. Breault described his efforts to contact Ross and referred to the deprogrammer as someone who "has detailed information on cult awareness groups and cultbusters" (Breault and King, 1993:137). Breault also said Ross knew that "something was about to happen real soon" on February 16, just two weeks before the ATF raid (Breault and King, 1993:315), and that Ross urged family members to "get Steve (Schneider) out as soon as possible" (Breault and King, 1993:317). Ross's advance knowledge of the ATF raid suggests he had more than a peripheral role as an advisor.

Ammerman (1995) provides more information about Ross regarding the negotiations which took place during the 51-day standoff. The FBI's crisis negotiators were working with the HRT and attempting to persuade the Davidians to surrender. She observes that while religious scholars and others were ignored, however, the negotiators "were still listening to Rick Ross. The FBI interview transcripts document that Ross was, in fact, closely involved with the ATF and the FBI. He talked with the FBI both in early March and in late March. He apparently had the most extensive access to both agencies of any person on the 'cult expert' list and was listened to more attentively" (Ammerman, 1995:289). Ammerman goes on to describe Ross's possible influence on the FBI's decision-making on the ground:

> In late March, Ross recommended that agents attempt to humiliate Koresh, hoping to drive a wedge between him and his followers. While Ross's suggestions may not have been followed to the letter, FBI agents apparently believed that their attempts to embarrass Koresh (talking about inconsistencies, lack of education, failures as prophet, and the like) would produce the kind of internal dissension Ross predicted. Because Ross had been successful in using such tactics on isolated and beleaguered members during deprogramming, he must have assumed that they would work en masse. Any student of group psychology could have dispelled that misapprehension. But the FBI was evidently listening more closely to these deprogramming-related strategies than to the counsel of scholars who might have explained the dynamics of a group under siege. (Ammerman, 1995:289)

Another ACM activist, Dr. Murray Miron, played a key role in the 51-day standoff. Murray, a psychologist and prominent member of the Cult Awareness Network (CAN), was asked by the FBI to examine letters written and sent out of Mount Carmel by Koresh. Miron concluded that the letters contained "all the hallmarks of rampant, morbidly virulent paranoia" (U.S. Department of Justice, 1993:175). But this assessment was steeped in ACM framing and rhetoric.[2] Indeed, it was Miron who told the FBI on April 15, four days before the deadly CS insertion and fire, that Koresh was "a determined and hardened adversary who has no intention of delivering himself" (U.S. Department of Justice, 1993:175). The FBI appears to have acted on Miron's assessment since they began planning to force the Davidians out by launching the CS gas attack a few days later. This plan was pushed through despite the advice of two other experts, James Tabor and Phil Arnold, to take a more patient approach and wait. Tabor and Arnold were convinced Koresh would come out after he finished writing his theological interpretation of the "Seven Seals" described in the Book of Revelation (Tabor, 1995). Their advice was ignored while the opinions of Miron and Ross were adopted, serving as a rationale for the fatal CS insertion by the HRT on April 19.

Media

Media sources played a critical role in promoting the claims of apostates and opponents of the Davidians. Chief apostate Marc Breault formed a partnership with the Australian TV reporter for *A Current Affair*, Martin King, to target Koresh through a carefully calculated set of interviews which were subsequently edited and run as a sensationalized exposé. Breault would later assert in his autobiographical account that the objective of this venture was to "expose (Koresh) as a sex-crazed despot" (Breault and King, 1993:256). Relying on Marc Breault as a confidant and advisor, King conducted and filmed interviews with a group of nine Davidian apostates in December 1991 and later with Koresh in Waco in January 1992. The filmed interviews were woven into a familiar anticult narrative and shown on Australian television for four nights, from April 15 to April 18, casting the Davidians as a "dangerous cult" and lodging a litany of claims against Koresh, including child abuse, planning a mass suicide, and brainwashing. During the same time, the *Herald Sun*, a Melbourne newspaper, covered the story in print. Breault then sent copies of the newspaper coverage and the filmed programs to allied opponents and authorities in the United States.

Not coincidentally, the *Waco Tribune-Herald* began its investigation of the Davidians the following month, in May 1992. The link between Breault and *Waco Tribune-Herald* reporter Mark England is chronicled in Breault's book. The seven-part series, "The Sinful Messiah," published by the Waco newspaper just prior to the federal raid, depicted Koresh as a fanatical cult leader who exercised mind control over his followers. The reporting by England relied substantially on Breault's own narrative of events, exhibiting a striking similarity to the garish paperback. Indeed, reporter England cited Breault as a source and quoted him numerous times throughout the series. The day after the government raid, England and fellow reporter Darlene McCormick ran an article titled "Experts: Branch Davidians Dangerous, Destructive Cult," which relied exclusively on deprogrammer Rick Ross and other key ACM figures to paint the group in the most threatening terms (England and McCormick, 1993). The reporters acknowledged that they had obtained their information from interviews with more than 20 "former members" and quoted a man "deprogrammed" by Ross. The transmission of the anticult frame was clearly evident as the report cited "former cult members (who) said Howell uses traditional mind-control techniques to entrap listeners" (England and McCromick, 1993:12A). The allegations instigated by Breault, King, Ross, and allied opponents were treated as undiluted fact by the Waco reporters, which then became sources for state agents in public claims against the group, particularly after the raid on Mount Carmel (Richardson, 1995; Shupe and Hadden, 1995; Wright, 1995b).

State Agents

In 1992, the Texas Child Protective Services (CPS) was contacted by an anonymous person—likely Marc Breault—alleging child abuse at Mount Carmel. In response to the anonymous tip, CPS caseworkers made three separate visits to Mount Carmel, interviewing adults and children, including Koresh and his wife Rachel. The children denied being abused or having any knowledge of others experiencing abuse. The adults emphatically denied using severe or abusive physical punishment in disciplining children and the caseworkers could find no evidence of abuse. Physical examinations of 12 Davidian children were conducted and the investigations did not turn up any meaningful signs of abuse or injury. Given the absence of evidence to support the child abuse allegations, CPS officials terminated the investigation after several months. However, this did not prevent the ATF investigator, Davy Aguilera, from inserting child abuse allegations into the affidavit for the search and arrest warrant for Koresh. Aguilera received this information from Marc Breault, who was the agent's principal source of intelligence about Koresh and the Davidians throughout the investigation.

ATF investigator Aguilera built his case against the Davidians relying heavily on apostate and opponent accounts. One cannot overstate the importance of this link between organized opponents and ATF. The claims of opponents became part of the evidence record in support of the federal warrants. Marc Breault was named as the source of embellished claims regarding illegal weapons, paramilitary training exercises on the grounds at Mount Carmel, 24-hour armed sentries, shoot-to-kill orders of any suspicious intruders, and efforts to engage in war against the American government (U.S. District Court, 1993:12). As stated earlier, Rick Ross and David Block were the ATF's sources for the alleged stockpile of weapons. The influence of other apostates (David and Debbie Bunds, Robyn Bunds, Janine Bunds, Bruce Gent) is also evident, as their claims appear in the federal affidavit as well.

ATF agent Aguilera also asked apostate Breault to submit a statement suggesting that the Davidians were manufacturing drugs. Though Breault was aware that the charge was false, he provided the ATF with the evidence that was used to claim a "drug nexus" to DOD officials and obtain military support and training for the raid. According to the McClennan County Sheriff's Department, Koresh found methamphetamine lab equipment upon taking possession of Mount Carmel in 1988 and reported it to authorities. An associate of the previous occupant, George Roden, was actually responsible for the drug lab equipment. The Sheriff's Department investigated the complaint and removed the equipment. Breault's statement to Aguilera implied that the drug lab might still be operational. The final congressional report on Waco concluded that "ATF agents misrepresented to Defense Department officials that the Branch Davidians were involved in illegal drug manufacturing" (*Investigation into the Activities of Federal Law Enforcement toward the Branch Davidians*, 1996:3) and exposed the deception in some detail (see pp.45–46). In fact, there was no evidence of drug manufacturing by Koresh and the Davidians. The building in which the lab equipment was found in 1988 burned to the ground in 1990, three years before the ATF raid.

Claims

While space does not permit a full examination of all the claims made against the Branch Davidians by opponents, a survey of some of the key claims should be sufficient to make our case. Many of these claims overlap and others have already been discussed at some length here and elsewhere (see Wright, 1995; 2005; 2011; Wright and Fagen, 2011).

Dangerous Cult

As mentioned previously, the Davidians were widely perceived to be a benign separatist sect by local residents over the many decades of their presence in the Waco area. Only in the early 1990s did usage of the derogatory term "cult" abruptly arise with regard to the Branch Davidians (Lewis, 1995; Pitts, 1995). Scholars argue that the term "cult" conveys a value-loaded set of disparaging stereotypes (Lewis, 1995; Pfeifer, 1992; Robbins, 1988), facilitating the claims-making efforts of organized opponents (Bromley, 1998a; Hall, 1995; Wright, 2011). It has evolved, in contemporary vernacular, as a term of derision or denigration and is no longer a neutral construct or description of a religious group (Richardson,

1993). The derogatory term has been applied intentionally as a strategy by anticult movement organizations and actors since the early years of the movement (Shupe and Bromley, 1987; Shupe and Darnell, 2006), and its evolved use in the popular culture can be attributed in no small part to ACM influence. ACM leaders and their allies have labored to control the naming of minority faiths in the public square, battling with scholars, civil liberties groups, interfaith organizations, and others over the scientific merits and ethical usage of the term, both here and abroad (Gunn, 2003; Introvigne, 2001; Richardson, 1993, 1999; Richardson and Introvigne, 2001; Wright, 2002b). The importance of this struggle over language—the labeling and framing of the targeted groups—cannot be overstated. State control and repression of "cults" is not likely to provoke public outcry or protest since the term connotes cultural illegitimacy. "Cults" have few institutional allies and little public support (Bromley, 1998b; Bromley and Breschel, 1992; Olsen, 2006). As discussed earlier, "cults" are *soft targets* for attacks, vulnerable to inflated claims by opponents and deep-seated suspicions harbored by public officials.

By casting the Davidians as a "dangerous cult," opponents gained a distinct advantage in their moral campaign to assail Koresh and mobilize state control actions. Breault's detailed account of "cultbusting" activities involving collaboration with allied opponents documents the successful hawking of the cult narrative to law enforcement and other government officials. The uncritical acceptance of this narrative was made clear in the days and weeks following the ATF raid on Mount Carmel, in which the Davidians were routinely referred to as a dangerous cult in news reports and by government spokespersons in ATF, FBI, the Department of Justice, and the White House. In effect, the unchallenged cult framing of the group by the organized oppositional network contributed to an exaggerated threat which was, in turn, used by state actors to justify the deadly paramilitary raid in order to serve the warrants.

Child Abuse and Sexual Abuse

The child abuse and sexual abuse claims have been widely examined and debated, though it is often difficult to separate the purported claims from the evidence. Koresh's doctrine of the House of David did lead to spiritual marriages with both married and single women in the group and with at least one underage girl. The underage girl was Michele Jones, the younger sister of Koresh's legal wife Rachel and the daughter of Davidians Perry and Mary Belle Jones. Koresh took Michele as a spiritual wife when she was 13, evidently with the consent of the Joneses. This means that Koresh was in violation of state law and could have been prosecuted for statutory rape in Texas. A six-month investigation of child abuse allegations by the Texas Child Protective Services in 1992 failed to turn up any evidence, likely because the Davidians concealed the spiritual marriage of Koresh to Michele Jones, essentially assigning a surrogate husband to the girl for the sake of appearances. A second allegation involved an underage girl, Kiri Jewell, who gave testimony in the House hearings on Waco in 1995. She claimed Koresh engaged in improper sexual touching and other behaviors that would have brought sexual assault charges against him. There is no independent corroboration of this incident, however, and Kiri's family was split over whether they believed her story.[3]

With regard to the allegations of physical child abuse, the evidence is less convincing. In one reported incident, former Davidians alleged that Koresh became irritated with the cries of his son Cyrus and spanked the child severely for several minutes on three consecutive visits to the child's bedroom. In another incident, Koresh was said to have beaten the eight-month-old daughter of another member for approximately 40 minutes until the little girl's bottom bled. In a third incident, a man involved in a custody battle visited Mount Carmel and claimed to have witnessed the beating of a young boy with a stick. According to this account, the beating lasted 15 minutes (see Ellison and Bartkowski, 1995:120–121). Finally, the FBI's justification for forcing an end to the 51-day standoff with the Davidians was predicated on the charge that Koresh was beating children inside Mount Carmel. In the immediate aftermath of the deadly conflagration, Attorney General Janet Reno told reporters that "We had specific information that babies were being beaten. I specifically asked (the FBI), 'You mean babies?' Yes, he's slapping babies around" (Verhovek, 1993). It was later learned that this charge was baseless. FBI Director William Sessions countered the attorney general's claim and told reporters that they had no such information about ongoing child abuse inside Mount Carmel (Labaton, 1993). A careful investigation of the other physical child abuse allegations also found the evidence to be weak and ambiguous, casting serious doubt on the charges (Ellison and Bartkowski, 1995).

Stockpiling Weapons

The search and arrest warrants obtained by ATF charged that David Koresh and others were in violation of federal firearms laws. The ATF was convinced that Koresh was converting legal semiautomatic rifles to fully automatic weapons and possibly gathering bomb-making materials. While these were valid concerns, a congressional investigation later found that the affidavit supporting the warrants "contained numerous misstatements of the facts, misstatements of the law, and misapplication of the law to the facts," as well as "substantial irrelevant and confusing information" (*Investigation into the Activities of Federal Law Enforcement toward the Branch Davidians*, 1996:12). The congressional report called the ATF investigation "grossly incompetent" and stated that the "numerous errors and misrepresentations" regarding the alleged federal firearms violations created "a seriously flawed affidavit" (p.12). Equally significant for our purposes, the warrants implied—through the claims of apostates and opponents—that Koresh was stockpiling weapons *in order to launch a war against the federal government*. It is this latter charge that helps to explain the rationale for the massive paramilitary response by the ATF. Evidently, the ATF believed erroneously that the Davidians were linked to the violent Christian Identity/Posse Comitatus groups that formed the vanguard of the antigovernment movement that emerged in the 1980s and early 1990s (Wright, 2005:84).

Davidian survivor David Thibodeau later explained in his autobiography that the group was buying legal AR-15 semiautomatic rifles and converting them into M-16s for a licensed gun dealer in the Waco area, Henry McMahon (Thibodeau and Whiteson, 1999:128–129). McMahon intended to sell the popular automatic weapons at gun shows for a significant profit before they became banned, and the Davidians saw this as an income-producing venture. However, McMahon "got nervous" after a compliance check by the ATF sometime in the summer of 1992, according to Thibodeau, and "canceled the contract, leaving us with an inventory of unlicensed guns" (1999:129). This unfortunate development left the Davidians vulnerable to the weapons stockpile charge and much more. The Davidians were strategically framed by opponents as a violent apocalyptic cult holed up in an armed encampment preparing for the final battle of Armageddon against the Antichrist government forces (Wright, 2005:83–84). This received narrative apparently negated any consideration of routine enforcement procedures and instead prompted an extraordinary military-like response. Because ATF accepted uncritically the opponents' narrative construction, the stockpile of weapons—in concert with other menacing allegations—the religious group came to be seen as a much greater threat than was actually the case. Essentially, the cluster of claims by opponents painted a picture of a domestic terrorist group.

Federal agents became convinced that the Davidians would not cooperate in an investigation, hated the federal government, were controlled by a fanatical cult leader, and would launch a "holy war" if challenged. This is readily apparent in the affidavit accompanying the warrants. What shapes and frames the "warrior cult" motif in the affidavit are the accounts by ex-members and detractors who provided ATF agent Davy Aguilera with embellished descriptions of life at Mt. Carmel. Here one finds stories of armed sentries, paramilitary maneuvers and training, weapons stockpiles, "shoot-to-kill" orders regarding intruders, discussions of an imminent war, contingency plans for mass suicide, the group's purported . . . contempt for gun laws, and Koresh's messianic claims (not to mention polygamy and the sect leader's conjugal unions with underage women). Without these lurid and dramatic tropes to magnify the alleged threat posed by the Davidians, it is questionable that the ATF would have taken such extreme measures. (Wright, 2005:84)

The characterization of the Davidians as "terrorists" was made explicitly by Breault in his own account: "The Branch Davidians were not an ordinary group of criminals. They were religious zealots who would think nothing of dying for their leader. In many respects, they were like terrorists" (Breault and King, 1993:297).

Mass Suicide/"Another Jonestown"

John R. Hall, in his excellent work on the Branch Davidian conflict, argues that organized opponents invoked "intrinsic narratives" about mass suicide and Jonestown "in ways that proved central to how the tragedy at Mount Carmel unfolded" (Hall, 1995:207). Intrinsic narratives refer to the "diverse stories that various social actors tell within emergent situations to which they are mutually oriented, but in different ways" (Hall, 1995:206). This approach can "help show how cultural meanings become nuanced, shaded, interpreted, challenged, and otherwise reworked by participants, and how such meaning-shifts affect the course of unfolding events" (Hall, 1995:206).[In situations of contested meanings and conflict, individuals and groups jointly compose narratives that import freighted meanings to legitimize and make sense of projects they are undertaking.]

Hall observes that apocalyptic sects have as a central tenet of their faith the belief in the return of Christ or the coming a new age, but that the particular details of how such a transformation will take place is not

certain. Much depends on "any given sect's response to their construction of the apocalypse" and may involve a whole host of possibilities.
It is just as likely to include "a retreat to an 'other-worldly' heaven-on-
earth, disconnected from the evil society in its last days" as an active
engagement in the struggle. No conclusions can be drawn in advance
about the trajectory of an apocalyptic sect because it is a product of the
interaction of the group with the wider society. Thus the fate of the Branch
Davidians should be viewed not as a fixed path but rather as a "product of religious conflict between a militant sect and opponents who,
wittingly or unwittingly, helped fulfill the sect's emergent apocalyptic
vision" (p.207).

In the Waco case, the organized opponents of Koresh continually invoked the claim that the Branch Davidians were "another Jonestown"
in a manner that actually shaped the interactional dynamic. The opponents of David Koresh, Hall states, "reinvoked and reworked narratives about mass suicide in ways that shaped the escalating trajectory
of conflict at Mount Carmel" (p.206). Hall notes that the mass suicide
discourse became a self-fulfilling prophecy carried out by federal agents
acting, in part, on unreliable information and advice by Breault, Ross,
the Gent and Bunds families, and other oppositional claimants. Indeed,
chief apostate Marc Breault declared in his book that Koresh was "planning a mass suicide somewhere around April 18 of this year (1992) . . . I
believe that over 200 persons will be massacred next month," he wrote.
"Every day brings us closer to another Jonestown" (Breault and King,
1993:290–291). After the ill-fated raid, the tragedy at Mount Carmel
continued to be shaped by the intrinsic narrative of opponents. Breault
and Ross continued to press the mass suicide claim, as did the Waco
news reporters. The trope of mass suicide emerged conspicuously in
the *Waco Tribune-Herald* series, "Sinful Messiah," and was invoked by
federal officials as a cause for concern during the 51-day standoff. Ross
recommended to federal agents during the standoff that they "drive a
wedge between Koresh and his followers" (U.S. Department of Justice,
1993:129), which was predicated on the mass suicide narrative. The
"stress escalation" strategy employed by the FBI (Wright, 1999:46–47)
appeared to follow the advice of Breault, Ross, and Miron. However, the
strategy backfired and only served to solidify the group's resolve and
confirm their worst fears that the hostile government operation was a
sign of the Endtime and that the Davidians might have to be martyred
for their faith (Wessinger, 2009).

Conclusion

The Branch Davidian case provides strong support for our model explaining government raids. Indeed, as perhaps the most researched case of a government raid on a minority religion in American history, it provides an ideal opportunity to explore in depth the merits and applicability of the proposed model. First, the model posits that the alleged threat posed by the religious group in question is largely manufactured as a product of a concerted antisubversion campaign by opponents (Bromley, 1998b: Hall and Schuyler, 1998:142). This proposition holds true as the Davidians were viewed as a benign sect for over a half century and only came to the attention of the public and authorities through the dogged claims-making of apostates and a coalition of organized opponents—anticult organizations and actors, distraught relatives, selected news reporters. The branding of the Davidians as a subversive organization ("dangerous cult") arose directly from oppositional or countermovement agitation and activity, as we have discussed. Second, the litany of claims lodged against the targeted group was inflated and often wildly so (e.g., drug manufacturing, child sacrifice, brainwashing, mass suicide, launching of a "holy war" against the government). Studies shows that organized opponents of the Branch Davidians employed a strategy of deviance amplification to incite public fear and alarm (Palmer, 2011a; Wright, 1995b; Wright and Fagen, 2011) and to leverage increased apprehensions to press for urgent action. This deviance amplification strategy was part of a "dispute-broadening process" in which disgruntled apostates and opponents were able to effectively redefine circumscribed conflict within a small sectarian community and project it as a much broader societal crisis (Bromley, 1998b). The putative danger attributed to the Branch Davidians was elevated exponentially by opponents and made to appear as an imminent threat to the larger social order. Such a menacing and looming threat demanded an extraordinary response in the form of preemptive social control measures, putting further pressure on authorities to act. Finally, organized opponents were able to persuade authorities of their exaggerated claims and eventually forge alliances with state agents to carry out their partisan campaign to suppress or dissolve the targeted religious group. The raid on Mount Carmel fulfilled the primary objectives of the oppositional network and beyond, culminating in the complete destruction of the Branch Davidian religious community.

In the Waco case, we can see clearly how this reflexive process unfolded leading to the ill-advised and lethal federal raid. Since the Waco raid was not typical in terms of its deadly denouement, perhaps a comment is in order here to explain why violence occurred. As Hall and Schuyler (1998:142) observe, violence is a more likely response when an apocalyptic group's sense of legitimacy is gravely threatened and under attack. The Branch Davidian case certainly qualifies as one in which the sect's legitimacy was under attack, both literally and figuratively. Reacting to the strategic attack launched by apostates and ACM activists, the paramilitary raid by the ATF Special Response Team (SRT) was a planned "takedown" of the Davidians; an operation that the Treasury Department rightly observes was "the largest enforcement effort ever mounted by ATF" (U.S. Department of Treasury, 1993:134). The egregious overreach of deadly force to execute the warrants in this case created a real mortal threat to the Davidian sect. As such, the exceptional case of violence can be readily explained as a consequence of the elevated conflict between a religious movement and a broad coalition of opponents in which the stigmatized "cult" was afforded little deference or opportunity to defend itself against the implementation of coercive control measures by the state. The investigative agency refused or ignored critical opportunities resolve this dispute peacefully. The ATF refused an offer by Koresh to inspect the Davidians' weapons, an offer which the congressional report later called "the first of a series of instances to proceed in a non-confrontational manner" (*Investigation into the Activities of Federal Law Enforcement toward the Branch Davidians*, 1996:13). The ATF also ignored opportunities to arrest Koresh outside Mount Carmel during undercover and surveillance operations and "instead were determined to use a dynamic entry approach. In making this decision," the government report states, "ATF agents exercised extremely poor judgment . . . and ignored the foreseeable perils of their course of action" (*Investigation into the Activities of Federal Law Enforcement toward the Branch Davidians*, 1996:3). Indeed, the high-risk, military-like raid on the Mount Carmel community, whose residents were predominantly children, women, and elderly people, was spectacularly misconceived. Finally, the congressional report observes that in face of knowing that the element of surprise had been lost and the raid compromised, the ATF raid commanders "recklessly proceeded with the raid, thereby endangering the lives of the ATF agents under their command and the lives of those residing in the compound" (p.3).

It is our contention that the violence in this case should be understood *not* as an intrinsic property of the religious group, but rather as a product of the heightened conflict in which the dispute settlement processes were controlled by oppositional coalitions (Bromley, 1998b:24). The ATF became allied with organized opponents in an attempted "takedown" of the Davidians and the repeated decisions of ATF agents to ignore nonviolent or nonconfrontational opportunities prior to the raid indicate a determination to use a violent approach. The trajectory of conflict culminating in violence then was largely shaped by the actions of the state. In the end, the besieged religious group, confronted with an array of oppositional forces undermining its capacity to survive as an autonomous organization, was willing to meet violence with violence. The Davidians believed the federal agents at Mount Carmel were trying to kill them and there is now substantial evidence to suggest that this perception was not unreasonable.

Armored vehicle used in Texas state raid 2008. Courtesy of Willie Jessop/FLDS

CEV and paramilitary unit FLDS 2008. Courtesy of Willie Jessop/FLDS

Authors at Damanhur 2009. Photo taken by Esperide Ananas.

Authors visiting 12 tribes community in Sus, France 2009. Photo taken by unidentified Twelve Tribes member

French raid on Ogyen Kunzang Choling 1997**. Courtesy of Ogyen Kunzang Choling

Ogyen Kunzang Choling leader sitting for picture (France) 2009. Photo taken by Stuart Wright

German raid on 12 Tribes 2013. Courtesy of Jean Wiseman/Twelve Tribes

German raid on 12 Tribes, mother crying. Courtesy of Jean Wiseman/Twelve Tribes

German raid on 12 Tribes, search of property. Courtesy of Jean Wiseman/Twelve Tribes

German raid team at Klosterzimmern 2013. Courtesy of Jean Wiseman/Twelve Tribes.

German raid team on the ground. Courtesy of Jean Wiseman/Twelve Tribes

Mandarom guest center 2009. Photo taken by Stuart Wright

Palmer at ISKCON center in Belgium 2009. Photo taken by Stuart Wright

U.S. Raid on Nuwaubian Nation 2002**. Permission from Nick Oza.

6

The United Nuwaubian Nation

Overview of the Raid

ON MAY 8, 2002, the FBI executed a massive paramilitary raid on the United Nuwaubian Nation, a Black Nationalist group in Georgia. The FBI's target that day was the Nuwaubian "compound" outside the sleepy rural town of Eatonton, about 70 miles southeast of Atlanta. The "compound" was hardly an armed fortress. It was an exotic fantasy theme park, called Tama Re, constructed to replicate an ancient Egyptian shrine, an incongruous sight among the farmlands and cow pastures of middle Georgia. The group had originally formed in Brooklyn, New York, in the 1970s, around their spiritual leader, Dr. Malachi Z. York, and moved to Georgia in 1993.

Tama Re was dominated by a black pyramid that rose 40 feet, flanked by a smaller golden pyramid. Tama Re's winding avenues were lined with pillars and statues of animal-headed gods. There was a five-foot concrete scarab beetle, a huge sphinx, and a museum of black history. A black Jesus was crucified on an ankh, crowned with the feathered headdress of the Plains Indian—a testament to Dr. York's eclectic creativity.

The state raid was planned and executed as a spectacular show of force. Three armored vehicles accompanied by over 300 agents from the FBI, ATF, and the local county sheriff's office burst past the armed guards and rammed through the flimsy painted obelisks that formed the front gates of Tama Re. The FBI's SWAT team, comprised of 80 agents, leapt out of trucks to make a "dynamic entry," armed with machine guns, semi-automatic Glocks, hand grenades, head masks, body shields, and tear gas. They were followed by a force of deputy sheriffs, snipers, and a rifle team. Two helicopters hovered over the theme park as armored trucks breached the front entrance to Tama Re. Agents descended from the two helicopters that hovered overhead, kicked in the residents' doors, and threw canisters of tear gas into their windows.

The FBI had been careful to maintain the element of surprise. Presumably, they had learned this lesson the hard way from the ATF's disastrous 1993 assault on the Branch Davidians outside Waco, Texas. Unlike the ATF in the Waco assault, the FBI came in fully prepared for fire and for collateral damage with ERS, fire trucks, and ambulances. Within three minutes the FBI had complete control of the perimeter and ordered the residents to lie face-down on the ground.

One reason there were no casualties at Tama Re was because its residents (unlike the Branch Davidians) did not shoot at the invading raid team or put up any resistance. They lay down meekly, facing the ground, their hands on their heads. Only 65 adults were present at Tama Re. Twenty-five were men, mostly elderly, and 40 were women. The more than 50 children who resided at Tama Re were seized and placed in custodial detention by state social workers.

The raid was deemed "successful" in that no one was killed but the results proved to be disappointing for the FBI and for the Bureau of Alcohol, Tobacco and Firearms. The ATF had participated in the raid and searched the "compound" for a stash of illegal weapons. The local sheriff, Howard Sills, told the media that he was aware of "numerous weapons ranging from handguns to assault rifles that had been confiscated." He claimed that "in York's bedroom alone, there were at least three assault rifles and other assorted handguns and what I would call regular long guns." Sills also noted that "the barn where the men lived . . . had a lot of weapons in it" (Osinski, 2007:241). But there was no mention in the news reports of the ATF finding a stockpile of machine guns or illegal weapons, as there surely would have if they were discovered. More to the point, there were no weapons charges once the case went to court.

The raid also failed to produce physical evidence of child molestation. Sheriff Howard Sills told reporter Rob Peecher of the *Macon Telegraph* why five "children," ranging in age from 14 to 16, were taken into protective custody: "We received information about these five children that was corroborated by others that caused us to seek out the protective order. We had an order from the juvenile court signed [by a judge] prior to going on the compound. The children, we suspect, are victims of child molestation" (Peecher, 2002). However, when these five teenagers were examined by doctors, social workers, and psychologists, no medical evidence was found that any of them had any sexual contact with Dr. Malachi York. Four tested positive for STDs.[1] The residents of Tama Re explained that some of the teens had flouted the commune's rules regarding sex and drugs by "partying" in the barn at night (Palmer, 2010b).

Earlier that morning of May 8, the group's leader, Dr. Malachi Z. York, was arrested by FBI agents in the parking lot of a supermarket in the nearby town of Milledgeville while he was shopping with one of his plural wives. The FBI raided York's house in Athens where they found and confiscated $400,000 in cash (Peecher, 2003). York and his main plural wife, Kathy Johnson, were charged with transporting children across state lines for sex, from New York to Georgia, in March and April 1993, the dates of the group's initial resettlement. It was also alleged that York had transported the children across state borders, from Georgia to Disney World in Orlando, "for purposes of having sex with them." York was charged with 74 counts of child molestation, 29 counts of aggravated molestation, 4 counts of statutory rape, 1 count of rape, 2 counts of sexual exploitation of a minor, 1 count of influencing a witness, and 5 counts of enticing a child for indecent purposes: altogether a 116-count indictment. York was denied bail, and his four top female administrators (also his "wives") were charged with eight counts of child molestation. The trial of Dwight York was held in January 2004, almost two years later. York was convicted of child molestation and racketeering and sentenced on April 22 to 135 years in federal prison.

History and Background of the United Nuwaubian Nation

Dwight York (Dr. Malachi Z. York to his disciples) was born in Maryland on June 26, 1945.[2] He spent his youth in New York, where, according to federal records, he became involved in youth gangs and drug dealing and established a criminal record (FBI Report, 1993). In 1964 he was charged with statutory rape, possession of a dangerous weapon, and resisting a police officer. He received a three-year prison sentence on January 6, 1965 but was paroled on October 20, 1967. Like Malcolm X, York converted to Islam while in prison. On his release he began to attend the State Street Mosque in New York under the Sunni Islam spiritual master Sheikh Daoud Faisal. Faisal was an outspoken figure who condemned the Nation of Islam (NOI) for their unorthodox recognition of Wallace Fard Muhammad as divine. Dwight York was also a card-carrying member of the Moorish Science Temple.

In 1967 York began to preach his own original theory about the nature of the Black Man. He rejected the notion of blacks as "Asiatics" espoused by most Black Moorish and Black Muslim groups, including prominent leaders like Noble Drew Ali and Elijah Muhammad. Instead, he proposed a noble lineage traced back to the Nubian kingdom in Africa, to the Sumerian and Egyptian civilizations, and finally to ancient astronauts from the planet "Rizq," who allegedly colonized our own planet (see Palmer, 2010b:16).[3]

He founded his first spiritual organization in 1967 when he and his youthful friends formed Ansaar Pure Sufi in New York City. He then went on to found (or in some cases, reconstitute) a series of exotic black spirituality movements that often mimicked others. York freely appropriated the texts, symbols, costumes, and rituals of the NOI, the Black Hebrews, the Five Percenters, and the Prince Hall Masonry (Palmer and Luxton, 1998:353–370). With each new phase, the identity of York's followers underwent corresponding shifts: from Black Hebrews, to "brown" Muslims, to Moors, to "red" Yamassee Amerindians, and even to "green" descendants of extraterrestrials. York's religious organizations have appeared on the streets of New York, Brooklyn, and other major U.S. cities under the following names:

1967	Ansaar Pure Sufi
1968	The Nubian Islamic Hebrew Mission
1969	The Nubian Islamic Hebrews
1973–1992	The Ansaaru Allah Community
1992	The Holy Tabernacle Ministries
1993	The United Nuwaubian Nations of Moors
1993	The Yamassee Native American Moors of the Creek Nation

The most stable phase of the movement was from 1973 to 1992, when York established a Muslim communal society in Brooklyn known as the Ansaaru Allah Community (AAC).[4] The AAC received commendations from New York's mayor in the 1980s for purging the streets of crime and drugs. Soon, however, it was under investigation by the New York Police Department, the Federal Bureau of Investigation, and the Bureau of Alcohol, Tobacco and Firearms for suspected arson, harboring criminal fugitives, welfare fraud, and purchasing and stockpiling illegal weapons (FBI Report, 1993).

In 1993 the group sold all its property in Brooklyn and moved to Georgia. There they purchased a building for their headquarters in Athens for $285,000, and bought 473 acres of land in Putnam County for approximately $1 million. York's disciples, no longer "Ansaars," now called themselves "Nuwaubians" and proceeded to construct an Egyptian village near the town of Eatonton, called Tama Re. Tama Re was designed as an Egyptian theme park, a moneymaking enterprise open for visitors, black or white, during the summer season. But it also functioned as a pilgrimage site, a utopian "Egipt in the West" that would be a center of pilgrimage for African Americans of modest means. The annual highlight of this pilgrimage was the June festival called "Savior's Day" that celebrated York's birthday. It proclaimed the birth of the Messiah and advertised the notion of Tama Re as a sacred "Land"—a safe haven for all black people in the impending apocalypse. This summer festival attracted many African Americans, from 2,000 to 5,000 between 1999 and 2001. For many of York's disciples, there was a sense of urgent millenarian expectation that fueled these pilgrimages. York had prophesied that in May 2003 a "Mothership" from the planet Rizq bearing the extraterrestrial ancestors of the Nuwaubian people would descend on Tama Re's 40-foot pyramid to carry away 144,000 elite members before the destruction of the world (see Palmer, 2010b:71–74).

When Dr. York and 100-odd disciples arrived in Georgia in 1993, they had hoped to make a fresh start, to leave behind the conflicts they had experienced in the State of New York during their Ansaaru Allah phase. But they would soon encounter an even more intense level of organized opposition in Georgia. The first news reports that appeared in the local newspapers portrayed the Nuwaubians in a light-hearted fashion as merely bizarre—as a "quasi-religious sect" from Brooklyn whose members dressed as cowboys, lived on a commune, and were building weird architecture. But as the construction progressed, the group began to experience a series of legal and bureaucratic obstacles to their utopian enterprise (Eckenrode, 2001; Pinzur, 2000).

The first serious conflict began in 1997 when the guards at the gate of Tama Re refused entry to a building inspector, "Dizzy" Adams, who had been sent to inspect their construction projects. The second conflict was over the zoning permit for the Ramses Social Club at Tama Re.

Another source of tension was the Savior's Day festival. Huge crowds of York's black supporters converged on this sparsely populated farmland of the Eatonton area for the week-long festival that in June 1997 and 1998 attracted up to 5,000 people. On the one hand, the festival brought in business for the local townspeople, generating revenue and boosting the economy. But on the other hand, the festival also raised fears that the sheer number of people (read: black people) posed a "security risk." York ignored concerns raised by detractors and declared Tama Re a "Sovereign Nation." On entering the gate, visitors had to buy "egiptian [sic] passports" and change their money into egiptian [sic] coins (Palmer, 2010b:72).

As thousands of African-American pilgrims converged on nearby towns during the summer festivals, some locals began to perceive them as trying to "take over" the county. Local journalists characterized the Nuwaubians as a "racist" group, and some of their Georgian neighbors referred to them derisively as "the Waubs."

In September 1999, the Nuwaubians sought to defuse the growing tensions by inviting distinguished black leaders to visit Tama Re and speak up on their behalf. First they hosted Rev. Al Sharpton, a nationally known civil rights leader, to deflect public concerns. Sharpton led a rally in Eatonton calling the actions of county officials "oppressive" for shutting down the club (McCain, 2002). Next they invited Tyrone Brooks, an Atlanta state representative and president of the Georgia Association of Black Elected Officials. Congressman Brooks befriended York and the Nuwaubians and became concerned that the state might take repressive actions against the group. Brooks regularly intervened in racially sensitive cases as a seasoned legislator and visited Tama Re multiple times. He went to Putnam County to mediate the dispute between local officials and the Nuwaubians (Palmer, 2010b:78). In 1999 Brooks warned Governor Barnes that "Dwight York and his group were being targeted for Waco-like racial violence" (Osinski, 2002). On April 27, 2001, Rev. Jesse Jackson, a distinguished civil rights leader and the founder of the Rainbow/PUSH Coalition, spoke at Tama Re. Jackson called it "the American Dream" and pledged his solidarity with the Nuwaubians in their ongoing zoning and building disputes. Jackson supported York and the community as this dispute seemed to take on elements of a racial conflict. The Nuwaubians believed they were being singled out for their race and religion. Some locals who were uncomfortable with the odd religious group expressed a preference that the group go back to New York. Dr. York's defiant attitude probably did not help matters. He held a press conference on September 15, 1999 in which he called white people "the Devil" and suggested that the Caucasians "go home to Europe."[5]

On June 22, 1999, Dr. York refused to comply with Superior Court Judge Hugh V. Wingfield III's order to appear in the Putnam County Court on a contempt motion filed by county officials. In response to York's refusal to show, the judge sent Sheriff Howard Sills to Tama Re to padlock several buildings even as thousands of visitors arrived to celebrate Savior's Day. The group was forced to hold its festival outdoors while Nuwaubian leaders led a chant, "We love sunshine" (Osinski, 2007:197).

In June 2001 Dr. York was ordered again to appear in court on contempt charges. Not coincidentally, the date again fell on the week of the Savior's Day festival. This time 700 Nuwaubians dressed in Moorish black tunics with embroidered fezzes surrounded the courthouse in Eatonton and organized themselves in patrols. A U-haul truck circled the square filled with Nuwaubians "ready to be deployed if their savior was taken into custody" (Moser, 2002).

The zoning and building inspection disputes were only a prelude the state's pitched battle against York and the Nuwaubians. Officials had been secretly building a case against York on multiple counts of child molestation since 1997. Sheriff Sills claimed he had been receiving "anonymous calls and letters" alleging that sexual abuse of children was going on at Tama Re. Sills worked closely with journalist Rob Peecher, who covered the Nuwaubian story for the *Eatonton Messenger* and the *Macon Telegraph*. Peecher's articles relied heavily on the antagonistic views of Sheriff Sills, who soon became the leading interpreter of events in the Nuwaubian conflict, and virtually the only source regarding Nuwaubian religious culture. Peecher could not interview the Nuwaubians directly since his stories had alienated members of the community. Peecher also claimed that he began to receive death threats from the Nuwaubians and was attacked by two "Waubs" in a supermarket.

In the media coverage of the raid on Tama Re, the actual purpose of the enforcement action was never clearly stated to the public. Charges of sexual abuse surfaced against York after the raid. These charges were based on statements from second-generation members who had grown up in the Ansaaru Allah Community but defected. The ex-members claimed York had sexually exploited minors of both sexes, between the ages of 4 and 18. Media reports broadcast these allegations before York had a chance to defend himself in court, thereby effectively stigmatizing the "cult leader" as a pedophile.

Organized Opposition

It is clear there was a network of organized opponents who worked together to put York in prison and dissolve the religious community. The network was composed of apostates and ex-members, county officials, local and federal law enforcement, and opportunistic journalists. This case represents a slight variation from our model in that there appears to be no direct participation by ACM organizations and actors. However, it is evident that organized opponents relied heavily on an anticult framing or branding of the Nuwaubians and their leader, Dwight York (see Palmer, 2010b: xv–xvi; Osinski, 2007:174–178). There is also evidence that prior to relocating to Georgia, a "counter-cult movement formed among orthodox Muslim groups in the Brooklyn area to oppose the AAC" (Palmer, 2010b:67). The religious countercult movement (CCM) labeled York's community at the time as a "dangerous anti-Islamic cult operating in America" (Palmer, 2010b:68). In 1988, an author linked to the countercult movement published a book entitled *The Ansar Cult in America* (Philips, 1988). We argue that the allegations and the stigma attached to York's community followed them to Georgia and provided a backdrop or "intrinsic narrative" (Hall, 1995) for later attacks on the group. The language and tropes of organized opponents borrowed generously from anticult and countercult framing in their campaign against York and the United Nuwaubian Nation.

Apostates

A network of apostates and ex-members, each of whom had his/her own reasons to oppose Dwight York, formed in May 2001. The network was led by York's disaffected son, Jacob York, who might be described as the chief whistleblower and "arch-apostate" in the campaign against Dr. York and Tama Re. The ex-member network was a critical catalyst in the oppositional coalition to challenge the Nuwaubian leader and the religious community.

Jacob York was raised in the AAC, but left in 1990 at age 16 with his mother, Dorothy Mae Johnson, Dwight York's first and only legal wife. She left in protest over her husband's financial mismanagement of Tama Re. Jacob later enrolled at Columbia University, where he began organizing dance parties for the students, inviting talented and promising hip-hop bands to play. By 1994 he was a successful music producer and agent. He became the manager of Li'l Kim, who would become a famous feminist *avant-garde* hip-hop artist.

Jacob had broken all ties to his father's movement as a young adult, but he was later approached by an FBI agent seeking information about Dr. York, the "cult leader," in the mid-1990s. On hearing of the controversy

surrounding Tama Re in news reports, Jacob decided to re-establish contact in 1995, when he visited his father at Tama Re (Interview with Jacob
York, 2003).[6] Jacob claimed he met another ex-member who showed him
a video of a young girl dancing naked, a girl who had been Jacob's childhood sweetheart when he was in the AAC. Afterward, he set about to organize an "underground railroad" to help members "escape." He opened
up an e-mail account so that members of the group who "wanted out"
could write to him for help. His sister joined him and the two siblings
established and operated a halfway house to rehabilitate disaffected Nuwaubians who had grown up in the commune setting and to teach them
how to adapt to secular society (Osinski, 2007:227).

In March 2001, Jacob learned through the ex-members' network that
one of the top administrators at Tama Re had defected. Abigail "Habibah"
Washington was an 18-year-old second-generation member and was one
of York's plural wives. She had also had given birth to two of his children.
Abigail left the community at Tama Re in February 2001 and moved back
to New York to live with her family. According to a statement she made in
April 2003, Jacob York approached her and invited her to go on a weekend
trip to Florida with a group of other ex-members. By this time, York was
actively playing the apostate role in attempting to broaden the disputes of
disaffected ex-members and pressing authorities for legal action. Jacob had
become the fiercest and most outspoken critic of the Nuwaubian leader.

On February 7, 2003, Abigail Washington was interviewed by WABC
New York and described how Jacob York had organized a private meeting
with ex-members who had all agreed to tell their story to the authorities.
She said that this had been the "turning point" in the case against York
and the Nuwaubians. Jacob also showed her videos on Jonestown and
Heaven's Gate and compared Tama Re to these groups, which had committed mass suicide. Jacob told Abigail that "we were a cult—we lived like
this" (quoted in Palmer, 2006:6).

Abigail was featured as the prosecution's star witness in the federal
trial against Dr. York, but she later recanted her testimony, saying she felt
threatened and intimidated. She was told by Jacob York that the only way
she could receive immunity from prosecution was to go to the FBI and
support the stories of other disgruntled ex-members.

> Jacob told me that there were certain [ex-members] who went to the
> FBI about certain things with myself, and there was no way I could
> disprove it. The only way was to go the FBI and seek immunity. At

that point I was afraid. No one really messes with the FBI. So I went the following day with Jacob. . . . The only [ex-]members I knew were disgruntled with Malachi. Nicole, Sakinah, Ahmal, Krystal—they all had issues against Malachi. They called in different people and we all called each other and we discussed how the story should go and backed each other's stories up. That's how the case sort of started. (Quoted in Palmer, 2010b:118)

Abigail also discussed some possible private motives of the ex-members:

Nicole had a lot of disgruntled [sic] issues—she had been kicked out and she felt it was wrong . . . she spent her whole life in the community, she had nowhere to go. Everybody started venting about different things they disliked— nothing to do with child abuse— things to do with growing up, mostly arguments with Malachi. Jacob brought up that he was in love with Nicole [and that] she was in love with his Father. Jacob fed off this anger; he felt his father was responsible for his mother's death, his brother's death. Jacob took that anger and said we should go to the government with that anger. (Quoted in Palmer, 2010b:118)

Abigail explained how the ex-members worked together to coordinate each other's accounts in order to "sound more believable":

If Nicole did an interview, she would call us, we would back her up . . . make her story sound more real, more believable. If we all prosecuted [incriminated] ourselves, then what we said about Malachi would sound believable. If we all back each other up, we can make it sound more believable. (Quoted in Palmer, 2010b:119)

Finally, Abigail stated that Jacob told the ex-members they could obtain substantial money and fame if they stuck to their stories: "Jacob said we would have a class action lawsuit worth millions of dollars. We would make movies, there would be books . . . everybody fed off that idea" (quoted in Palmer, 2010b:119).

The actions of apostates were well known among members at Tama Re. In April 2004, an article appeared on a Nuwaubian website called "Conspiracy and Conspirators."[7] This posting stated that Jacob York "masterminded a conspiracy" by forming a network of ex-members "with disgruntled issues" [*sic*] to put Dr. Malachi Z. York in jail for life and seize the land belonging to the Yamassee Nation. The tone is vituperative and the prose riddled with errors but it does invite an examination of the claims by a handful of former members who defected during different tumultuous phases of the Nuwaubian movement and came together to lodge grievances against their leader.

The claims of apostates and ex-members provided the substance of charges that the state needed to launch the raid. Since there was no forensic evidence of child victimization or illegal weapons, these claims were vital to the federal case. Pauline and two other former plural wives of Dr. York, Nicole and Sakinah, were among the original women who joined the network of opponents and among the first introduced to the FBI by Jacob York. Years later the ex-wives appeared on the Montel Williams Show, in an episode entitled "Cult Survivors Speak Out," to tell their story. The show aired on February 10, 2007.

Montel Williams introduced Pauline to the audience as one of Dr. York's plural wives, who bore him three children. She told viewers that she joined York's movement when she was 16, when it was still called the Ansaaru Allah Community, and she worked as a writer and editor in their publications office. Pauline claimed she was "kicked out" of the AAC because she was sick and unable to work:

> I had prestige in the community as one of his wives and mother of hischildren. But then he put me out. I was pregnant with my third child . . . I was very ill and couldn't work. He saw I was of no use to him and put me out – no money, no milk for the children, no Pampers. I had to go on medical assistance. I was suffering from stress. We were living in Liberty, N.Y. (That was while he was "The Lamb"). . . . I had a nervous breakdown. (Quoted in Palmer, 2010b:122)

Pauline sent the very first letter to Sheriff Sills in 1997 alerting him of sexual abuse "out at the compound." But this young woman was never at Tama Re and could not have been an eyewitness to such events. Indeed, Pauline admitted to Montel that she never actually "saw with my own eyes anything happening with the children"; she said that she "heard rumors." Rather, she inferred depredations from a previous time. Sick and pregnant with her third child, she stated she saw little kids coming out of his room late at night (in New York) and felt a sick feeling in her stomach: "I just knew he was messing with those kids."

The two other former wives who appeared on the Montel Williams show, Nicole and Sakinah, both described how they were brought into the Ansaaru Allah Community by their mothers as children, and how they each bore a child by Dr. York. Both girls were over the age of 17 when they gave birth, but they insisted that Dr. York had molested them when they were still under legal age.

Sakinah was the author of a letter sent to Sheriff Sills in 1998 that contained a diagram of the "compound." According to the "Conspiracy and Conspirators" posting on the Nuwaubian website, "Sakinah . . . came to the 404 Shady Dale Rd. property days before the May 8, 2002 raid, wired (wearing a wire). She was the one who walked through every building and gave the FBI items to place in their affidavit to get the illegal search warrant."

State Agents

Howard Sills took office as the sheriff of Putnam County in 1997. His first encounter with the Nuwaubians occurred in 1997 when the guards at the gate of Tama Re refused entry to a building inspector, proclaiming that Tama Re was a "sovereign nation"—and therefore Sheriff Sills had to accompany him on his next visit. Sheriff Sills' interpretation of the situation was curiously cast, comparing it to the deadly federal siege at Waco: "Mr. York was begging for a Waco. He asked for it! They *wanted armed conflict* over something as innocuous and routine as a building permit!" (Interview, Sheriff Sills, 2003). However, this situation was resolved peacefully when the inspector returned with the sheriff.

Sheriff Sills's second encounter occurred a year later when a television show sparked the zoning conflict. Sills was watching an Atlanta TV news report in 1998 that featured the lively dance parties taking place in the Ramses Social Club at Tama Re. Sills realized the barn in which they were held did not conform to zoning regulations (Barry, 2004). The building inspector had given the Nuwaubians a permit to use the metal building as a storage facility but the structure had been modified with bathrooms, lighting, and sound equipment for their social club. The group was fined $45,750 for violating building codes. Sills sought an injunction to prevent the use of the Ramses Club. The Nuwaubians applied for a zoning permit to build a theme park around the same time and were denied.

Sills claims in December 1997 that he heard about child molestation from a woman who had left the compound, and in 1998 he started to receive anonymous phone calls complaining about child molestation. In the spring of 1998 Sills received an anonymous letter making the same claims. The sheriff's office opened an investigation in September 1998 when another anonymous letter arrived which included a diagram of Tama Re's residences, showing the buildings where the boys and girls slept (the anonymous letter was from Sakinah). Shortly afterward, Sills was contacted by Jacob York. Jacob York coordinated an effort to bring 12 ex-Nuwaubians to the sheriff's office. Together this group of ex-members conveyed stories of child abuse, child molestation, financial improprieties, and other alleged violations. This group is also the likely source of allegations about child pornography and stockpiles of illegal weapons which surfaced during the raid but did not materialize in the evidence. Sills contacted the FBI to report on these charges. Sills later told Susan Palmer, "We found we had the biggest case of child molestation in the history of the United States; big in terms of the number of victims, but also big in terms of the timeframe" (Interview, Sheriff Sills, 2003).

1997 was also the year that 39 members of Heaven's Gate committed mass suicide in Rancho Santa Fe, California. York's writings about extraterrestrial ancestors arriving in a Mothership to carry away 144,000 elite members of the Nuwaubian Nation before the destruction of the world certainly fanned the fears of local residents. The sheriff began receiving calls from townspeople expressing apprehensions that the Nuwaubians could be "another Heaven's Gate." The reaction led some residents to surf the Internet for more information about "cults." They soon found internet sites featuring anticult (ACM) and countercult (CCM) sources on York. According to journalist Osinski:

> Some people in Putnam County started surfing the Internet and they called (Sheriff) Sills in alarm over what they found. While clicking around in the general area of cults, they discovered that there was one in their back yard. Some cult-watch websites had general information about the Nuwaubians, or the latest version of Dwight York's formerly Muslim cult. These people called Sills to ask him what he was going to do about it. (Osinski, 2007:125)

In an interview with Susan Palmer in 2003, Sheriff Sills made the following comment about this incident:

> When they started to talk about the Mothership coming to take away 144,000 chosen ones to the planet Risq . . . well, that's when

people saw them as an alien cult, like Heaven's Gate. I began to receive calls asking if they were a cult and if they were going to commit mass suicide. (Quoted in Palmer, 2010b:77)

Sheriff Sills began his own research into "cults" and learned about a new religious community in Oregon in the 1980s called the Rajneeshees, named after their leader the Bhagwan Shree Rajneesh. Like York, the Bhagwan was accused of leading a "sexually oriented cult" and was a "self-proclaimed god" (Osinski, 2007:125). The Nuwaubians allegedly had other similarities to the Rajneesh community. They talked about setting up their own government and using festivals to encourage out-of-state visitors to register to vote. According to Oskinski (2007:125–127), residents of Wasco County in Oregon also feared a political "takeover" of local government by the group as well. This wasn't the worst of it; actions by rogue leaders in the Rajneesh community deepened the sheriff's fears even more. Several Rajneeshees sprinkled salmonella on the salad bars in the area, causing more than 700 residents to become ill. Apparently, these efforts were undertaken to deplete the ranks of local voters so they could install their own members as elected officials.

Sheriff Sills traveled to Wasco County, Oregon, in 1998 to meet with local police and prosecutors. Officials told Sills that the county had spent millions of dollars to fight off a "political invasion of the Rajneeshees, challenging the cult's voter registration tactics and their commercial expansion plans" (Osinski, 2007:127). Wasco county authorities told Sills that the most effective strategy against the religious group was land-use or zoning laws. The county's strategic use of zoning laws shut down operations and sources of revenue for the Rajneeshees. "Hold fast to your land use laws," Sills was advised by an Oregon prosecutor (Osinski, 2007:127). The sheriff returned to Putnam County with his worst fears confirmed. Sills believed that "the buildup of the Rajneeshee cult was eerily similar to the early years of the Nuwaubian cult in Putnam County" (Osinski, 2007:126).

The sheriff's inquiries also turned up a copy of the 1993 FBI intelligence report on Dr. York and the Ansaaru Allah Community. The report listed suspicions of arson and one former member was tied to murder. The FBI report also cited the Nuwaubian Nation as a "potential terrorist threat" (McCain, 2002). The framing of the Nuwaubians as a "terrorist" threat was groundless but contributed to an inflated perception of violence posed by the group. As early as 1997, federal agents were asking Putnam County building inspector "Dizzy" Adams if he saw "stockpiles of weapons"; York was being investigated by the FBI's antiterrorism unit (Osinski, 2007:123). The federal agent who opened the investigation of York, Tom Diehl, told reporter Osinski that he was looking into "possible connections to Middle East terrorist groups" (Osinski, 2007:215). Agent Diehl also told the reporter that they could be facing "another Waco" (p.215). FBI agent, Jalaine Ward, requested and received a hostage negotiation team "in case of resistance that included the taking of hostages" (Osinski, 2007:237).

In 2001 Sheriff Sills began to work closely with the FBI in planning the raid. It was clear from the raid planning that authorities expected to confront a violent, terrorist-like group. Law enforcement officials repeatedly referred to Tama Re as a "compound." Sheriff Sills invoked the Waco narrative, implying that the religious group could be armed and prepared for a shoot-out with law enforcement, or even capable of committing mass suicide. The ATF participated in the federal raid with the expectation of finding a suspected "stockpile of illegal weapons" (Palmer, 2010b:90). Indeed, the massive raid team arrived at Tama Re with "body bags and refrigerator trucks" (Palmer, 2006).

Because the Nuwaubian community was difficult to infiltrate with informants and isolated on a large tract of private land, the FBI relied on Sheriff Sills to conduct surveillance in the weeks leading up to the raid. The FBI believed that the presence of federal agents might alert locals and possibly the Nuwaubians to the intended enforcement action. The raid was scheduled for May 8, 2002. The sheriff's surveillance team included three deputies, whom Sills called his "three marines," dressed in camouflage with faces painted dark (Osinski, 2007:232), as well as a local news reporter for the *Macon Telegraph*, Rob Peecher.[8]

The surveillance team secured an observation post, organized a rotation of deputies, and utilized a scanner and other high-tech listening devices. Apparently, the surveillance operation was nearly exposed when a neighbor boy stumbled on to the deputies. The boy was captured and returned to his home. In another confirmation of official's expectation of a violent confrontation, Sheriff Sills told the boy's mother, "people are going to die if you say anything" (Osinski, 2007:233).

The exaggerated perception of "another Waco" didn't materialize. When the massive raid force arrived at Tama Re with armored vehicles, tear gas, and helicopters with mounted guns, there was no resistance by the Nuwaubians. The sect members lay on the ground as they were ordered and Tama Re was secured within three minutes. According to news coverage of the raid, federal agents seized 20 weapons (McCain, 2002), but these were later reported to be handguns and rifles, not illegal weapons, properly registered (Palmer, 2006). The weapons cache agents expected to find also did not materialize. Twenty guns found in a community of 500 people is hardly a "stockpile" of any kind. If one calculates the number of guns per person in this community, it works out to be 4 percent. We don't have comparable data for Georgia in terms of guns per capita, but according to *Guns and Ammo* magazine, 40.3 percent of residents in Georgia are gun owners (Tarr, 2013). Ironically, it seems that guns were more available or "stockpiled" in the surrounding region than at Tama Re.

Media

By 2001, the Nuwaubians had been the target of hundreds of news stories excoriating York and the group (Palmer, 2010b:82). Even the *New York Times* had covered the story of escalating tensions surrounding this "black sect in Georgia" (Lassette, 1999). The *Macon Telegraph* featured a story with the headline, "The Nuwaubians: Who Are These People?" (Pinzur, 2000). Patricia Mays of the Associated Press called the Nuwaubians a "cult" like Heaven's Gate and the People's Temple: "This group has a combination of all those schools of thought," she quoted Sheriff Sills as saying (Palmer, 2006). One news reporter for the *Macon Telegraph* made a stunning confession after interviewing some of the alleged victims, stating "through all of it I kind of got to hate the Nuwaubians. It was hard to maintain my objectivity."[9]

The sources for these news stories, however, were problematic since neither York nor Nuwaubian members spoke with the press. Thus, the sources for journalists almost always came from their critics—fearful townspeople, local officials, Sheriff Sills, and apostates/disaffected ex-members. As such, the framing of the conflict in Putnam County by television and print media was severely skewed. Journalists painted almost uniformly negative portraits of Dr. York. From the beginning of the Nuwaubian saga in Georgia, even before the child molestation allegations surfaced, there was close cooperation among county officials, law enforcement, and the media to cast the group as a potential threat.

One of the most significant journalists to cover the conflict was Bill Osinski, who worked for the *Atlanta Journal-Constitution* during this time. Osinski not only covered the story for the Atlanta newspaper, he later authored a book on the case which we have cited generously in this chapter. The title of his book, *Ungodly: The Story of Unprecedented Evil*, conveys the journalist's complete abandonment of even the pretense of objectivity. It uncritically embraces apostate accounts and reports Sheriff Sills' views as unmitigated fact. The book also provides incomplete citations and references, making statements or assertions difficult to verify. But what the book does provide is a definitive picture of how a key news reporter covering the Nuwaubian conflict constructed and framed the story.

Osinski describes York's Black Nationalist movement as a criminal enterprise and York as a charlatan, a cheat, and a dangerous cult leader who poses the threat of child abuse, sexual abuse, and violence. The primary material on which the book is based includes interviews with apostates/disaffected ex-members, local and county officials—especially Sheriff Sills—and court documents. Osinski does not consider that his interview sources might be embellished or distorted. He does not seem to be aware of the research literature that shows that apostate accounts are often unreliable (Beckford, 1985; Bromley, 1998a, 1998b; Foster, 1981, 1984; Johnson, 1998; Lewis, 1986, 1992; Mauss, 1998; Miller, 1983; Palmer, 1998, 1999; Wright, 1995b, 1998; Wright and Ebaugh, 1993). Some of these accounts may be true, or some portions of them true, but Osinski doesn't exercise any healthy skepticism as an investigative journalist. He certainly doesn't demonstrate any awareness of the problem of false allegations of child sexual abuse in the absence of forensic or medical evidence (Coleman, 1989; Coleman and Clancy, 1990; Nathan, 1991; Nathan and Snedeker, 1995).

At times, the journalist seems to channel Sheriff Sills and it is not clear if statements that appear in the book are his or the sheriff's. For example, following the forced closure of the Ramses Club in 1998, Osinski writes, "Sills delivered a message: The law in Putnam County would not look the other way for York. There would be no 'hands-off policy,' as there had been in Brooklyn. There would be no 'safe-streets' commendations from politicians. . . . The lights in Club Ramses would never go on again" (p.119). The muscular tone of this excerpt suggests the bravado of Sills, but no credit or citation is attributed. This style of writing pervades the book. Osinski's reporting takes on a cheerleading quality with respect to the sheriff and county officials, while the tone turns caustic and opprobrious when the subject is York and the Nuwaubians.

The journalist also invokes the intrinsic narrative of the "violent cult" throughout the book. For example, in assessing recorded tapes by Dr. York about escalating tensions between the Nuwaubians and local authorities, he writes:

One of the tapes was of a speech being made by Dwight York. In it, York repeatedly stated that his cult (*sic*) was a sovereign nation, and his farm in Putnam County was their homeland. York made what seemed to be a clear call to arms when he stated on the video, "When they come, and they will come, we have to be ready." (2007:118)

York's alleged statement on the video ("When they come . . . we have to be ready") can be interpreted in many ways. It is anything but "clear," as the journalist suggests. There is no mention of arms, no reference to a violent confrontation. But throughout the book, Osinski summons Waco as an unsubtle portent of things to come and at one point refers to the Nuwaubian religious community as "foot soldiers for an armed insurrection" (Osinski, 2007:221). The reading of armed violence into York's statement by Osinski seems to say more about the journalist than it does about York.

In one of the few parts of the book where Osinski attempts to discuss research on NRMs, he reveals a direct influence of ACM ideology and framing. The author discusses briefly the works of Margaret Singer, Flo Conway and Jim Seigelman, and Rick Ross to explain the defining characteristics of "cults" and their behavior. For example, Osinski retrieves Singer's list of "main factors that work together to make the cult member feel trapped—Deception, Debilitation, Dependency, Dread, and Desensitization" (Osinski, 2007:177–178). Guilt and shame keep people in cults, according to Singer. Osinki concedes, however, that "Singer never directly studied the Nuwaubian cult" (p.178). But Osinski is evidently not bothered by Singer's dearth of research on the Nuwaubians because "she served on the board of an institute founded by an anticult activist who did," former deprogrammer Rick Ross (p.178). Osinski observes that Ross "gave a speech in Atlanta on the topic of violent cults. Afterward he was approached by two women who identified themselves as former Nuwaubians and told him that 'something awful was going to happen' on the Putnam County land owned by York" (p.178). Curiously, the investigative journalist never thought to ask at what kind of gathering an avid anticult activist like Ross would be speaking. After the meeting, Osinksi observes, Ross "started monitoring York and the Nuwaubians" (p.178).

Osinski further opines that there are similarities between the "suicide cults of Heaven's Gate and Jonestown" and York's group, according to "cult researchers Flo Conway and Jim Siegelman in their book, *Snapping*" (Osinski, 2007:175). There is a parallel, he observes, to a phenomenon

identified by Conway and Siegelman as "the Death Spiral." "They identified a pattern of escalating chaos in their study of apocalyptic cults, satanic sects, and radical paramilitary survivalist sects, particularly in the
story of David Koresh and the Branch Davidians at Waco, Texas" (p.175).
Osinki follows this facile synopsis with a quote from Conway and Seigelman: "Repeatedly, we watched the same spiral dynamic draw everything
into its path—individuals, families, communities, the media, law enforcement, and higher government officials—into a vortex that exploded in
fury and left a trail of death and destruction in its path" (p.176). Osinksi
is convinced that he has tapped into a treasure trove of profound insights
about "cults." We quote Osinski below to convey his received understanding of cults, particularly the parallels between York and Koresh, clearly
shaped and abetted by ACM ideology.

> In the case of Koresh, Conway and Seigelman described him as
> a "strange attractor, a one-man energy center." Koresh sealed his
> group off from the outside world, preached frequently about the
> coming Armageddon, amassed an arsenal of weapons, beat his fol-
> lowers and starved and sexually abused their children—all things
> that York did to some degree. Koresh foretold of a coming holy war
> between his cult and the surrounding world, and prepared for that
> war by stockpiling weapons, burying a school bus on his com-
> pound and stocking it with a year's worth of food, and prepared his
> followers for an apocalyptic end. (Osinski, 2007:176)

Despite some factual errors and unfounded assertions in Osinki's (and
Conway and Seigelman's) description of events at Waco, the journalist is
not deterred. Why did all these cult members participate in such strange
behaviors? Osinski offers a formulaic ACM riposte: "the followers must
forfeit their free will in deference to the cult's godhead" (p.177).

As we indicated at the beginning of the chapter, while direct participation by ACM actors was not part of the oppositional coalition, the influence of ACM framing on journalists and other opponents of York was
clearly evident.

Claims

The claims invoked by organized opponents of the Nuwaubians follow a
familiar pattern. They evoke the fears and threats effectively disseminated

by ACM (and CCM) already embedded in the public consciousness. These include child abuse and sexual abuse, cult brainwashing, stockpiling weapons, mass suicide, and terrorism, among other things.

Child Molestation and Sexual Abuse

The most serious and damaging allegations against York and the Nuwaubians pertained to child molestation and sex abuse. The accusations were lodged by former members who contacted Putnam County Sheriff Howard Sills through anonymous phone calls and letters. Sheriff Sills, with support of county officials, launched an investigation into these charges and he also contacted the FBI. Sills was later approached by Jacob York, the chief apostate and instigator of the network of ex-members, offering to put him in touch with alleged victims of abuse. The network of ex-members worked closely with Sheriff Sills and the FBI in building a case against the Nuwaubians. The claims by apostates and ex-members led Sheriff Sills to describe it as "the biggest case of child molestation in the history of the United States." But the raid and subsequent custodial detention of Nuwaubian children produced no forensic or medical evidence of sexual abuse.

In the 2004 trial of Dr. York, there were 14 witnesses called to testify about alleged abuse. Six of the young women who were subpoenaed insisted they had never said they had been abused. Apparently, they changed their stories (Palmer, 2010b:110–112). One alleged victim, Suhaila Thomas, refuted the FBI report, claiming she had never been sexually abused by York. Thomas admitted she had met with FBI agents for four to six hours during their investigation but denied she had ever told them that she had been molested (Torpy, 2004a). Five other alleged victims also denied they had been molested by York. Twenty-one-year-old Sakinah Woods told the jury, "It seemed [the FBI agent who questioned her] wanted me to say something that didn't happen. They kept asking me over and over and I kept telling them, 'no, no, no'" (Torpy, 2004b). Affidavits filed by some of these young women later charged that they were threatened by FBI agents to make false statements. One said she told FBI investigators "what they wanted to hear because I felt that I would go to jail if I didn't go along with what they were saying" ("Nuwaubian Nation of Moors Cult Founder Malachi York Accuses FBI of Coercing Witnesses," *Macon Telegraph*, July 15, 2009). Another alleged victim swore in an affidavit that an FBI agent told him if he cooperated and made certain statements he could get his mother out of prison. But seven other alleged victims testified in court that York sexually abused them. One alleged victim, Abigail Washington, testified that she was abused and then later recanted her testimony. Then sometime later she recanted her recantation. Both prosecutors and defense attorneys claimed that the inconsistencies in the witnesses' statements supported their side of the case. In the end, the jury found York guilty on six counts of child molestation charges.

While we do not wish to go on record condoning or trivializing sexual molestation of minors, we are concerned that even those accused of pedophile crimes have the right to be presumed innocent and receive a fair trial. In York's case, it is very difficult to assess his guilt or innocence due to a number of obstacles. First, the court records of York's trial are sealed so we cannot read the victims' statements. Second, many of York's teenage wives were uncertain as to whether they were of legal age of consent when they were allegedly molested. Certainly, everyone agrees that York was a polygamist and many of his wives were teenagers, but his defense attorney, Adrian Patrick, argues that the government's case against York might have fallen apart if the RICO charges had not been added.[10] The inconsistencies in the testimonies of the witnesses were troubling for the jury.

Brainwashing

Numerous charges of brainwashing were leveled at York and the Nuwaubians. Even before Sheriff Sills arrived in his new office, his predecessor Sheriff Gene Resseau was contacted by family of Nuwaubian members to say "their children had been brainwashed and had joined a cult" (Osinksi, 2007:124). In preparation to take action against York, FBI agent Tom Deihl arranged for FBI profilers to search York's property. After seeing Tama Re, Diehl told a reporter that it "made believers out of the specialists. They saw people who were like *zombies*" (Osinski, 2007:215, emphasis ours). The metaphor of "zombies" recalls the common ACM claim that brainwashed cult members are robbed of their free will and cannot think for themselves. ACM activist Rick Ross told reporter Osinksi that "York's followers were also paralyzed, in terms of their own ability to think, or act" (p.178). On Ross's "Cult News" website a few months before Dr. York's trial, Ross wrote that "the Nuwaubians, like other 'cult' members, . . . are deeply 'brainwashed.'" Ross went on to say "the children of this faithful remnant remain prisoners of the 'cult' until their parents break free from the mental and

emotional bondage wrought by York" (Ross, 2003). At York's bail hearing, one unidentified FBI agent testified that "Mr. York controlled every
aspect of his followers' lives" (McCain, 2002).

Stockpiling Weapons

The claims about stockpiles of weapons and "illegal" weapons were marshaled to fuel the threat of "cult violence." These claims were packaged
with deliberate invocations of "another Waco" and the use of militaristic
terminology—"compound," "foot soldiers," "fortress"—to refer to the Nuwaubians and their community. However, the claims of weapons stockpiles proved to be hollow. No illegal weapons were found and no weapons
charges were filed. This didn't alter the perceptions of government officials who continued to perpetuate an image of the Nuwaubians as an
armed and violent group. At the 2004 trial of Dr. York, authorities produced a dramatic show of force that received considerable media attention.
According to the *Athens Banner-Herald*, "the court facility. . .was ringed
with dozens of law enforcement personnel, from black SWAT-outfitted
Glynn County police officers to machine gun–toting Federal Protective
Service officers" (Palmer, 2010b:108).

Mass Suicide

The Nuwaubians were linked explicitly to two religious groups involved
in collective violence, Heaven's Gate and the Branch Davidians. The com-
parisons were drawn to herald the imminent threat that the Nuwaubians
might commit mass suicide. Thus, a call for immediate and forceful action
would be in order. The added and embellished threat of mass suicide elevated the putative danger of the "cult" and hence, increased pressure on
authorities to "do something." For the record, the evidence supporting
mass suicide in the Heaven's Gate case is not a matter of dispute. But in
the Branch Davidian case, there is compelling evidence that the sect was
the casualty of an overly aggressive paramilitary assault by federal agents,
not mass suicide (*Investigation into the Activities of Federal Law Enforcement Agencies toward the Branch Davidians*, 1996; Wright, 1999, 2005,
2009). It is unfortunate that both Sheriff Sills and FBI agent Tom Diehl
would invoke "another Waco" when it is quite plausible that the actions
of law enforcement were largely to blame for the deaths of the Branch
Davidians. After the deadly April 19 assault at Waco, Justice Department
and FBI officials publicly declared that their actions were taken to "save
the children," even though all the children died in the attack. The use of

the child-saving narrative to rationalize a high-risk, paramilitary raid on a religious community was exactly what the joint county-federal raid team was proposing in the Nuwaubian case.

Terrorism

While claims of mass suicide were presented as an internal threat to members within the group, the charge of terrorism signaled an *external* threat indicating that the group could turn violent toward its neighbors or the surrounding society. The claim of terrorism was packaged together with the stockpiling of weapons to enhance the level of threat posed by the group. The 1993 FBI report on the Nuwaubians listed the group as a "potential terrorist threat" (McCain, 2002). The report cites confidential informants and calls for a "full domestic terrorism investigation" (Palmer, 2010b:65). York was subsequently investigated by the FBI's antiterrorism unit (Osinski, 2007:123). The FBI agent who opened the investigation of York, Tom Diehl, told a reporter that he was looking into "possible connections to Middle East terrorist groups." Anticult activist Rick Ross compared York to Charles Manson and stated that the Nuwaubian leader might stage his own "Helter Skelter" (Ross, 2003). Prior to the 2002 raid, an FBI agent requested a hostage negotiation team "in case of resistance that included the taking of hostages" (Osinski, 2007:237).

Conclusion

Dwight York and the United Nuwaubian Nation were prime candidates for a countersubversion campaign by organized opponents and the state. York was a defiant Black Nationalist with little tolerance for critics, traditional religion, and the "white power" structure. He was a charismatic figure who was not constrained by normative expectations and pursued spirituality as an ongoing experimental journey. As Max Weber tells us, charismatic authority is "specifically outside the realm of everyday routine and the profane sphere. In this respect, it is sharply opposed both to rational, and particularly bureaucratic, authority and to traditional authority" (Weber, 1968:51). It is also inherently unstable and can only be maintained in its pure form for a relatively brief time. Indeed, charisma can "exist only in the process of originating" (Weber, 1947:364). As Roy Wallis (1982:73) observes, charismatic authority can result in a very fluid kind of movement due to "the changing millennial vision of its founder." Dwight

York's critics interpreted his perpetual shifts in the character and form of religion as an indication that he was a trickster and a fraud. Though this kind of fluidity is entirely consistent with Weber's conceptualization of charismatic authority, it also made York vulnerable to charges of gamesmanship and fakery. The additional tensions brought about by race in the rural, Bible Belt South only exacerbated the suspicions and conflict surrounding this strange black NRM with its pyramids, flamboyant apparel, and UFO beliefs.

Given the convergence of these factors, a targeted campaign by apostates/ex-members was readily joined by local and county officials, law enforcement, and opportunistic journalists. York's unconventional marriage and sexual arrangements were readily construed as abuse and they gave some disaffected second-generation members powerful ammunition to bring allegations forward. The black "cult leader" with multiple wives, concubines, and a loyal following, living in a separatist community with walls and guards and proclaiming his small parcel of land a "sovereign nation" mobilized a fierce reaction. Of course, we do not have sufficient information to assess the validity of the child sexual abuse charges against York. But even so, our model outlines how claims by opponents can follow a pattern of "deviance amplification" and expand into something much larger. A loose coalition of opponents formed not only to lodge claims about possible child sexual abuse but also to frame the Nuwaubians as a dangerous, violent group of "terrorists" capable of mass suicide or "another Waco." The threat was perceived as so imminent and perilous that it necessitated a massive paramilitary response by over 300 law enforcement agents. Like the other cases we have studied, the government raid on the Nuwaubians was grossly disproportionate to any real threat posed by the group and another example of apparent overreach by authorities.

7

The Fundamentalist Latter Day Saints

Overview of Raid

ON APRIL 3, 2008, a joint task force of five Texas state and county law enforcement agencies accompanied by the Department of Family and Protective Services (DFPS) raided the Fundamentalist Church of Jesus Christ Latter Day Saints (FLDS), a Mormon polygamist sect, near the small town of Eldorado. The Yearning for Zion (YFZ) Ranch was home to 800 members of the FLDS. Authorities claimed they had evidence of a "widespread pattern and practice" of child sexual abuse and underage marriage. The massive state raid, involving a force of over 100 law enforcement agents, was triggered by phone calls to the Newbridge Family Shelter hotline in San Angelo, Texas, only 30 miles away, on March 29 and 30. The calls were made from a 16-year-old girl inside the YFZ community who alleged she was raped and beaten by her 49-year-old spiritual husband (Wright and Richardson, 2011a).[1]

The young girl identified herself as Sarah Jessop and claimed to be the seventh wife of a man she identified as Dale Barlow. According to court documents, she told volunteers at the Family Shelter that her husband choked her, hit her in the chest, and forced himself on her sexually. One of the beatings was so severe she was left her with broken ribs and she had to be taken to the hospital. Sarah said she was forced to marry at 15 years of age, had an eight-month old infant, and was several weeks pregnant at the time of the phone calls. The frantic young mother said she was not allowed to leave the Yearning for Zion Ranch by herself. She requested help from the domestic violence shelter and child protection officials to escape the ranch and flee the abusive relationship.

Four days later the Texas state raid was launched to rescue Sarah, arrest Dale Barlow, and collect evidence of child sexual abuse against the accused. After an extensive two-day search of the YFZ Ranch, however, DFPS and police were unable to find the young girl or the alleged perpetrator. Despite the failure to find any of the parties to the putative crime, child protection authorities took 439 FLDS children into state custody.[2] It was the largest state custodial detention of children in U.S. history. Officials defended the action asserting that all of the FLDS children were at risk of child abuse (*Original Petition for Protection of Children, District Court of Schleicher County, Texas, 51st J.D., Cause 2902, 2008*). This assertion would prove to be legally problematic for state officials. But the raid on the FLDS community and seizure of materials did produce evidence of underage marriage. Eleven FLDS men were later charged with sexual assault of a minor (underage marriage) and other related charges.

Texas officials soon learned that the caller was not Sarah Jessop, as the woman claimed, but a mentally disturbed 33-year-old woman from Colorado Springs, Rozita Swinton. Ms. Swinton had been arrested previously for making false charges of abuse to the police. In fact, Ms. Swinton had been linked to at least ten incidents of false claims to child protection and law enforcement agencies across the country since 2006 (Wright and Richardson, 2011b:2–3). Embarrassed officials scrambled to avoid a public relations disaster when they realized the raid was based on fraudulent charges by a woman with a history of mental instability and a criminal record. Stephanie Goodman, the chief spokesperson for Texas's social service agencies, told news reporters, "it doesn't matter," although the calls "got us to the gates, it's not what caused us to remove the children" (Garrett, 2008).

The Texas state raid on the FLDS was predicated on 16 phone calls placed between March 29 and April 5 to authorities, as well as more than 30 hours of recorded phone calls made to FLDS apostate and anticult movement (ACM) activist, Flora Jessop. Jessop encouraged Swinton to contact the domestic violence center in San Angelo (Garrett, 2008). But the caller was not a member of the FLDS, much less an abused spiritual wife at the YFZ Ranch. Moreover, Dale Barlow, the man accused of abusing her, had never been on the Yearning for Zion Ranch in Texas. Barlow was a member of the FLDS community in Colorado City, Arizona. He had been convicted on sexual abuse charges in 2007 and was on parole. State authorities confirmed that Mr. Barlow was in Arizona during the time the caller claimed to be abused. It appeared that Ms. Swinton culled Barlow's name from news article in fabricating the perpetrator.

FLDS parents of the seized children filed an appeal of the District Court's ruling giving protective custody to the DFPS. The appeal was made to the Texas Court of Appeals, Third District, in Austin. On May 22, the appellate court found that the district court erred and that the Texas authorities did not carry its burden of proof required by law. The court ruled that the state would have to hold hearings for *each* of the 439 children to determine if their physical health or safety were in danger. The DFPS appealed to the Texas Supreme Court, but to no avail. The Texas Supreme Court held that the removal of the children was unwarranted and ordered the children returned to their parents (*In re Texas Department of Family and Protective Services*, 2008).

The criminal trials of the 11 FLDS men began in November 2009 in Schleicher County, Texas. The trials were conducted consecutively and covered a period of two years and four months. Nine of the men were convicted of sexual assault, one pled guilty to three counts of bigamy, and one was convicted of performing an unlawful marriage of his 12-year-old daughter. With the exception of Warren Jeffs, the other men received sentences ranging from 7 to 75 years. Jeffs was convicted on two counts of sexual assault and given a sentence of life plus 20 years.

History and Background of FLDS

Mormon fundamentalism is rooted in the Church of Jesus Christ of Latter Day Saints (LDS). The FLDS is part of a larger sectarian movement that split from the LDS church when it abandoned the practice of polygamy (plural marriage or "The Principle") established by its founder, Joseph Smith. The sectarian schism originated with the Manifesto of 1890 issued by LDS Prophet and President Wilfred Woodruff reinterpreting Smith's prophetic vision and renouncing plural marriage. The LDS church was under pressure to repudiate polygamy and was offered statehood by federal authorizes in exchange for their cooperation. The territory of Utah and the LDS community were also threatened with military assault if they refused. The church fathers conceded and formally proclaimed its fealty to the institution of monogamy. The term "fundamentalist" applies to those who continue to practice plural marriage and who believe that they adhere to the more pure doctrines of their founder before the church caved in to the pressure of the federal government to conform to national mores and religious standards.

Today, substantial Mormon fundamentalist communities can be found in various parts of the intermountain West in the United States, in Sonora and Chihuahua, Mexico (where some Mormons fled at various points in history to escape prosecution in Utah; Bennion, 2004), as well as Bountiful, British Columbia, which is home to approximately a thousand FLDS in Canada's only openly polygamous community (Campbell, 2009). Although Mormon fundamentalists are a diverse group, the FLDS is most often the target of ex-member acrimony and media attacks. All of the fundamentalist sects emerged as a result of conflicts over power and leadership in the original Short Creek, Arizona, community (later called Colorado City), which was first settled in the late 1920s by Leroy S. Johnson and other polygamist families. Power struggles arose among a group called the five "apostles of God" whose primary duty was to keep polygamy alive after it was renounced in 1890 (Bennion, 2011). There are approximately 20,000 FLDS members in Utah, Arizona, Texas, Colorado, South Dakota, and British Columbia.

The Apostolic United Brethren (AUB) is a group that split from the FLDS shortly after Joseph W. Musser (one of the five apostles from the Short Creek community) was to step into John Y. Barlow's shoes as the leader of the FLDS after his death in 1949. Musser, unable to take over this post due to medical issues, assigned Rulon Allred to take his place. Since many followers did not agree with Musser's choice, Musser broke off from the group with his own modest following leaving Leroy Johnson to lead the sect now known as the FLDS (Driggs, 2011). As of 2005, the AUB has been under the leadership of Lemoine Jenson. Its membership is estimated to be between 5,000 and 8,000 members.

The Kingston clan split from the Short Creek community following the death of J. Leslie Broadbent, the priesthood president, in 1935 and formed its own community in northern Utah. This Mormon fundamentalist sect embraced the claim of Elden Kingston that he had been chosen as Broadbent's Second Elder and rightful successor. Kingston claimed that an angel visited him in a cave in northern Davis County, Utah, and directed him to establish the United Order. Kingston responded to the call by forming the Davis County Cooperative Society in 1941. In 1977, the Kingstons formally renamed the group the Latter Day Church of Christ. It is one of the five major Mormon fundamentalist groups today. The sect has approximately 1,200 members.

Centennial Park split from the FLDS and formed in 1986 after the death of Leroy Johnson and the appointment of the new FLDS leader Rulon Jeffs. The split was based on disputes over leadership and authority. Jonathan Hammon and Alma Timpson led a group of dissenters who rejected the autocratic "One Man Doctrine" that gave complete authority and control to a single leader (Driggs, 2011; Hammon and Jankoviak, 2011). Jeff's claim to exclusive prophetic authority was rejected by Hammon and Timpson, leading to the founding of Centennial Park, also called the Second Ward. Centennial Park is located in Colorado City very near the FLDS community. The membership of Centennial Park is approximately 1,500.

Finally, the LeBarons fled to Mexico to escape prosecution by the U.S. government in the mid-1950s. Infighting over who would lead the group prompted the LeBarons to officially split from the AUB and create the Church of the Firstborn of the Fullness of Times, which is now known as the LeBaron group (Bennion, 2011). The membership of the LeBaron group is approximately 1,000. Despite the split, the LeBaron Group and the AUB have much in common, including more modern gender norms and not necessitating followers to practice polygamy as a requisite to gaining access to the eternal life in the hereafter (Bennion, 2008, 2011).

The twin FLDS towns of Colorado City, Arizona, and Hildale, Utah (they straddle the Arizona-Utah border), constitute the largest single gathering place for Mormon fundamentalism. More than any other fundamentalist group, the FLDS has been the target of intense efforts at social control, including excommunications by the LDS Church (Cragun, Nielsen, and Clingenpeel, 2011), charges of violations of the Mann Act for allegedly transporting women across state lines for immoral purposes, and state raids on the community in 1944 and 1953. The 1953 raid was a large-scale raid involving a force of more than 1,500 police and social service personnel, wielding 122 warrants for FLDS members. Arizona state officials seized 263 FLDS children and placed them into protective custody. For two years following the 1953 raid, the FLDS endured a protracted series of hearings in juvenile court in Phoenix (Evans, 2011). In the end, all but one of the women who were underage at the time of marriage returned with their children to the community. The raid failed to stop the practice of plural marriage among the FLDS. Indeed, the 1953 Arizona raid created somewhat of a public backlash and media disaster for state officials as public opinion turned against the government for the mass seizure of children. The *Los Angeles Times* and the *Arizona Republic* "condemned the way it exemplified totalitarianism in the isolated landscape of northern Arizona" (Bradley, 2011:19). Arizona's Young Democrats organization assailed the raid as "odious and un-American," accusing Governor Howard Pyle, who organized the raid, of using it for self-serving, political purposes (Bradley, 2011:19). As a result of this backlash, Arizona officials took a much different and more cautious approach toward the FLDS after 1953. Officials made efforts to build relationships within the community and address potential violations of *individuals*, rather than conducting sweeps of the whole community (Bradley, 2011:30–31).

In the 55 years between 1953 and 2008, Mormon fundamentalism evolved to become a distinctive religious culture. This prolonged period of solitude and seclusion without government intrusion would probably have continued had the FLDS not decided to found a new community in West Texas. Problems for the FLDS arose after the death of its prophet Rulon Jeffs in 2002 and passing of the leadership to his son Warren. Warren Jeffs' leadership "marked a significant shift in FLDS practices and policies by which he sought to solidify his power and authority" (Wright and Richardson, 2014:88). Jeffs called for a greater centralization of power in the person of the prophet. One key shift in policy was a return to the marriage of underage girls. Jeffs reversed a long-term trend of women waiting later to marry (Bradley, 1993:100). He apparently sought to establish the Texas community to shield this controversial practice from outsiders and even from others in the main community at Colorado City.[3] At the time of the purchase of the YFZ Ranch in 2003, the legal age of marriage with parental consent was 14 (see Richardson and Schreinert, 2011; Wright and Richardson, 2014). Only in 2005, two years after the FLDS community was established, did the Texas legislature raise the legal age of marriage with parental consent to 16. The legislator who introduced the bill, Harvey Hilderbran, represented Schleicher County where the FLDS community was located. In a press release accompanying the passage of the bill, Hilderbran made clear why the bill was introduced: "I want to keep Eldorado, Schleicher County, and all of Texas from becoming like Colorado City, Arizona, and Hilldale (*sic*), Utah, where this cult came from" ("Governor Perry Signs SB 6 into Law," *Eldorado Success*, June 9, 2005).

Organized Opponents

Research shows that from the beginning of the establishment of the new FLDS community in Eldorado in 2004, FLDS apostates, anticult actors, local media, elected officials, and others worked together as a loose coalition of opponents to press claims, incite public opinion, broaden disputes, and amplify perceived threats with the intent to force state action (Wright and Richardson, 2011b; Richardson and Schreinert, 2011). Curiously, Texas state police investigating the fraudulent complaint made little effort to corroborate the authenticity of the caller who claimed to be Sarah Jessop. That the hoax calls were believed so readily by Texas authorities, predicated on such weak and unsubstantiated evidence, requires explanation.

Richardson and Schreinert (2011) argue that raid on the FLDS community in Texas was not simply a single act that developed as a response to a series of hoax phone calls. Rather, evidence indicates that the presence of this controversial group had been flagged by local and state authorities years before and that "officials had been preparing for a confrontation for an extended period" (Richardson and Schreinert, 2011:225). Some of the plans for a confrontation began almost as soon as the public became aware of the group's move to Texas in 2004. Consequently, it appears that child welfare workers, law enforcement, elected officials, and other moral gatekeepers already concerned about the presence in this West Texas community of the LDS splinter group were predisposed to believe the most sensational tropes and narratives about the sect, making verification of the hoax calls unnecessary.

Apostates

The most important and active anti-FLDS apostate in the development of the Texas state raid was Flora Jessop. Jessop was more than an outspoken critic of the sect; she had carved out a role as a "career apostate" (Bromley, 1998b; Brown, 1996; Wright, 1998). According to news sources, Rozita Swinton placed her first call to Flora Jessop on March 29, claiming to be the abused polygamist wife of an FLDS member at the YFZ Ranch. Jessop apparently believed Swinton's story, telling the *Colorado Springs Gazette* that "she [Swinton] honest-to-God sounded like a sixteen year-old or younger child in need of help" (Newsome, 2008). Jessop admitted to crying over the stories that Swinton conveyed and said she was "amazed at how much Swinton knew about the sect" (Newsome, 2008).

Flora Jessop was the critical link between Swinton and Texas child welfare authorities. Jessop encouraged Swinton to call the Newbridge Family Shelter hotline in Texas following their extended conversations. Swinton made calls to the domestic violence shelter the same day. More importantly, on the following day, March 30, Jessop contacted Texas authorities directly and gave them more than 30 hours of recorded phone calls with Swinton (Garrett, 2008). This may also help to explain why Texas state officials made no effort to verify the authenticity of the caller. Flora Jessop had a record of involvement with prosecutors and child protection officials in Arizona and Utah and had cultivated extensive networks and contacts with child-saver's organizations. Details of her association with county and state officials, including the Utah attorney general's office, are well documented in her autobiography (*Church of Lies*). She was likely seen as an informed source on the FLDS by child protection workers. Thus Jessop's direct involvement with Texas authorities was seen as a kind of validation of the caller's credibility.

Flora Jessop was born into a polygamous family in Hildale, Arizona, one of 28 children. She fled the FLDS at the age of 16 after being sexually abused by her father (Jessop and Brown, 2009). After a series of difficult challenges adjusting to life outside the sect, she found her calling and passion as a "professional ex" (Brown, 1996) contesting the FLDS. According to the *Los Angeles Times*, Jessop "devotes almost every waking moment to exposing the church as a hotbed of child abuse and helping the community's girls and women escape from the polygamous life she fled" (Heller, 2004).

In 2001, Jessop founded Help the Child Brides, a nonprofit organization designed to provide assistance to underage brides in the FLDS who were allegedly forced into polygamous marriages. This organization has its own website that features narratives of ex-members as well as various books and articles critical of the FLDS. She is also executive director of the Los Angeles–based Child Protection Project, another nonprofit organization offering financial assistance to young people who have left polygamy. In addition to these roles, Jessop has also written a provocative biography about her own experiences in the FLDS (Jessop and Brown, 2009), including a detailed description of her involvement with law enforcement and child protection workers in Arizona with the intent to expose the FLDS as a "dangerous cult."

Flora Jessop's public campaign against the FLDS has at times earned her sharp criticism. The *Phoenix New Times* described Jessop as "a publicity-hungry fanatic whose demands to have control over someone else's children are becoming eerily similar to the dictatorial attitude of her sworn nemesis, Warren Jeffs" (Heller, 2004). She has been called a "vigilante" by church members and a "rock star" by supporters. Jessop is well known for overstating her claims against the FLDS. On one television news show in Los Angeles she told an audience that the FLDS was "not a religion" but actually a form of "terrorism" (Heller, 2004). Arizona Attorney General Terry Goddard has questioned her aggressive approach, complaining that she has "gotten nastier and nastier" and stated that she has "fanned fears" without good reason. The attorney general told the *Los Angeles Times* that Jessop's tactics have actually "undermined the state," and he accused her of being "misguided and devious" (Heller, 2004). Arizona state congresswoman Linda Binder, also a public critic of the FLDS, told a news reporter that the problem with Jessop's methods is that "she wants to go in there guns ablazing, get everybody out" (Heller, 2004). Binder's statement was made four years before the massive paramilitary raid in Texas.

Jessop provides a thorough account of claims-making activities in her book, which documents the amplification of ostensible threats posed by the FLDS. Jessop also reveals how she managed to enlist news media and state officials early on in the oppositional campaign.

By March 2004 Warren Jeffs had started putting up buildings on his Texas property near the town of Eldorado. And it was in March that I was on ABC's *Primetime* after journalist John Quinones went *of course* with me to Colorado City. A lot of people saw that show—including people in Eldorado, Texas, who were beginning to get worried about what these people from Utah had in mind. I was no longer fearful of the media. I'd learned that they could help me get my message out there. Right away, I started contacting people in Texas, including newspaper editors and other journalists. I made a trip out to Eldorado to warn people about what was coming. The local papers started interviewing me for a series of stories they were writing on the FLDS compound. . . .

In April, I held a news conference in Eldorado. It was attended by government and law enforcement officials from Texas and Arizona—including Mohave County, Arizona, supervisor Buster Johnson, whose district included Colorado City.

And it was covered not only by media in the Southwest but also by the *New York Times* and ABC's *Primetime*.

I told them my story. I told them about sexual abuse, forced marriages, child abuse, tax evasion, welfare fraud, and child labor. I told them exactly who had purchased the land that Warren was now calling YFZ, LLC, a limited liability corporation. . . . The FLDS members believed that Zion would be their place of refuge when the sins of the wicked destroyed the world. The name chilled me to the bone. I wondered what Warren might be planning next. (Jessop and Brown, 2009:450–451).

Jessop's cultivation of media connections provided critically important public venues to disseminate and expand upon the victimization narrative, building unfavorable, even hostile, public opinion toward the FLDS. By her own account, she started contacting newspaper editors and reporters in Texas, issuing press releases, and holding press conferences. Her efforts yielded almost immediate results: the *San Angelo Standard-Times* published a series of news articles on the FLDS in March 2005 quoting Jessop extensively (Anthony, 2005; Phinney, 2005). Jessop was the primary source for the news stories and Jessop's own biographical account was reproduced, solidifying her role as a whistleblower and expert on the FLDS. The local news stories featuring Jessop's inflated claims became part of a larger public perception and narrative that facilitated an inhospitable political climate for the FLDS and mounting public pressure on officials to take action.

Other key FLDS apostates include Carolyn Jessop, Rebecca Musser, and Ross Chatwin. Carolyn Jessop was a conspicuous figure during and after the raid. Her biographical account of life in the FLDS, aptly titled *Escape* (Jessop and Palmer, 2008), gave her credibility with news media. Carolyn Jessop has been a persistent and harsh critic of the FLDS for years, though not as aggressive or tenacious as Flora Jessop. Carolyn Jessop took an active role in the attempted "rehabilitation" of the FLDS children after they were taken into state custody by Texas officials (Adams, 2008). In the days and weeks following the raid she appeared in numerous interviews on television retelling her story about her own "escape" from the group.

Rebecca Musser is the older sister of Elissa Wall, another apostate who wrote her own book, *Stolen Innocence* (Wall with Pulitzer, 2008). Musser was married to the FLDS founder Rulon Jeffs in her late teens and evidently was pressured to marry Warren Jeffs after Rulon's death. She refused the marriage and eventually left the group. Musser formed a close relationship with Schleicher County Sheriff David Doran in the months leading up to the raid. She was accused by church members of helping law enforcement officials obtain a search warrant for the YFZ Ranch. Doran denied the charge, saying only that he "networked with Becky; she is not my confidential informant" (Perkins, 2008). Doran told reporters that "Becky helped us with questions concerning this group that would assist law enforcement" and that "she assisted child protection services with their investigations" (Perkins, 2008). Musser's role in the oppositional coalition was made even clearer when she became an expert witness for the state in the prosecution of FLDS defendants charged with sexual assault. One defense attorney called her "a very effective witness."[4]

Ross Chatwin is a discontented ex-member who was excommunicated from the group and became embroiled in a property dispute. In the years prior to the Texas raid, Chatwin was engaged in a dispute with sect leaders. He was described by one news source as the "most visible rebel" contesting the FLDS, denouncing Warren Jeffs and likening him to Adolf Hitler ("We Fear Another Waco," 2004). Chatwin accused the FLDS leader of a litany of crimes, including "brainwashing," rape, murder through a "blood atonement" doctrine, and stockpiling weapons in a cave, among other things. Chatwin also became a popular figure in the media after the raid, granting many interviews, expressing grievances, and pressing claims against the FLDS and Jeffs (Hunsicker, 2008; Winslow, 2008).

ACM Organizations and Actors

Flora Jessop's explicit ties to ACM organizations and actors provide a fuller and more complete picture of the emergent oppositional network in this case. Connections to ACM organizations can be found on Jessop's Child Protection Project website (www.childpro.org/). Under the "Resources and Links" page, there is a listing of organizations identified as contacts for information. The listings include five prominent anticult/countercult organizations: 1) Apologetics Index: Apologetics Research Resources on Religious Cults, Sects, World Religions, and Related Issues; 2) International Cultic Studies Association (formerly the American Family Foundation; publishes the ACM-based *Cultic Studies Review*); 3) Steven Hassan's Freedom of Mind Center; 4) Meadow Haven (a cult rehabilitation center billed as "a resource for cult survivors to transition into society"); and 5) Religion News Blog, operated by the Apologetics Index group mentioned above. The CPP website explains the rationale for these listings as follows: "Often we combine resources with other organizations while working on certain projects in which *we all share a common goal*" (emphasis ours). The common goal is not difficult to ascertain; all these organizations depict NRMs as "cults" and exercise considerable time and effort in exposing alleged misdeeds. Some also offer assistance in "cult counseling," "recovery," and "rehabilitation" services.

On Flora Jessop's Help the Child Brides website, one can find a link to Rick Ross's Institute for the Study of Destructive Cults, Controversial Groups and Movements. Rick Ross has been a highly visible figure in the ACM for decades. Ross was a professional deprogrammer until he was successfully sued by one of his victims following a failed deprogramming in

Washington state in 1995 (see Shupe and Darnell, 2006). The victim, Jason Scott, had converted to a Pentecostal church, prompting his parents to hire Ross. Scott was forcibly abducted and restrained, taken across state lines, and confined in a remote cabin for days before escaping. The jury in the U.S. District Court of Washington found in favor of Mr. Scott and awarded him $2.5 million in damages from Ross. The lawsuit ended Mr. Ross's career as a deprogrammer and in 1996 Ross began promoting himself as a "cult expert," "consultant," and "lecturer," founding the virtual institute hosted on his website.⁵ Ross's website features an archive of news articles highlighting alleged crimes and abuses of cults, as well as self-serving interviews with him and other ACM leaders. The FLDS has the distinction of being the most prominently cited group in Ross's archive with over 800 news articles.

Jessop's ties to Ross range beyond the mere website links, however. In the same *San Angelo Standard-Times* articles featuring Jessop in March 2005, Ross is also interviewed. It appears that Jessop recommended Ross as an expert on cults to the news media and possibly to government authorities in Texas. Ross and Jessop are quoted in tandem and the anti-cult narrative is faithfully executed for readers. Ross is simply described as a "New Jersey expert on fringe religious groups who has studied the FLDS for 20 years" (Anthony, 2005:2). The reporter apparently makes no effort to corroborate Ross' claims; Ross is a self-proclaimed "expert" who possesses no educational credentials to substantiate any expertise. In the news story, Ross invokes a stereotypical ACM frame to describe the FLDS: "There is [an] eerie quality [about them]; what some would call brainwashing" (Anthony, 2005:2). Predictably, Ross expands the threat further, offering the reporter a comparison between the FLDS and Jonestown, and likening FLDS leader Warren Jeffs to Jim Jones:

> What he [Jeffs] seems to be doing is cocooning," Ross said, comparing the situation to that of Jim Jones, the San Francisco preacher who in the 1980s [sic] fled with his cult to Nicaragua [sic] as legal scrutiny increased. Jones and his followers later committed mass suicide when legal pressures continued. (Anthony, 2005:4).

Without any evidence to support this assertion, Ross expands the putative threat from "brainwashing" and "cocooning" to "mass suicide." Incredibly, the reporter—who factually misstates both the time in which the People's Temple fled (it was in the 1970s) and the country where the group established its community (Guyana)—makes no attempt to question Ross about the strained comparison. The readers of the newspaper are left with an exaggerated and unsupported allegation by an alleged "cult expert" who is actually part of the oppositional coalition.

Another link posted on Jessop's Child Protection Project website is to Steve Hassan's Freedom of Mind Center. Hassan, like Jessop, is a former member of an NRM (Unification Church) and a longtime career apostate. His Freedom of Mind Center is an established ACM organization. Hassan is also a former deprogrammer who lists his credentials as an "exit counselor," consultant, and "expert." Like Ross, he has frequently appeared on newscasts shortly after incidents such as raids or criminal charges are made against minority religions. Like Jessop and other apostates, Hassan authored a book (*Combatting Cult Mind Control*; Hassan, 1988) that plays to the victimization narrative and accuses new religions of brainwashing and mind control. Hassan has been a key figure in the reframing of deprograming as a type of counseling and facilitation of recovery (Wright, 1998).

News coverage of the post-raid management of sect children in state custody reveals the involvement of another anticult activist, Janja Lalich. Lalich is listed on the Cultic Research website (www.cultresearch.org) as the "founder and director of the Center on Influence and Control." She is also faculty member at California State, Chico. Lalich coauthored an oft-cited book with the matriarch of the anticult movement, Margaret Singer, titled *Cults in Our Midst: The Hidden Menace in Our Everyday Lives* (Singer and Lalich, 1995). According to a 2008 report by the *Salt Lake City Tribune*, Lalich "went to Texas last summer to help caseworkers" with the FLDS children in state custody (Adams, 2008). Reporter Brooke Adams posted on her blog that Lalich "participated in a two-day training seminar for shelter providers and CPS workers involved in the YFZ Ranch case" (Adams, 2008). Lalich's role in advising and assisting child protection workers after the FLDS raid is significant for several reasons. First, Lalich brought a decidedly anticult framing to the shelter, stating in one interview with the press that the FLDS was "abusing hundreds and hundreds of women and children" (Bryner, 2008). Second, according to news reports, Lalich apparently came to this conclusion by interviewing a career apostate and anti-FLDS activist, Carolyn Jessop (Adams, 2008). Lalich and Jessop are subsequently coupled in media interviews and together they warn readers of the perilous threat posed by the FLDS. Jessop told reporters, "Once you go into the compound, you don't ever leave it." Jessop's warning was buttressed by Lalich, who provided a subversion narrative about "cults" and explains how "fear" is the motive for loyalty to the group.

This news story, in turn, was prominently featured on Flora Jessop's Help the Child Brides website within a few days of its appearance in print.

One health professional with ties to the ACM who was identified in court documents was Bruce Perry. Perry is a psychiatrist and senior fellow at the Child Trauma Academy in Houston. According to CBS news coverage of the custody hearings of FLDS children, Perry was identified as one of the state's "experts" and described as "an authority on children in cults" ("Polygamist Sect Kids to Undergo DNA Tests," 2008). Perry was also a key figure in the disastrous Branch Davidian raid in 1993. He led a child trauma team into Waco to evaluate the Branch Davidian children after the raid. Some of Perry's evaluations of the children were criticized for a blaming-the-victim approach and for not recognizing the trauma caused by the government's own actions (Coleman, 1994).

Perry was also hired to evaluate children seized in a government raid on The Family International in Australia in 1993. Perry was referred by an Australian ACM group and submitted an expert opinion based on his evaluation to the court (Perry, 1994). Another psychiatrist hired by the defense castigated Perry's findings, noting that Dr. Perry never actually examined any of the children in question. His evaluation was merely based on materials provided by anticult groups. Perry offers an evaluation in this case that adheres to a generalized anticult template cloaked in psychosocial rhetoric. The observations by the defense attorney's psychiatrist are worth quoting at length here.

> Dr. Perry displays an outrageous methodology from the outset, when on page two he claims to have studied groups which engage in "coercive, destructive" practices and says they are "similar to those described by the COG." He goes on to mention "pan-sexuality," and even "torture." The reader of this report is given no data to support such descriptions of these other groups, but is apparently expected to accept such claims at face value, and then accept the notion that the Family is "similar" because someone has said so.
>
> Dr. Perry, in describing what he has done in studying other groups, claims to have performed *on specific individuals* "comprehensive psychosocial review, psychological evaluation, quantification of symptoms, multiple non-structured contacts including repeat observations under a variety of situations, structured psychiatric interviews and interviews with important collateral contacts." (page 2). I believe Dr. Perry should be required to explain

why he has been willing to reach such damning conclusions about the Family and the children of its members, when *he performed none of these evaluations* on any Family members.

Instead, Dr. Perry has apparently based his opinions on nothing more than "reviewing pertinent materials." The idea that he can, from reading documents, determine in a professional and competent manner, what is in the best interests of a child, is a grotesque distortion of the legitimate process of evaluating a child and his or her living situation. (Coleman, 1994:2)

The medical examinations of the seized children by state health professionals in Australia produced no evidence of sexual abuse as claimed by opponents and child protection officials. Perry's long-distance evaluations were evidently unconvincing; the New South Wales Supreme Court ruled that the raid and forced custodial detention of the children were illegal and cleared the way for defendants to seek damages against the state (Nicholas, 1999; Richardson, 1999).

Perry's ties to the ACM are not insignificant. Among other activities, he has been a featured speaker at several anticult conferences, is listed in the International Cultic Studies Association directory and profiles section, and has published an article in the International Cultic Studies e-newsletter on the Branch Davidian case (Perry and Szalavitz, 2007). Perry has been a reliable and credentialed voice in the health professional field for the anticult framing of NRM children seized in raids.

State Agents

Law enforcement and child protection officials proved to be critical allies in the opponents' campaign against the FLDS. According to pleadings filed by attorneys for the 11 indicted FLDS men in Schleicher County criminal court on July 12, 2009, an investigation by Texas Ranger Leslie Brooks Long led to phone calls to Mohave County Sheriff Alan Pashano in an attempt track down Dale Evans Barlow in the days before the raid (Floyd and Sinclair, 2009). Shortly afterward, the Mohave County Sheriff's Office notified Schleicher County Sheriff David Doran that Barlow had not left Mohave County since 2007 and had never been to the YFZ Ranch. Sheriff Doran conveyed this information to Ranger Long. Officer Long also instructed Schleicher County Deputy George Arispe to contact the local medical center to verify the claim by the 16-year-old pregnant caller that she had been treated for broken ribs and physical abuse. But the medical center had no such record of treating a person fitting this description (Floyd and Sinclair, 2009).

Moreover, anti-FLDS activist Flora Jessop, who first received the calls from Swinton and sent the recorded calls to Texas, told news sources that Swinton alternately claimed to be Sarah, Sarah's twin sister Laura living in Colorado City, and Laura's friend (Mitchell, 2008; Rizzo, 2008). Texas officials were aware of the multiple inconsistencies in the recorded calls. Despite these bewildering discrepancies, Ranger Long filed an affidavit in support of an arrest and search warrant in connection with an alleged sexual assault of a minor named "Sarah Jessop" by "Dale Barlow" (*Affidavit for Search and Arrest Warrant, No. M-08–001 S, The State of Texas, County of Schleicher, April 3, 2008*). Curiously, Ranger Long failed to inform Judge Barbara Walther, who signed the warrant, that 1) the Mohave County Sherriff's department confirmed that Barlow had never left Arizona, 2) that the local medical center had no record of treating a pregnant 16-year-old girl for physical abuse, and 3) that there were numerous other holes and contradictions in Sarah Jessop's account.

The state's uncorroborated and conflicting information in this case should have raised serious questions among law enforcement investigators. There were clearly insufficient grounds for rushing forward into a high-risk, paramilitary raid on such weak evidence. Why were officials seemingly locked into a "preordained road" (as ATF officials were in Waco) to conduct a raid?

Local officials also conducted surveillance of the YFZ Ranch, paid frequent visits to the ranch, deployed informants, gathered damaging information (though often unverified), and essentially orchestrated a range of activities in preparation for the raid. Indeed, NBC News reported shortly after the raid that "State troopers put into action *the plan they had on the shelf* to enter the 1,700 acre compound" ("Texas Authorities Defend Sect Raid," 2008, emphasis added). The reference to the raid plan "on the shelf" strongly suggests that state officials had already determined their method of enforcement. Other statements by government officials revealed that they were only waiting for a "complaint" or "spark" to mobilize the state control machinery against the FLDS community (Johnson, 2008; Neil, 2008).

Flora Jessop's ties to ACM activists and child protection advocates in Texas were essential to the actions taken by DFPS. This became evident in the aftermath of the raid as DFPS officials expressed a strong anticult framing of the group. Beyond the issue of underage marriage, officials labeled the FLDS a "cult" and repeating inflated claims routinely offered up by ACM activists (brainwashing, stockpiling weapons, mass suicide, forced servitude). This connection between state agents and ACM activists was supported by accounts of independent child protection workers who were brought in to counsel the FLDS children in the weeks following the raid. Linda Werlein, chief executive officer of the Hill Country Community Mental Health and Mental Retardation (MHMR) Center in Kerrville, Texas, led a team of approximately a dozen social workers to San Angelo to assist DFPS after the raid. However, Ms. Werlein was distressed by what she observed and later told the *Las Vegas Review Journal* that "much of what she was told by [DFPS] officials turned out to be wrong" (Smith, 2008). She stated in a sworn affidavit that DFPS officials misrepresented evidence of child abuse. "My staff and I soon learned," she said, "that each and every thing that we were told was either inaccurate or untrue" (Smith, 2008). Wanda Brown, the Hill Country Community MHMR Director of Nursing, stated in a sworn affidavit that "These women and children show absolutely no signs of abuse. The only signs of abuse I saw took place in the pavilion where there were women and children were being held like prisoners of war" (Smith, 2008). Ms. Brown condemned the way in which the DFPS was treating the FLDS women and children, even employing the term "abuse" to describe what she saw.

We reached Linda Werlein after reading her account in the news coverage and she agreed to be interviewed. She repeated the previous statements and expressed concern that DFPS workers were making unfounded abuse claims.

In our work, we know the difference between nurturing mothers and non-nurturing mothers. We get children in our clinic who have been abused and we know what that child looks like. Now I know that's not scientific; I know it's anecdotal. But we did not see children who were being abused. (Interview with Linda Werlein, 2008)

Ms. Werlein and her staff found no evidence of the abuse DFPS officials claimed was pervasive and began asking for sources of evidence. Upon questioning officials about the charges, she said they became defensive and labeled her and her staff "sympathizers." She and her staff were even "kicked out" of the pavilion at one point because officials deemed them too sympathetic toward FLDS mothers. "Well, we were just out-and-out told that we were to do their bidding," she said. "It was made really clear to us that if we were too sympathetic we would be kicked out, and at one point we were." They were later asked to return but were clearly chastened by those in charge.

Further into the interview, Ms. Werlein said that the state's investigation was being guided by outside "cult experts" for whom she attributed much of the misinformation and confusion. She keenly observed that the so-called experts had no expertise on the FLDS but rather on "cults" as a generic category.

> I was interested in asking people about their sources. Where are you getting this information? Like they had information that they (FLDS) had tunnels underneath the houses. Now I know Eldorado as one of the towns in the nineteen counties we serve and I said, "Have you ever been there?" to this one lady. And she said, "No, why?" I said good luck on finding a tunnel, it's solid rock out there. I know they searched for tunnels and there were none.
>
> I was told it was an investigation, and the "experts"—and I never knew who they were—they said they understood and studied a lot about this group. And it turned out they were experts on "cults" generally and not on the FLDS group. . . . When I would ask specific questions, they would just quote the experts and then say, "You don't understand." (Interview with Linda Werlein, 2008)

Ms. Werlein said that she did not know the identity of the cult experts and officials did not use their names. However, she clearly describes the situation at the detention site in San Angelo. Her observation of the relationship between the cult experts and state social workers at the pavilion supports the thesis advanced here that an oppositional alliance had formed involving collaboration and coordination between the parties. We know from other sources already cited that Flora Jessop, Carolyn Jessop, Janja Lalich, and Bruce Perry were extensively involved in the evaluation and treatment of the FLDS children in state custody. There may have been others who were not identified by name who were involved in the brief "rehabilitation" of the FLDS children in San Angelo.

Media

Media sources played a vital role in promoting the claims of apostates and opponents of the FLDS. The *San Angelo Standard-Times* gave apostate Flora

Jessop considerable coverage in her dispute-broadening campaign as early as 2005. As previously mentioned, the San Angelo paper published a series giving Jessop an unchallenged voice as both victim and expert. Through Jessop, the paper also furnished a platform for former deprogrammer and ACM activist Rick Ross to trumpet grossly exaggerated claims about the FLDS, giving Ross unwarranted standing as a "cult expert." These embellished claims were not balanced by more nuanced or alternative views by veteran scholars of new or nontraditional religions (of which there are many), historians of religion, church-state scholars, disinterested observers, or even by some modest background inquiry into the substantial body of research literature on such groups. This glaring omission of basic journalistic standards suggests that reporters became allies in the opponent's crusade.

Jessop also managed to collaborate with a reporter for ABC's *Primetime* for a story on the FLDS, giving Jessop a national stage to press claims and "warn authorities" of the dangers of the "cult." As documented in her biography, she learned to use media "to help me get my message out there," to contact newspaper editors, conduct press conferences, give interviews, provide media contacts to other ACM activists and networks, and work with allies to mobilize public opinion and state officials against the targeted sect (Jessop and Brown, 2009:450–451). News stories comparing the FLDS to the Taliban, al-Qaeda, domestic terrorists, the People's Temple, and crime syndicates were widely disseminated. This distorted, one-sided account engineered by Jessop and fellow antagonists became part of the larger public narrative defining the FLDS as a dangerous threat requiring social control actions by the state.

Claims

Ostensibly specific claims made against the FLDS reveal the use of a common template by opponents in which only some of the charges stick and most others are marshaled to stir public concern, amplify threat, engender fear and suspicion, and place pressure on authorities to take action.

Child Abuse and Sexual Abuse

While many of the child abuse claims lack support, some of the claims regarding underage marriage were indeed true. Eleven FLDS men were convicted of sexual assault and charges related to underage marriage. In no way do we condone the practice of underage marriage. But it is instructive to examine some context and history here as well. According to Bradley (1993:100), by the late 1980s, the average age of marriage for FLDS women

had reached 19 as these women were expressing more interest in waiting to marry and obtaining higher education or professional training outside the community. Underage marriages were becoming less common.
But when Warren Jeffs assumed the leadership in 2003, after the death
of his father Rulon, he reversed this trend. Evidence from testimony in
the 2011 criminal trial in Texas support Bradley's finding that the FLDS
was moving away from the practice of underage marriage prior to Warren's brief reign. In the criminal trial, former FLDS member Ezra Draper
testified that "FLDS men began taking brides younger and younger after
[Warren] Jeffs took over" (Weber, 2012). Jeffs was convicted on two sexual
assault charges and sentenced to life plus 20 years, essentially guarantee-
ing that he would never be released from prison. Though the FLDS appear
to be divided over Jeff's status following his conviction, his permanent detention combined with other developments in the post-raid environment
of the FLDS community have led to the emergence of a rival leader insti-
tuting a change in policies regarding marital consent and women's roles
(see Wright and Richardson, 2014). It remains to be seen what leadership
faction will prevail and what direction the FLDS will take in the future.

The claim by DFPS that there was evidence of "widespread pattern and
practice" of child sexual abuse and underage marriage is probably overstated. According to its own report issued more than six months after the
government raid ("Eldorado Investigation," December 22, 2008), all but 15
of the 439 cases (96 percent) were "non-suited" (i.e., parents had taken appropriate action to protect children from abuse). Eventually, all but one of
the FLDS children taken into state custody were returned to their parents.
Of the more than 40 young women between the ages of 12 and 16 taken into
custody, 15 were suspected of being sexually abused; 5 were determined to
have become pregnant. But the sweeping generalization that all FLDS children were in danger of sexual abuse was unfounded. There was no evidence
of widespread abuse of boys or prepubescent girls, who made up the vast majority of sect children. The appellate court ruled that the state had no such
evidence in mandating that the FLDS children be released to their parents.

Brainwashing/Mind Control

Years before the raid on the FLDS community in Eldorado, apostates and
ACM activists were pronouncing sect members to be brainwashed. In
2004, excommunicated member Ross Chatwin described, in hyperbolic
fashion, the FLDS regimen as "one of the most effective brainwashing
schemes since Hitler" (We Fear Another Waco," 2004). In 2005, former

deprogrammer Rick Ross invoked the brainwashing motif, comparing Warren Jeffs to Jim Jones, the leader of the People's Temple who engineered a mass suicide in Guyana in 1979 (Anthony, 2005). In 2006, apostate Laurie Allen told *Deseret News* that the FLDS was less about religion and more about "the denigration of women and mind control" (Winslow, 2006). Allen produced a documentary film, *Banking on Heaven*, that was panned by *Variety* magazine as "amateurish and more agitprop than balanced reportage" (Winslow, 2006). Former deprogrammer and anticult activist Joe Szimhart told ABC News, "I have no doubt that they've (FLDS members) have been brainwashed" (Friedman, 2008). Carolyn Jessop told MSNBC a few days after the raid that the FLDS practiced "mind control" on its members: "With this level of mind control, it's something you're born into and it's generational. The babies born into this don't stand a chance" (Celizic, 2008). Larry Beall, a Utah psychologist and the state's "cult expert" in the criminal trial of the first FLDS defendant, Merrill Jessop, told a reporter for *Time* magazine that "the FLDS is a cult involved in plain ole brainwashing since birth" (Hylton, 2008).

Mass Suicide/Collective Violence

Widely publicized allegations of mass suicide and violence were made routinely against the FLDS by opponents. In 2004, Flora Jessop told a British journalist that FLDS members "are prepared to die for their leader" ("We Fear Another Waco," 2004). Jessop also claimed in the same interview that the FLDS had a "fallout shelter" packed with emergency supplies and stockpiles of weapons. In 2006, Ross Chatwin warned that FLDS would be another Waco: "It's ready to blow," he proclaimed. "It's going to turn into another Waco" (Walters, 2006). In a guest editorial for the London's *Daily Mail*, Carolyn Jessop described a grim joke she and her sister told while growing up: "Don't drink the punch," they would say, a reference to the mass suicide at Jonestown (Jessop, 2008). Another apostate, Elaine Jeffs, was quoted in Laurie Allen's film (two years before the raid) as saying "what I'm afraid of is another Jonestown or another Waco" (Winslow, 2006). Several days after the raid, Texas authorities told the *Fort Worth Star-Telegram* that sect members resisted efforts by investigators to enter the temple on the YFZ property, "raising fears of a Branch Davidian–style standoff" (Hanna, 2008). During the execution of the search warrant at the YFZ Ranch, state officials also claimed to find "a cyanide poisoning document," though no explanation was offered for the outlandish claim and the news report went on to suggest the claim was baseless: "Nothing in the eighty-page list of items seized indicated that members of the sect planned to use cyanide," it said (Blaney and Roberts, 2008).

Conclusion

The Texas state raid on the FLDS in 2008 provides strong support for our model. At Eldorado we find yet another case in which a government raid was based largely on orchestrated activities and inflated claims by a network of opponents. The polygamist Mormon sect was an easy target for opponents with their odd beliefs, strange dress, and unconventional marriage practices.

In the years leading up to the Texas raid, we can document the collaboration of chief apostate Flora Jessop with anticult actors such as Rick Ross and with local and national news media, which she conveniently describes in detail in her autobiography. Jessop learned to use media opportunities to broaden personal disputes, make exaggerated claims, and herald an array of threats posed by the FLDS. Jessop linked reporters to other disgruntled ex-members for interviews and stories. She also developed networks and contacts among child protection officials in Utah, Arizona, and Texas, largely through her nonprofit organizations. She assisted staff in attorney general's offices in Utah and Arizona regarding investigations of FLDS members. Most importantly, it was Jessop who forwarded the fraudulent calls by Swinton to Texas officials and linked the parties together, which served as the legal basis for the 2008 raid on the YFZ.

By the time of the Texas raid on April 3, authorities had access to a network of mobilized opponents who assured them that the FLDS was a perilous threat that necessitated drastic action. After the raid, DFPS social workers relied on "cult experts" in San Angelo to interpret and discover hidden abuses. Court hearings to remove the sect children relied on Dr. Bruce Perry as court expert and "authority on children in cults" to aid the state's effort to obtain conservatorship. A parade of apostates— Flora Jessop, Carolyn Jessop, Ross Chatwin, Rebecca Musser, Elissa Wall, Laurie Allen—furnished TV and newspaper interviews to solidify the ACM framing of the raid.

Anticult narratives depicting the group as "terrorists" or brainwashed cultists on the verge of mass suicide and/or stockpiling weapons in a cave were designed to inflame prejudice and instill fear toward the group and pressure law enforcement to take action. Once the group was defined as a "dangerous cult," the state's justification for a massive paramilitary raid became self-evident. In turn, the raid became an instrument of repression, having ramifications well beyond the ostensible intent to enforce the law. Sexual assault of a minor is a serious crime, but absent the grossly exaggerated claims of violence made by opponents against the FLDS, might law enforcement have opted for a less dangerous method than a raid?

The question of *selective enforcement* must also be raised here. Did it matter that the sexual assault allegations were made against a minority religion labeled a "cult"? This question is put into sharp relief when one considers that roughly a year after the Texas raid, the *Houston Chronicle* reported that "nearly half of all Texas children killed by abuse belonged to families previously investigated by Texas Child Protective Services—a statistic that has shown no improvement since 2004 despite efforts to save more children" (Langford, 2009:A6). Between 2004 and 2009, 1,227 children died of abuse in Texas, and 516 of those children came from families with CPS histories. Another *Houston Chronicle* report found hundreds of incidents of mistreatment and abuse of children at state residential treatment centers from mid-2008 through April 2010 (Langford and Ramshaw, 2010). But no criminal indictments were sought against the perpetrators, and their names were kept secret by DFPS. This deplorable lack of action by the state points to a troubling double standard. The post-raid claim by Texas authorities that the extreme enforcement action was necessary to "save the children" at Eldorado doesn't comport with their record on other cases throughout the state. There was no history of child deaths at the YFZ Ranch, yet the state of Texas spent an estimated $14 million on the FLDS raid (Moritz, 2008). Might the state have better spent hard-earned taxpayer dollars in the ordinary supervision of children under the care of the chronically underfunded DFPS?

8

The Church of Scientology

SINCE THE 1960s the Church of Scientology has been the subject of countless investigations in various countries and the target of many state-sponsored raids. These raids have been launched in at least seven countries and have covered a span of almost 50 years. While most of the other minority religions featured in this study were raided as parts of investigations involving one or two specific criminal allegations such as child abuse or sexual abuse, in the case of Scientology claims have extended over a wide variety of charges. Indeed, the Church of Scientology has the dubious distinction of being the most raided NRM in modern history. Scientology presents a more complex and challenging case than the others we have studied. The raids on Scientology cover a much greater time span, take place in a greater array of countries, involve more diverse charges, and occur with more frequency than any other new religion. For this reason it is important to examine the entire scope of raids on the church.

The raids on Scientology are divided into two periods, the early raids (1963–1989) and the later raids (1990 to the present). We focus in this chapter on the early raids principally because almost all the government raids on Scientology after 1990 occurred in France and coincide with the heightened transnational mobilization of the ACM. Since we devote a separate chapter to raids in France exclusively in the next chapter, which includes an analysis of the Scientology raids in the later period, we concentrate here on the early raids in the United States, Australia, and Canada. We think the raids on Scientology in the early period inform a more comprehensive understanding of government actions toward the church, setting the stage for the surge in the later period. What our investigation shows is that the unique aspects of Scientology, its use of the E-meter, its therapeutic claims, the fees for services it demands, the confession of intimate secrets in auditing—these aspects have, since Scientology's beginnings, generated passionate opposition.

Coalitions of opposing groups and individual critics of Scientology have formed and attempted to control the expansion of this NRM, to prosecute its leaders, or to gain compensation for its "victims." Since the beginning of the conflict in the 1960s, these opposing parties have been formidable. They include the American FDA, IRS, and FBI; the Australian judiciary, mental health authorities, and the Australian Medical Association; the Royal Canadian Mounted Police and the attorney general of Canada. Over time, we see the rise of local anticult groups and movements that tended to exert more pressure and more influence on these governmental bodies. By the 1990s we find a powerful government-sponsored anticult movement at the heart of France's National Assembly, and a well-organized international coalition of local anticult groups that work in tandem to fight "harmful cults."

The earliest raids in the United States (1963) and Australia (1965–1969) focused on issues of alleged medical fraud, specifically with regard to the church's claims concerning the therapeutic and healing benefits of Dianetics, and their use of the mysterious machine called the "E-meter."[1] These raids in the 1960s predate the formation of the ACM, though we do find some semblance of organized opposition in Australia. The 1977 raids in the United States followed a scandal involving a secret operation by a special branch of the church, the Guardian's Office (GO), to infiltrate the Internal Revenue Service and other government institutions in the United States and the United Kingdom, in order to steal, copy, alter, or destroy incriminating documents about Scientology or unflattering portraits of L. Ron Hubbard, its leader. The 1983 raid in Toronto involved similar allegations of efforts by the local branch of the Guardian's Office to gain illegal access to government records concerning Scientology. We find evidence that this raid was planned in coordination with ex-members and anticultists and its aim extended beyond simply prosecuting those Scientologists who purloined documents.

The majority of raids on Scientology since 1990 have occurred in France. This latter period is one of heightened mobilization and transnational expansion of the ACM. Since 1990, the church has been the target of 21 police raids (some of them multiple simultaneous raids) in France alone. Some of the raids described above and the ensuing legal conflicts have been documented and analyzed elsewhere (see Evans, 1974; Lewis, 2009; Melton, 2000; Urban, 2006). But in this chapter we offer a more detailed and comparative analysis of Scientology's history of raids on an international scale leading up to the heightened ACM mobilization.

History and Background of Scientology

Scientology was founded by Lafayette Ronald Hubbard (1911–1986) who was born in Tilden, Nebraska. He was a successful and prolific science fiction writer in the 1940s and 1950s, and Hubbard gained the support of John Campbell. Jr., the editor of *Astounding Science Fiction* magazine in promoting his new book, *Dianetics: the Modern Science of Mental Health*, before and after its publication in 1950. Hubbard then founded the Dianetic Research Foundation, and after unsuccessfully trying to control "heretics" and "revisionists," in 1952 he added several new dimensions to Dianetics which transformed it from a popular psychotherapeutic system or a psychic science into a highly original new religious movement. By adding the concept of the thetan (the immortal, omniscient beings that underlie our limited human consciousness), reincarnation, and a creation myth involving extraterrestrials, the religion of Scientology was created. The first Church of Scientology was founded February 18, 1954 in Los Angeles.

Scientology's main goal is to erase *engrams* (trace memories of traumatic events) buried in the *reactive mind* (similar to Freud's unconscious) with the assistance of a trained auditor who can read the E-meter, a machine that measures galvanic response. The advanced Scientologist who has succeeded in erasing all engrams collected in this lifetime, is considered to have "gone clear" and achieves the status of an "operating thetan" (Wallis, 1977). Over the years, Scientology has proven to be a highly successful movement in terms of international growth. It has consistently evoked controversy, and Hubbard and its ministers have been accused of brainwashing and exerting draconian control over members, of splitting up families through its elite Sea Org operation, of extorting money from converts, and of misrepresenting itself as both psychotherapy and a religion in order to succeed as a business.

The Raids in Australia, 1965–1969

On December 22, 1965, at 4.55 p.m. the Church of Scientology in Melbourne was raided by two officers from the attorney general's office and three policemen. They arrived at the church's Spring Street center just before closing time. While the church's secretary, Mr. Gogerley, was busy cooperating with the officer in charge of the search, policemen sent to the rear of the building claimed they witnessed Scientologists frantically burning papers in two rubbish bins. A detective said he observed a file being passed through the window of a car. After an hour and a half of searching, the officers seized thousands of files, which were then transported to the attorney general's office (*Sydney Morning Herald*, Dec. 22, 1965).

The Influence of Organized Opponents

The very first comprehensive government investigation in the Church of Scientology's practices was in Australia in the early 1960s. It is significant that the Melbourne raid was carried out only a few hours after Scientology had been outlawed in Victoria, as a result of the passage of new legislation called the Psychological Practices Act.

According to Australian scholar Bernard Doherty, there was no organized anticult movement in Australia until after the Jonestown tragedy in 1978, though a few isolated and short-lived anticult groups did exist from the early 1960s. The first was the Committee for Mental Health and National Security, started by apostate Phillip Bennett Wearne in 1963 as a part of Wearne's campaign against Scientology. Three anticult groups formed in the wake of Jonestown; the Concerned Christian Growth Ministries (CCGM), a Jewish exit-counseling ministry established by Melbourne Rabbi Raphael Aron, who later founded Cult Counseling Australia (CCA), and the Cult Awareness and Information Centre (CAIC), formed by ex- Jehovah's Witnesses and Mormons (Doherty, 2014).

The government investigation into Scientology practices that was launched in 1963 was spurred by complaints from a loose coalition of ex-members (headed by Wearne), health professionals, government health authorities, and distraught relatives of Scientologists. Roy Wallis referred to the Australian campaign against Scientology as a "moral panic" and observed that the "press, medical and psychiatric agencies, professional bodies and disgruntled former Scientologists joined forces to promote government action against Scientology" (Wallis, 1977:215). In his research, Doherty (2014) has documented specifically the role of tabloid media in this oppositional campaign. For example, he notes that "from 1960 to 1964 the now-defunct Melbourne tabloid newspaper *Truth* ran a series of unflattering stories about the Hubbard Association of Scientologists International (HASI), christening the group 'bunkumology' and opining that it was 'time they were put out of business'" (Doherty, 2014:38–39). According to Doherty, calls for actions against Scientology were also made by the British Medical Association's Victorian branch secretary, leading Australian psychiatrists, and popular Roman Catholic radio personality Father Leslie Rumble (Doherty, 2014:39).

The role of the Catholic radio icon Father Rumble was not insignificant. The intensity of early attacks on Scientology in Australia were heightened by thinly veiled religious or theological motives. In this regard, one finds at the heart of the attacks a more traditional countercult orientation. The religious countercult quality of the anti-Scientology campaign became evident with the publication of the Anderson Report.

Responding to the coalition of forces demanding state action, Australian MP, the Honorable J.W. Galbally, introduced a bill to restrict the teaching and practice of Scientology for payment or remuneration. Galbally outlined a series of accusations aimed at Scientology which he referred to as "a group of charlatans who for monetary gain are exposing children of tender age, youths and adults to intimidation and blackmail, insanity and even suicide, family estrangement and bankruptcy" (quoted in Doherty, 2014:39). A formal Board of Inquiry was appointed to study Scientology practices, conducted by Kevin Anderson, Queen's Counsel. After hearing 151 witnesses within 159 days, some of whom were disaffected ex-members, distraught relatives, and mental health professionals, the Board published a report in 1965 titled "Scientology and Religion."[2] The blatant Christian bias of this report, commonly referred to as the Anderson Report, was more than apparent. The report infers that, in order to qualify as a "religion," a group must adhere to Christian beliefs:

> The essence of Hubbard's axioms . . . is that the universe was created not by God, but by a conglomeration of thetans . . . many of the theories he propounds are almost a negation of Christian thought and morality. (Quoted in Possamai and Possamai-Inesedy, 2009:350)

The Anderson Report contained strong, value-laden language in its criticism and condemnation of Scientology that exhibited inflated claims of threat, providing a captivating illustration of deviance amplification:

> Scientology is evil; its techniques evil; its practices a serious threat to the community, medically, morally and socially. Its founder

is Lafayette Ronald Hubbard. . . . whose sanity is to be gravely doubted . . . and) with the merest smattering of knowledge in various sciences, has built upon the scintilla of his learning a crazy and dangerous edifice. (Quoted in Evans, 1974:83)

On the basis of this damning report, the Psychological Practices Act was passed in Victoria in 1965. This new law made the teaching and practice of Scientology's ideas or methods a *criminal* offense.[3] Moreover, sections 31 and 32 of the Psychological Practices Act made it an offense for anyone to charge a fee or accept compensation for even practicing Scientology, or to advertise its services. Scientologists could be fined up to £100 for a first offense, and £250 for a second offense, and they could receive up to a two-year jail sentence. The very same afternoon that the Psychological Practices Act was passed, the Melbourne police obtained a warrant from the attorney general to seize Scientology files and records (*Sydney Morning Herald*, Dec. 22, 1965).

It is interesting to note that the main issue that emerged after the raid was the confidentiality of sensitive material that was contained in the files. For officials from the Crown Law and Health Department, their main concern was to protect the privacy of clients of Scientology—the "preclears" whom they perceived as Scientology's gullible victims. Kevin Anderson, Queen's Counsel, presented his report before the Parliament in September 1965, and he argued that the 400-odd seized files contained the intimate secrets of clients and that these might be used for blackmail or extortion or to force people to sign up for more expensive courses (*The Australian*, Dec. 22, 1965). The MP, Mr. Galbally, backed by a psychology professor, recommended burning the files in order to prevent blackmail or other negative consequences. Under the new bill, anyone holding Scientology records[4] was required to deliver them forthwith to the attorney general's office to be "destroyed or otherwise as the Attorney-General thinks fit" (*Sydney Morning Herald*, Dec. 22, 1965).

Anderson admitted in his report to the state government that there was no actual evidence that "blackmail, in the legal sense, had been practiced." Nonetheless, he was apparently influenced by rumors that Scientology extorted money from its members through veiled threats to expose their discrediting secrets. Thus, Anderson argued that "the basis for such criminal activity exists in the files of the organization [since] the existence of these files containing the most intimate secrets and confessions of thousands of individuals is a constant threat to them and a matter of grave concern . . . more serious because copies of these reports are also held in England" ("Scientology Files to Be Examined," *The Herald* [Melbourne], Dec. 22, 1965).

By the end of December 1965, the files had still not been consigned to flames. The Chief Secretary of the State Department, Mr. Rylah, said that the 400-odd personal files were still being studied by officials of the Crown Law and Health Departments, who would report to him "in due course." Some in the media then proclaimed that it was very disturbing and quite wrong that any government department should have the power to look at these files. One newspaper editorialized that "government prying into the secrets of Scientology's unfortunate victims, who included many school children and university undergraduates, could have serious consequences" (*The Australian*, Dec. 22, 1965).

Brainwashing: The First Application of the Psychological Practices Act

The first application of the Psychological Practices Act was made in November 1965, in the case of Anthony Raper, a 38-year-old Scientologist who was found guilty on two charges of fraudulent conversion of trust monies on behalf of Scientology, totaling £4,170, between June and October 1962. The Crown passed a sentence of three years in prison for each charge, concurrently. But on review at the appeals court, it was decided that Raper was a "victim of brainwashing."

Raper's lawyers had argued that his client was, at the time of the offenses, enrolled in a course in Scientology and had therefore "suffered physical injury through being hypnotized and *his mind was not his own*" ("Court Sympathy for Scientology Victim," *The Melbourne Age*, 1966; emphasis ours). Judge Amsberg referred the case to the minister for justice and promised that if Mr. Raper's condition was found by the minister to come under Section 27 of the Mental Health Act, he would recommend Raper's release from prison as soon as psychiatrists certified him cured and restored to mental health.

In the Quarter Sessions of January 28, 1966, Judge Amsberg commented on the Raper case, saying it was one of the most difficult he had ever encountered on the bench. On the evidence, the jury's verdict of guilty had been the proper one, he acknowledged, but since "Scientologists leave a trail of devastation in mental health wherever they go, and sully everything they touch," he felt the "deepest sympathy" toward the brainwashed prisoner, and concluded, "Scientology seems like an evil cloud" ("Court Sympathy for Scientology Victim," *The Age*, 1966).

Eighteen years after the passage of the Psychological Practices Act, in 1983, the High Court of Australia decided that the Church of Scientology was a religious institution. Subsequently, this decision was challenged by Nicholas Xenophon, an Independent senator in the Commonwealth Parliament who declared on November 18, 2009, that the Church of Scientology was a "criminal organization." But the Senate rejected his call for a parliamentary inquiry, insisting its proper role was to inquire into matters of public policy and administration, and not into specific organizations: "It is a very dangerous thing for us to have what could be seen as a witch hunt against an individual organization, be it a religion, a trade union, a community organization or a company" ("No Inquiry into Church of Scientology," *The Herald*, Dec. 7, 2009).

Scientology Prohibition Act 1968

Following the passage of the Psychological Practices Act 1965, legislators turned their attention to the perceived "evils" of Scientology specifically. After robust debates throughout legislative sessions in Western and South Australia, both governing bodies passed versions of the Scientology Prohibition Act 1968, which banned the practice of Scientology and outlawed possession of its instruments and materials. On November 15, 1968, just two days after the Scientology Prohibition Act was given the Assent of the Governor in Victoria (Western Australia), a police raid was launched on the Hay Street headquarters of the Hubbard Association of Scientologists International (HASI), also known as the Church of the New Faith. On January 28, 1969, a second raid was launched involving five detectives and the inspector of police. The local newspaper reported that the police "searched the premises for about an hour and took away stationery, records, and electrical equipment" ("Police Seize Scientology Material," *The West Australian*, Jan. 29, 1969). However, these raids were given little media coverage. It appears that they may have been a prelude for something bigger.

On February 14, 1969, a much larger raid team involving 25 police stormed the Adelaide headquarters of the church in South Australia confiscating E-meters and thousands of documents and files. The homes of at least four church officials were also raided and documents seized there as well ("Detectives Raid Cult HQ, Seize Papers," *The Advertiser*, Feb. 15,

1969). Police used a five-ton truck to carry away the bulk of confiscated material. State Attorney General Mr. Millhouse told reporters that the warrants had been issued because he had reason to believe that "Scientology records were being kept on the premises" ("Detectives Raid Cult HQ, Seize Papers," *The Advertiser*, Feb. 15, 1969). However, no charges, arrests, or prosecutions were ever recorded.

On April 11, 1969, 15 members of HASI were prosecuted and convicted of violating the new act in Western Australia and fined £200. But the church appealed the convictions and on December 3 the convictions were dropped due to what Doherty (2015) refers to as a "shoddy" prosecution case.

The 1963 FDA Raid in Washington, D.C.

In January 1963 the Food and Drug Administration (FDA) raided the Scientology headquarters in Washington, D.C.[5] Around two dozen law enforcement personnel, including FDA agents, U.S. Marshals, and deputized longshoremen carrying drawn guns, burst into the building, followed by the press (Evans, 1974:81). The raid was a complete surprise to the Scientologists. Those who were eyewitnesses to the raid described the experience in sworn affidavits:

> The FDA agents burst into the church offices . . . and threatened all in sight; observed absolutely no courtesies except for not actually shooting the guns they carried. . . . Showing no legal warrant, the agents . . . pounded their way up stairways, bursting into confessional and pastoral counseling sessions, causing disruption and violently preventing the quiet pursuit of the normal practice of religious philosophy. They seized all the publications and all the confessional aids called E-meters they could find. . . . The agents removed from the church . . . some tens of thousands of copies of over twenty Church books, texts, recorded sermons; even the Church archives were sacked. . . .
>
> When ministers of the Church asked that their property be handled more carefully, the "deputies" from Baltimore gave only sneering illiteracies for answer. (Garrison, 1974:143)

Photographs of sober-faced Marshals trudging out of the building with armloads of E-meters appeared on the front pages of newspapers across the nation the following day. Four trucks filled with three tons of literature were then ushered back to the FDA depot in Baltimore by armed police on motorcycles (Evans, 1974).

Background of Conflict

At the time, the FDA was a federal agency under the U.S. Department of Health, Education and Welfare (now the U.S. Department of Health and Human Services). Its mission is to monitor the food and drugs bought and sold by producers and consumed by American citizens. One of its tasks has been to investigate quack medicines and unorthodox gadgets used in alternative healing circles.[6] Thus, the purpose of the raid on Scientology was to investigate the E-meter. In the early 1960s the FDA had filed a "libel of information" with a U.S. district court, after which Judge William B. Jones ordered a warrant authorizing the seizure of the E-meters and of "an undetermined number of items of written, printed or graphic matter" ("A Conspiracy Revealed," *Freedom Magazine,* 1995).

In Scientology's system, the erasing of "engrams" (trace memories of traumatic events) is vaunted to result in dramatic improvements in a person's health. Thus, it appears that the FDA decided to launch a raid to investigate what they assumed were unwarranted medical claims. The FDA then filed suit against the Founding Church of Scientology, claiming the E-meter was a fraudulent healing device (Atak, 1990).

Aftermath of Raid

The outcome of this raid was that the FDA found no evidence in the seized documents to support their allegations of fraud. When the case went to court, the harshest thing that could be said about the E-meter was that it was "unscientific." But the FDA also complained about its price, since it cost $5 to manufacture, but was sold at $50 to members. "Such profitability," the commissioner reported drily, "while not at all conclusive, is indicative of a commercial enterprise" (Evans, 1974:82).

The problem with launching a malpractice suit predicated on the use of the E-meter, as applied in Scientology auditing sessions, is that the apparatus is essentially an "innocuous gadget . . . not a device for treatment of illnesses, whether physical or psychological" (Evans, 1974:82). At worst, the E-meter might be criticized as an unreliable aid to diagnosis.

But it took nine years of protracted legal battles and the expenditure of millions of dollars in legal fees for the church and FDA to reach a final settlement in 1971.

The FDA was forced to return the seized E-meters in October 1973, but the court ordered the Church of Scientology to pay the warehousing costs of the confiscated items held over the previous nine years, plus all the legal fees of the government's prosecution efforts (MacKaye, 1973). Moreover, the church had to pay the salaries and travel expenses of FDA agents who would occasionally visit to ensure compliance with the court's order. The court also ruled that every single E-meter (and all Scientology literature describing the E-meter) must bear the following warning label:

> This device has been condemned by a United States District Court for misrepresentation and misbranding under the Food and Drug laws, that use is permitted only as part of religious activity, and that the E-meter is not medically or scientifically capable of improving the health or bodily functions of anyone. . . . each user, purchaser, and distributer of the E-meter shall sign a written statement that he has read such a warning and understands its contents and such statements shall be preserved. (*U.S. v Hubbard Electrometer*, 1971)[7]

The Church of Scientology now includes such a disclaimer on each E-meter.[8]

The 1977 FBI Raids in Los Angeles and Washington, D.C.

On July 8, 1977 the Church of Scientology's headquarters in Los Angeles (Hollywood) and in Washington, D.C. were simultaneously raided. The L.A. raid was particularly spectacular, for it involved 156 FBI agents, more than had ever been deployed in a single raid in the United States. This raid lasted 21 hours, and the agents filled a 16-ton truck with documents and other items (Urban, 2006).

The newspapers broadcast the results of the raid, stating that the seized documents revealed illegal activities against the United States government, against "alien governments," and against individuals considered to be "enemies of Scientology" (Beresford, 1980a). Two British politicians who were part of the official British government's inquiry into Scientology were said to be targets, along with officials belonging to the

National Association for Mental Health (NAMH) and World Federation for Mental Health (Marro, 1977).

Various conspiracies hatched by Scientologists were outlined in the *New York Times*, the *Washington Post*, and the *Guardian* ("Dianetic Sect Said to Spy on AMA," *New York Times*. Nov. 2, 1979). The *Guardian* described an "Operation Freakout," a plan to frame journalist Paulette Cooper for her incriminatory book, *The Scandal of Scientology*, on false bomb-threat charges. The plan also involved an attempt to frame Gabe Cazares, the outspoken critic and mayor of Clearwater, Florida, on false hit-and-run charges (Beresford, 1980b).

The government raids on the Los Angeles and Washington, D.C. headquarters were prompted by documentary evidence that Scientology's "Guardian's Office" had infiltrated the FBI and other government agencies and had stolen, reproduced, or altered their files on the church.

The Guardian's Office had been established inside the church in 1966 as a defensive response to external harassment and discrimination. Aside from experiencing the scrutiny of U.S. federal agencies, the 1963 FDA raid, and pressure from the Internal Revenue Service demanding the church pay millions of dollars in back taxes, Scientology leaders became aware that FBI agents had secretly infiltrated Scientology's organization (Urban, 2006).

As early as 1960, L. Ron Hubbard had proposed that Scientologists should infiltrate government departments by taking secretarial or bodyguard positions or other jobs (Urban, 2008). The GO was a stealth unit, set up in 1966 at the Saint Hill Manor, in England. Its initial mission was to protect the interests of the Church of Scientology and gather information on agencies and individuals deemed as its enemies, and to monitor heretics and notable apostates. Hubbard's wife, Mary Sue Hubbard, was appointed as the GO director.[9] The GO functioned as an intelligence bureau and planted members in key positions within federal government agencies in order to obtain confidential material. The Guardian's Office itself had its own secret intelligence bureau at the top of its organizational structure.

In the mid-1970s the GO launched its secret operation known as "Operation Snow White." Its origins were probably in L. Ron Hubbard's Guardian Order 732, which called for the removal and correction of "erroneous" Scientology files by "legal means." This directive was liberally interpreted by GO staff members. Nonetheless, Hubbard himself was later named by federal prosecutors as an "unindicted co-conspirator" for his part in the operation (Marshall, 1980). Operation Snow White employed up to 5,000 covert agents, who carried out a series of infiltrations and thefts from 136 government agencies, foreign embassies and consulates, and private organizations in over 30 countries. This operation was described in the *New York Times* as "the single largest infiltration of the United States government in history" (Labaton, 1993).

Aftermath of Raids

Scientology leaders declared that the files seized from the church in Washington, D.C. and Los Angeles were taken unlawfully ("Stolen Documents Reported Found in FBI Raids on Scientologists," *New York Times*, July, 10, 1977). Scientology's lawyers argued that in order to prepare for an August 8, 1977 hearing on the legality of the raid, they must be able to see the documents. By July 20, a Washington judge ruled that the documents should be returned temporarily to the church, and that none of the documents could be shared with other branches of the government unless that specific branch was investigating Scientology. On July 27, 1977 a judge in Washington ruled that the warrant authorizing the raid was too broad, and as such violated the church's Fourth Amendment rights ("FBI Raids on Church Are Ruled Improper," *New York Times*, July 28, 1977). But in August this ruling was overturned, and when Scientology took the case to the Supreme Court in 1978, the high court refused to hear the case ("Court Refuses to Act in Church of Scientology Appeal," *New York Times*, Mar. 21, 1978).

Eleven officials and agents of the Guardian's Office were indicted in the trial, including Jane Kember, the international head of the Guardian's Office, and Hubbard's wife, Mary Sue Hubbard. In the end, the defendants were convicted of relatively minor crimes but public revelations of the actions of the Guardian's Office opened the church to broad censure from both religious and secular leaders ("Convictions of 9 Scientologists in Plotting Thefts Are Upheld," *Washington Post*, Oct. 3, 1981). The incident became a decisive moment in the church's life and led to the emergence of new leadership and a major international reorganization.[10]

The 1983 raid in Canada, six years later, was in part prompted by documents that had been uncovered in the Washington, D.C. raid, apparently stolen from the attorney general's office in Ontario, Canada. These indicated that the Guardian's Office Worldwide had launched a similar "Snow White" operation in Canada (Morgan, 1999).

The 1983 Toronto Raid

The Toronto raid must be analyzed as a response to the findings of the L.A. raid, but also it is clear that authorities relied on the burgeoning Canadian anticult movement, which shaped the issues that resulted from the raid. The 1983 raid on the Scientology center was not the first government action taken against a "cult" in Toronto. In 1971 there had been a surprise investigation on a Toronto group called PSI (People Searching Inward).[11] This action was taken as a response to allegations of "brainwashing" which were launched by a local anticult movement organization.[12]

On March 3, 1983 in the afternoon over 100 Ontario Provincial Police (OPP) officers arrived in three chartered buses to raid the Church of Scientology's headquarters at 696 and 700 Yonge Street in Toronto. They wore orange armbands and carried battering rams, sledgehammers, axes, tape recorders, video cameras, and fire extinguishers. The church president, Caroline Charbonneau, was guided by the agents around the building while the staff was told to stay at their desks. OPP officers removed around two million pages of documents according to Scientologists; however, new reports estimated it was closer to 250,000 pages of documents (Stephens, 1983). The raid involved officers from the Tactical Rescue Unit, a paramilitary police unit.[13] Journalists were also present, invited along by the OPP to document the raid. Representatives from the Canada Revenue Agency were also present.

A journalist described this event as "the largest police raid in Canadian history" (Kavanaugh, 1992). Phil Caney, Ontario Provincial Police spokesperson, explained that 100 officers were needed because of the 75 rooms and many exits. When asked why the police had taken the unusual step of alerting the media to the search ahead of time, Caney explained, "this is a much larger than normal execution of a warrant and it is on the main and important street in Toronto, and we felt the media had a right to know what was going on. . . . We are called to account for our actions. We wanted to be able to show what we did, we did properly" ("100 Police Raid on Scientologists," *Montreal Gazette*, Mar. 4, 1983).

Scientologists, however, seized this opportunity to talk to the media. Staff members complained to the reporters that the police had smashed a glass door and destroyed another with a sledgehammer. Eyewitness Scott Carmichael described his reaction in this way: "I was in a room near the reception center when I heard a loud noise. I thought it was a bomb. Then I saw all these officers walking into the room. It was wall-to-wall police. It was a bad scene" (Nellis, 1983).

OPP Commissioner James Erskine held a press conference at the force's Harbour Street headquarters simultaneously to the execution of the raid. He read out a statement that explained the raid as the culmination of a two-year investigation into the church's alleged involvement in tax fraud, into "misrepresentation" of Scientology's courses to consumers, and into a "conspiracy to commit indictable offenses where perceived necessary" in order to protect the interests of Scientology (Nellis, 1983).

Organized Opposition

The Church of Scientology in Canada was founded in Toronto in 1955 and was incorporated in 1967. By 1983 the church claimed an active membership of 5,000 in Ontario and 10,000 nationwide. But it was not recognized as a church in Ontario, and Scientology's application to perform marriages had been denied.

A police investigation of the church was conducted between 1972 and 1977, spearheaded by Sergeant John Falliss of the Toronto Metropolitan police, working in tandem with Sergeant Ciampini of the Ontario Provincial Police. According to a Scientology source, "undercover agents were sent as plants into the church in 1981, and they went through our garbage. We had already had journalists in 1969 and 1970 doing undercover research for their media stories before the 1972 investigation. These police agents were disclosed after the raid."[14]

A study of the events leading up to the 1983 raid reveals a number of cooperating parties, including anticultists, ex-members and apostates, the Toronto Metropolitan police, the OPP, journalists, and the American FBI and Internal Revenue Service. Scientology leaders believe the psychiatric establishment may have been involved as well. Scientologist Bob Dobson Smith told the press, "I wouldn't be a bit surprised if the raid was the result of a conspiracy between police and the psychiatric profession. Psychiatry has raised a hue and cry against our religion and our reforms" ("Secret Probe Sparks Raid on Scientology," *Toronto Star*, July 7, 1992).

OPP Commissioner James Erskine stated in a press conference that the police had worked closely with the attorney general's office in planning the raid (Maychuk, Dutton, and Ferri, 1984). Ontario police investigators had kept their operation secret since they were worried they had been infiltrated by Scientologists ("only those who had to know did know") (Maychuk, Dutton, and Ferri, 1984).

The president of the Toronto church, Caroline Charbonneau, blamed the raid on disgruntled ex-members. She claimed in a press conference that former members who had been ousted for violating church polices had "gone to the government and complained about acts which they themselves have committed" (Maychuk, Dutton, and Ferri, 1984).

According to a Scientologist who had worked on the defense in the ensuing trial, there was a group of prominent apostates who assisted the authorities in the pre-raid investigation. Nan McLean was a career apostate who had been treated badly by Bryan Levman, head of Toronto's Guardian's Office. She became an unnamed informant for police Sergeant John Fallis, and she and journalist Paulette Cooper worked closely with the FBI to identify and interpret documents seized in the 1977 U.S. raid. Nan McLean's departure from Scientology was not amicable. After she left the church, members of the Guardian's Office staged a mock funeral for her. She subsequently became an "exit counselor" and worked with various antagonists and parents of Scientologists.[15]

Gerry Armstrong was a Canadian apostate who has been invited as a "cult expert" to speak to audiences in Germany and France. He worked closely with Sergeant Ciampini of the Ontario Provincial Police and with the IRS. Scientologists claim, "we got him on videotape explaining how he planned to take over the church in Canada after it was taken out."[16] He was told by the authorities that if he helped them take down Scientology, they would let him take over and reform the church.

David Mayo was another important apostate who assisted the OPP. He had acquired a senior tech position in the Florida church but then was expelled for "squirreling" (altering or adulterating L. Ron Hubbard's technology). In the early 1980s Mayo founded his own rival church in California, "The Advanced Abilities Center." Scientology attorneys sued David Mayo for copyright violation ("that's how we preserve the purity of LRH's legacy"). Mayo was interviewed by Ciampini, who in turn helped to locate witnesses to testify against Scientology.[17]

Scientology leaders in Toronto claim that the OPP and attorney general's office were receptive to a scheme devised by apostates Emile Gilbert, Alan Buchanan, and David Mayo to stage a coup against the church in Canada.[18] The trio was accused of trying to take over its leadership in order to restore a philosophy they believed was the pure, unadulterated version of L. Ron Hubbard's original vision. Scientology leaders claim that the three apostates tried to make a deal with the Attorney's Office so they could seize control of the Church of Scientology after it collapsed and install former members in new positions. According to church officials, "There were thirty to thirty-five people ready to take over."[19]

From an outsider's perspective, however, it appears far more likely that government officials and police were indifferent to the relative orthodoxy of Scientology's teachings, but were rather humoring the apostate reformers in order to gain their cooperation in the investigation and to gather as much incriminating evidence as possible. A Scientology source offered the opinion that the covert and ultimate aim of the investigation was "to destroy the church" rather than to prosecute its leaders:

> The 1978 Joint Report by Metro Police Sgt. John Fallis and OPP Officer Al Ciampini detailing their investigations prior to the raid in 1983 brought up incidents that the Church was later prosecuted for—but the question is, why did they not go ahead and prosecute those individuals . . . Marian Evoy and Bryan Levman at that time? It was Levman who had organized all the illegal activity. But who, in the end, gets prosecuted? The church as a whole and people who were in junior positions. The reason is, they were waiting for a wider net, hoping for a new law that would give them the chance to shut the church down.[20]

Rise of Canada's Anticult Movement and the Quest for a New Law to Fight "Cults"

Hexham (2001:184) notes that "from 1977 onwards, parent's groups, often encouraged by university chaplains, formed across Canada to promote deprogramming and to encourage legislators to pass restrictive laws against [new religious recruitment and evangelism]." Anticult groups were formed in the major cities of Canada, and in Toronto the Council on Mind Abuse (COMA) had a strong presence on the University of Toronto campus and in the media.

As a response to the "cult scare" (Bromley and Shupe, 1981) that followed the Jonestown tragedy in October 1978, the attorney general of Ontario established a commission to investigate new religious movements and to write a major report on "Mind Development Groups, Cults and

Sects in Ontario." COMA lobbied for the investigation and endorsed the attorney general's actions. The famous Canadian black civil libertarian Daniel G. Hill led the commission. Members of the burgeoning anticult movement in Canada were hopeful that the results of Hill's research would influence the government to broaden the law so as to guard against "dangers of cults." But when the Hill Report appeared in June 1980, its findings argued that whereas some individuals may suffer harm through their affiliations with NRMs, these movements posed no threat to the general public. Daniel Hill and his team of investigators debunked ACM claims and condemned the practice of deprogramming as a violation of human rights and civil liberties (Hill, 1980). They advised the Ontario government to "ignore calls for anticult legislation and other measures aimed at restricting religious liberty" (Hexham, 2001:281).

But in 1984, a new law was passed that provided fresh opportunities to prosecute NRMs. The new law, titled the "Dredge and Dock Law," was named after a famous legal case involving the Canadian Dredge & Dock Company. It addressed the issue of who is responsible for crimes involving company members. It decided that the company would be held responsible if individuals in executive positions commit crimes. In a landmark decision, the Supreme Court of Canada adopted the English identification doctrine for liability, which states that culpability for acts and mental states of a corporation can be represented by employees and officers on the basis that they are the "directing mind" of the corporate entity (Tully, 2005). This notion of corporate liability was used in the court case against top Scientology officials in the Guardian's Office.

Eighteen months after the Toronto raid, in 1984, the charges were filed: 11 counts of theft and breach of trust against the church and nine of its members; 4 counts of theft of documents, 4 counts of breach of trust, and 7 counts of possession. The documents in question were allegedly stolen during the 1970s from two Toronto law firms, the OPP, the Metro Police, the Ontario Medical Association, the College of Physicians and Surgeons, and the Canadian Mental Health Association (Priest, 1991).

The Church of Scientology on Trial

The Church of Scientology trial in Toronto opened in April 1992. The Church of Scientology itself was charged with possession of property obtained by criminal theft and breach of trust. The theft charges involved nine counts of theft of documents worth over $200, and seven counts of possession of stolen documents (Hallechuk, 1990). Nineteen former members faced criminal charges. Five Scientologists stood trial on breach of trust charges and accused of infiltrating the police force and the attorney general's office. The Toronto Sun described the trial as "a bewildering array of jargon and terminology." Crown Attorney James Stewart, in his opening remarks, told the court that Scientology's "spy ring" extended into the RCMP, the OPP, the Metro Police, and even the Ontario attorney general's office.

Bryan Levman was the star witness for the prosecution and testified under a grant of immunity. He was the director of the Guardian's Office in Toronto in the mid-1970s, and he defined his mission as "protecting Scientology from its enemies" (Dunphy, 1992a). He admitted to planning and directing numerous "break-ins" and "intelligence operations." He described in his testimony how he was promoted to the Guardian's Office by Mary Sue Hubbard in 1973 when he was shown a secret policy directive from Mr. Hubbard outlining how the GO should "deal with Scientology's enemies." Levman explained that Jane Kember, head of the British-based Guardian's Office, was concerned that "the Ontario Attorney General's Office was investigating us, and the Ontario Provincial Police and the Metro [Toronto] Police. She wanted us to get the files" (Claridge, 1992a). He also mentioned a "target list of possibly a few dozen agencies and individuals church officials wanted us to spy on" (Dunphy, 1992a).

The techniques used by the Guardian's Office, according to Levman, included "ripoffs" ("basically walking into various offices . . . of enemies, looking through their files and copying them") and "agents" ("getting a job within the targeted organization and when the opportunity is right you get the information . . . any way you can") (Demara, 1992).

Levman laid forth the rationale behind these activities. Under the "Fair Game Law" Hubbard had proclaimed, "I am not interested in WOG [non-Scientology] morality" and had authorized attacks on Scientology's enemies. Levman explained, "we all felt there was an insane segment of society that wanted to destroy Scientology and I was doing my part to save the planet" (Demara, 1992).

Other ex-Scientologists from the Guardian's Office testified under a grant of immunity. Marion Evoy told the court that the Royal Canadian Mounted Police was targeted for infiltration because Hubbard "believed the Mounties were part of a worldwide conspiracy . . . run by a band of former Nazis who had taken over Interpol" (Dunphy, 1992b).

Kathy Smith testified that she had infiltrated the Ontario Provincial Police and worked as a mail clerk at their Toronto offices on Harbord Street between 1974 and 1976.[21] When hired by the OPP, she had sworn an oath of secrecy concerning the confidentiality of the documents she would be handling. "I did not intend to honor the oath," Smith confessed in court. "I would take files I thought would be of interest to the church. I would put them in a straw bag I carried in the summer and give them to my case officer who would then go off and return them within an hour. Other tines I would photocopy documents and hand them over" (Darroch, 1992). In the evening she would go to the "garden" (the secret room where the stolen documents were filed) and would file the papers she had stolen. Sometimes she and the other secret agents would meet there to practice how to handle "worst-case scenarios" if they were caught stealing documents (Darroch, 1992). Another ex-member described how agents were sent to the Scientology headquarters in the United States to "receive training in lock-picking" (Dunphy, 1992c).

Another witness described how she had made trips to the attorney general's office archives and stolen a file that dealt with the flow of intelligence information between Ontario and the United States (Dunphy, 1992d).

In defense of the church, a senior Scientology official, Mark Rathbun, testified in court that they had fired between 700 and 800 staff members for "crimes" during the Ethics Mission's cleanup in 1982. He blamed the people working in the Guardian's Office for perpetrating the crimes without the church's knowledge (Dunphy, 1992e). Scientologists today insist that the Guardian's Office, under Jane Kember, developed into a secretive, renegade organization that acted against the church's best interests and betrayed the directives of L. Ron Hubbard.[22]

The "Breach-of-Trust" Conviction

In June 1992, the jury found the Church of Scientology itself and three of its members guilty of breach-of-trust charges. The three members had been acquitted of 10 of the original 12 charges, since a judge ruled that the evidence was seized unlawfully in the raid—although the search warrant was (paradoxically) considered still valid.[23] Two other members were also acquitted and three charges against the church were dropped. In an early conviction in 1985, ex-Scientologist Nanna Anderson had pleaded guilty to photocopying files from the Ontario Medical Association, and the judge had granted her an absolute discharge ("First Conviction in Scientology Case," *Montreal Gazette*, Dec. 16, 1985).

This was an unprecedented decision. For nine years the lawyers on both sides of the case had presented arguments for whether or not a church could be prosecuted on criminal charges and whether the Charter of Rights and Freedoms prevented or permitted such litigation (Kavanaugh, 1992).

Scientology's lawyers appealed the decision, arguing that an incorporated nonprofit religious association should not be held responsible for criminal acts committed by individuals within its ranks. But in 1997 the appeals court upheld the 1992 conviction of the Church of Scientology (and one of its officers) on two counts of breach of trust.

In a 143-page ruling, a three-judge panel admitted that the liability did, in fact, infringe on the guarantees of religious freedom within the Charter of Rights and Freedoms. But it held that the infringement was permissible under Section 1 of the Charter, as a "reasonable limit" in a free and democratic society.

In an insightful speech, Judge Marc Rosenberg freely acknowledged that "the mere prosecution of the church would stigmatize the parishioners and members and divert funds from religious purposes to defense of the charge." But he also noted that the objective of applying the liability to religious corporations "relates to a fundamental tenet of our society—namely that no person is above the law." In upholding the $250,000 fine imposed on the church, Judge Rosenberg said sternly that "the offences represented a deliberate attempt to undermine the effectiveness of the law-enforcement agencies" (Claridge, 1997). The legal battle in Canada over the espionage activities of the Guardian's Office continued on for many years (Claridge, 1992b).

Conclusion

We note that the issues raised and debated in the wake of these international raids have been quite diverse. In the 1960s, the U.S. authorities suspected the church of tax fraud and of pseudo-therapeutic medical practices. The Australian concern focused on the un-Christian nature of this new "cult," and on the vulnerability of its clients to potential blackmail. The 1977 raids in the U.S. and 1983 raids in Canada targeted the infiltration and theft of official government documents thought to be damaging to the church by GO agents. We also see that in Canada timely innovations in the law were exploited to convict the entire corporate body of the Church of Scientology of breach of trust.

It is worth pointing out that the Hill Commission in Canada found that NRMs posed no threat to the public and discouraged anticult initiatives. The Canadian press, in contrast to the Australian (and more recently the French) press, exhibited a certain tolerance for Scientology as a possibly authentic religion despite its lack of legal recognition as such. Canadian journalists have consistently referred to Scientology as a "church" with "parishioners," rather than as a "cult" with "victims."

There is ample evidence that ex-members and other adversaries played a major role in the Toronto raid and the ensuing court processes that led to the church's conviction. However, it appears that these individuals were used as pawns in an ambitious and long-range plan to discredit and financially destroy the Church of Scientology in Canada. This network of interested parties, the OPP, the attorney general, the FBI, the IRS, and the Toronto Metropolitan Police (with possible input from the Ontario Medical Association, the College of Physicians and Surgeons, and the Canadian Mental Health Association) launched a coordinated plan that involved false promises to apostates, "divide-and-conquer" tactics for miscreants inside the Guardian's Office, and plea bargains and immunity for the star witnesses, many of whom were the authors of the crimes.

The legal troubles besetting the Church of Scientology in multiple countries in the early period made it more vulnerable to the claims of wrongdoing by opponents in the ensuing years. While the government raids and seizure of materials in the United States, Australia, and Canada were also fraught with legal problems once they were reviewed by the courts, nonetheless, the damage was done. Scientology, certainly culpable of some of the charges, was soiled. The church became an easy target for better-organized opponents who possessed ample ammunition to make claims and press authorities to launch new investigations or raids in the coming years.

9

Raids in France

FRANCE IS A unique case in the study of government raids on NRMs. The distinctiveness of France is tied to several factors including cultural and historical elements (*"laïcité"* and French nationalism) and the state regulatory structure governing *"sectes."* We explain the significance of these features in the following pages, but in short, we contend that powerful anticult organizations in France have faced few barriers of church-state separation and have become an arm of the state regulatory apparatus. ACM organizations are state supported and funded. Unlike North America, where ACM organizations are third-party interest groups or movements lobbying government officials to act, in France they are empowered by the state. As such, they have extraordinary authority and influence leading to extreme measures of social control.

Countermobilization against NRMs in France has essentially assumed the form of state mobilization. Social movement scholars emphasize the importance of accounting for actions and counteractions among states, movements, third parties, and countermovements in assessing movement trajectories (Goldstone, 2003; McAdam, Tarrow, and Tilly, 2001). States, of course, have a pivotal role because they can lay claim to the legitimate use of force against movements and other challengers. If and when countermovements become institutional allies of the state, the result is a hostile climate for new movements seeking a foothold in society. Such has been the case in France where anticult associations have been recognized as "public service" organizations by the national government, thereby becoming eligible for public funding and support. In concert with an official state monitoring office, the interministerial missions created by the National Assembly (MILS and MIVILUDES), an activist countercult crusade among some Catholic priests (Palmer, 2011b), and support for anticult legislation by the Catholic Church (Duvert, 2004:48), the ACM campaign against NRMs has achieved unprecedented success.

One consequence of this distinctive institutional alliance between the state and anticult organizations and actors has been the disproportionate and unparalled concentration of government raids on minority religious communities. Nearly half of all government raids on NRMs we were able to document occurred in France. Table 9.1 shows that French authorities conducted 57 raids on 17 different NRMs between 1971 and 2012. The raids escalated dramatically in the 1990s, consistent with the pattern seen in other countries; 88 percent of these raids ($N = 50$) were launched from 1990 onward. Twenty-one of the 57 French raids (37 percent) targeted one specific NRM, the American-based Church of Scientology. We will explain the French government's targeting of the Church of Scientology in this chapter. But the particular enmity shown toward Scientology by the French does not alone explain the elevated rate of raids experienced by new or nontraditional religious communities. The reach of state control over NRMs in France has been extensive, relentless, and sweeping. So why France?

In our model of countermovement mobilization outlined in chapter 2, we assume third-party/countermovement actors are *outsiders* attempting to press government officials to act on their behalf. The success of the model is largely contingent on the ability of core opponents (ACM actors, apostates, concerned relatives) to make inroads into government in order to effect legislation or public policy. In the case of France, we find the *nonpareil* for ACM countermovement effectiveness, since the impediments typically encountered by third-party outsiders are eliminated. For reasons unique to France, ACM organizations and actors have been integrated into the state machinery and thus become *insiders.* This troubling political alliance has resulted in what Palmer (2011b) calls a "government-sponsored war on sects." As James Beckford has acutely observed, "it is now necessary to think of France as the only Western country with an official mission to combat cultism. France is not content merely to monitor and, on occasion, to sanction religious movements that might break the law but it also campaigns actively against the work of most minority religious groups" (Beckford, 2004:29).

There are historical and cultural forces that help to explain French intolerance toward minority religions. France's severe, sometimes draconian, treatment of its religious minorities since the 12th century (e.g., Jews, Albigensians, Cathars, Huguenots, and Protestants) is well

Table 9.1 Government Raids on NRMs in France, 1971–2012

Group Targeted	Year(s)	No. of Raids
1. Scientology (Paris, Lyon, etc.)	1971–2009	(21)
2. Raelians (Perigord)	1973, 1979, 1991, 2001	(4)
3. ISKCON (Paris)	2005	(1)
4. Longo Mai (Castellane)	1989	(1)
5. The Family (Aix, Equilles)	1991–1993	(2)
6. Horus (Drome)	1991–1997	(6)
7. Mandarom (Castellane)	1994–1995, 2001	(4)
8. Twelve Tribes (Pyrénées-Atlantiques)	1996–1997, 2002	(3)
9. Ogyen Kunzang Choling (Castellane)	1997	(1)
10. R. Steiner/Waldorf schools (Anthroposophy)	1999	(6)
11. Terranova (Aveyron)	2000	(1)
12. Le Patriarche/Dianova (Toulouse)	2001	(1)
13. Les Gens de Bernard (Toulouse)	2007	(1)
14. Communauté des Béatitudes (Blagnac)	2008	(1)
15. Domaine de Chardenoux (Saône et Loire)	2010	(1)
16. Centre de Biodynamisme (Nyons)	2011	(1)
17. Amour et Miséricorde (Dijon)	2012	(1)
	Total	57

documented in history books and museums. More recently, the problems arising from the influx of Muslim immigrants from North Africa, incidents of *islamophobie*, unemployment and discrimination against Arabs in the workplace, and the Paris car bombings and ghetto riots, have been major topics in the media. Freedom of expression for French citizens who happen to be Muslims or Sikhs is also limited, due to the ban on headscarves and turbans and a shortage of mosques and *gurdwaras*.

But in order to properly understand the discrimination against new or alternative religious communities in France over the last 25 years, we must examine France's state-sponsored anticult movement and its rapid growth in the wake of the 1994 Solar Temple tragedy. Due to the powerful influence of anticult organizations like MILS, MIVILUDES, UNADFI, and CCMM, intolerant attitudes towards minority faiths have become official policies, institutionalized at the highest levels of the French government. Minority faiths such as the Jehovah's Witnesses, Soka Gakkai, and Scientology have gained legal recognition in other countries, but in France they are labeled and persecuted as *sectes*. Thus, France stands out among the other Western countries as a strikingly unique example of intolerance towards religious minorities.[1]

In its 1999 annual report on France, the International Helsinki Federation for Human Rights (1999) made this blunt observation: "While other countries abroad recommended dialogue with so-called sects, France has chosen open confrontation." The U.N. Special Rapporteur on Freedom of Religion or Belief, Ms. Asma Jahangir, in her 2005 report, condemned France's treatment of religious minorities, highlighting the "stigmatization of members of certain religious groups or communities, including those whose members have never committed any criminal offence under French law." Jahangir also criticized France's government-sponsored anticult mission, MIVILUDES, and expressed her hope that its future actions "will be in line with the right to freedom of religion and belief and avoid past mistakes."

Though France has a constitutional separation of church and state, there is no "wall of separation" as in the United States, and both the residual influence of the Catholic Church and the deep-rooted tradition of *laïcité* (radical secularism) tied to French nationalism (*la République*) have worked hand-in-hand to reject *les sectes* as an alarming threat to society. According to Beckford (2004:28), "the ideology of *laïcité* regards religion as, at best, acceptable in the private sphere although fundamentally incompatible with the institutions of a secular Republic and, at worst, antithetical to the capacity for rational free-thinking and to the primary loyalty of French citizens to their country." The advocates of *laïcité* hold that it is indispensable to the resolution of political and social conflicts that threaten the unity of France (Altglas, 2010; Hervieu-Léger, 2001; Luca, 2004). Indeed, for the French, *laïcité* means something quite different from mere secularization (declining religious belief, practice, or participation): "It refers to a strongly positive commitment to exclude religion from State institutions and, in its place, to inculcate principles of nonreligious rationality and morality" (Beckford, 2004:32). The conflict between secular Republicanism and the Catholic Church has cooled largely because the latter no longer engages in tasks that impinge upon the state nor does it challenge Republican values that stress individual rights, respect for law, and French nationalism. But NRMs are another matter. Beckford (2004:37) summarizes the problem adroitly: "NRMs constitute a threat not simply to individual recruits but to the very fabric of the French Republic by eroding the common faith in reason and by substituting an inchoate confusion of irrational meaning systems. There can be no justifiable freedom of religion for NRMs because, by definition, they extinguish freedom of thought for individuals."

The widely held suspicion towards sects in France was exacerbated by a disturbing event that occurred on October 4, 1994, when an esoteric group of Neo-Templars that called itself *l'Ordre du Temple Solaire* (Solar Temple) set fire to three ski chalets in Switzerland and Quebec. Fifty-three people died a violent death. Some were shot in the head as "traitors," others dressed as medieval Knights Templars were drugged and immolated as the chalets exploded and were consumed in flames. While the core group members volunteered for this "mission," there were apparently many unwitting participants in this ideologically driven mass suicide that was planned by the two grandmasters (Mayer, 1996).

Suddenly the Order of the Solar Temple was known throughout France as a dangerous *secte* that brainwashed its members to embrace a carefully orchestrated ritual suicide with sanctimonious arrogance. What surprised the public was that many of these dead *secte* members had been distinguished, respectable French citizens. Among the dead were wealthy Swiss businessmen, like Camille Pilet, or family members of ski champion Jean Vuarnet, orchestral conductor Michel Tabachnik, and several millionaires. Moreover, this wasn't a youth *secte* like some of the other groups. Most of the OTS members were middle-aged and some elderly. Their social status and maturity made their willingness to embrace the Solar Temple's radical apocalyptic, suicidal ideology all the more incomprehensible and terrifying.

The Guyard List

Shortly after the OTS mass suicides/homicides in 1994, the French National Assembly voted to establish a commission to investigate the *secte* phenomenon. A few months later, the Commission released the Guyard List (named after the president of the commission, Jacques Guyard) of 172 dangerous sects. The final Guyard Report issued in 1996 recommended the creation of a government monitoring agency to study the problem and warn the public of potential dangers. According to Palmer, the Guyard Report was a catalyst for the explosive growth in France's *antisecte* movement and established the "*secte* problem" as "an urgent item on the government's agenda" (Palmer, 2011b:10).

In their research, the Commission kept their sources of information secret, but judging from their findings it appears reasonable to assume that the Commission relied on three kinds of experts: ex-members of *sectes*, anticult activists, and the files of the Renseignements généraux (RG), France's secret police.[2]

Many groups, appalled to find their name on what they called the "*liste noir*," protested that they were not a "*secte*." But since there was no set of characteristics, no precise definition of a *secte* given in the report, it was impossible to contest their presence on the "*liste*." The Guyard Report described *sectes* in vague terms, as groups focusing on gaining financially, breaking up families, abusing their members physically and psychologically, recruiting children, espousing "antisocial" ideas, disturbing the public order, having "judiciary problems," and attempting to "infiltrate" organs of the state. Since the Guyard Report was based on data gleaned from the secret files of the Renseignement généraux, the source of the data could not be revealed, nor its accuracy double-checked. Even to inquire about it could be construed as an act of treason.

Despite the fact that the Guyard Report had no legal status, it had an enormous impact on the social status of minority religions and their adherents. According to French sociologist Veronique Altglas (2008), "It became an official and prevailing reference, leading the public to think there was a legal definition."

The Interministerial Observatory on Sectes (1996) and MILS (1998)

The *Observatoire Interministériel sur les sectes* (Interministerial Observatory on *Sectes*) was set up by Prime Minister Alain Juppé in May 1996. Its mandate was to observe and find more effective tools to "fight *sectes*." Training and "cult awareness" programs were set up for the police, state prosecutors, judges, and teachers. The minister of the interior, Jean-Pierre Chevènement, sent out a circular memo to police chiefs on November 7, 1997, urging them to "fight against reprehensible actions of sectarian movements," and asked UNADFI and CCMM to assist him in raising public awareness of the dangers of *sectes*. Chevènement also called for the mobilization of all state officials against *sectes*, to unite in exchanging information, heightening vigilance, and making work, school, and health inspections. He called the effort a "national priority" (Palmer, 2011b:17).

Even the Ministry of Justice sent out a circular December 1, 1998 to the public prosecutor's office, calling on all prosecutors and judges to support antisect associations such as UNADFI and CCMM to help combat "attacks on persons or private property committed by groups of a sectarian nature" (Palmer, 2011b:17–18).

In 1998 the Observatoire was replaced and given a new name, *Mission interministérielle de lutte contre les sectes* (MILS). Deputy Alain Vivien became its director, and its headquarters were housed in the prime minister's offices.

The 1999 "Sectes and Money" Report

On December 15, 1998 a third parliamentary commission was set up to "*lutter*" (fight against) the cults—this time to investigate the finances, property, and fiscal standing of *sectes*. This commission published a report in 1999 called "*Sectes* and Money" (*Rapport parlementaire français sur l'argent des sectes*), written by deputies Jacques Guyard and Jean-Pierre Brard, who had already been involved in the writing of the Guyard Report in 1995.

The "*Sectes* and Money" report provided an overview of the "*secte* problem" in France. It described a *secte* as "an association for pseudo-religious activities, [and] . . . commercial activities such as selling books or seminars." Since most *sectes* in France fall under the rubric of associations, according to the law of 1901, or of *cultes*, according to the law of 1905, the report proposed to tighten up the restrictions for associations in general. The purpose was to refuse all *sectes* the right to enjoy the status of an association "*cultuelle*" (which offers a form of *culte*, or public worship) by alleging that *sectes* were not "real religions." The report dealt with how *sectes* make money through exploiting the channels of education, health care, and sales motivation seminars, and recommended various measures to exclude them from these fields. The report also recommended that taxes be increased to 60 percent on member's gifts and donations. The possibility of financial abuse or fraud perpetrated by *sectes* was raised (although the commission admitted that few such groups had been prosecuted to date and not many found guilty).

The 1999 report focused on the larger, wealthier international groups like the Jehovah's Witnesses and Scientology. The state claimed these groups might use excessive or dishonest means to obtain donations, which then were transferred out of the country and beyond the reach of French tax authorities.[3] The report concluded with a recommendation that the anticult activities of MILS should be expanded, that there should be more cooperation with anticult groups like UNADFI, and that special anticult initiatives by each branch of the government should be instituted.

It should be noted that there was a flurry of "tax raids" or surprise investigations by *le fisc* (*l'Adminstration fiscale* or fiscal control) after the National Assembly published its report in 1999. Tax raids were launched on new religions' headquarters, new inflated tax bills arrived unexpectedly, and various yoga and meditation centers were audited by *le fisc*. Religious, philosophical, and psychotherapeutic groups that had previously enjoyed cordial relations with their local mayor and neighbors were bewildered to find they were suddenly barred from participating in customary annual public functions. Rental contracts with hotels where religious groups held their annual conferences were cancelled at the last minute, simply because the manager had discovered their name on the Guyard List. Their stalls in marketplaces for the sale of crafts, farm produce, and books were confiscated. Adepts were systematically "unmasked" by their local UNADFI chapter, which sent out faxes warning their employers. Hundreds of professionals lost their jobs or were denied promotions. Spouses involved in divorce disputes lost custody of their children or visiting rights, due to their affiliation with a known *secte* (Palmer, 2002).

As French scholars like Nathalie Luca and Danièle Hervieu-Léger have pointed out, the French people are highly suspicious of the promotion and commodification of religious or symbolic products. "The idea that money could be associated with religion is today, in the French context, something that scandalizes people" (Hervieu-Léger, 2001:119). This sentiment is rooted in the historical context of the Catholic Church's practice of selling indulgences. Luca observes that this was a part of the reforms of the Church required by the French, "which has established free availability of symbolic products" (2004:69). "The idea of paying for spiritual services is something new in France. It upsets a nation deeply influenced by a culture that denies the possibility of a link between spirituality and money" (Luca, 2004:70). Financial practices of some NRMs, such as Scientology, have "reawaken(ed) an issue addressed some time ago to deal with the economic puissance of the Roman Church" (Luca, 2004:70).

MIVILUDES and the Advent of "Dérives sectaires"

In 2002 the earlier government-sponsored anticult "ministry" was disbanded and MIVILUDES was formed under the Chirac government.

MILS had been criticized for its head-on fight (*lutte*) against *les sectes*. So MIVILUDES devised a more circumspect, sophisticated mission: the "vigilance and fight against *dérives sectaires*" (Palmer, 2002).

"*Dérives sectaires*" may be translated as "sectarian drift," "sectarian danger," "sectarian deviancy," "sectarian harm," and even "derailment" or going off the rails. On first glance, the *dérives sectaires* option appears to be a more even-handed approach to the public management of so-called cults. It sidesteps the problematic exercise of labeling groups and defining the characteristics of a *secte*. It poses (at least on the surface) a less direct challenge to religious free-dom. Certainly, it appeared to make a good impression on the UN's Special Rapporteur, Asma Jahangir, who wrote in her September 2005 report that she had the impression that France was becoming "more tolerant" of *sectes*.

In May 2005, Prime Minister Jean-Pierre Raffarin issued a circular declaring that the 1996 Guyard List should no longer be used to identify *sectes*, and he recommended that his civil servants should avoid depending on generic lists of groups. The second president of MIVILUDES, Jean-Michel Roulet, concurred that the Guyard List was "completely obsolete," but also conceded that it "allowed us to determine and delay the phenom-enon . . . in an erroneous and incomplete way" ("Le nouveau président veut aider les victimes à dénoncer les sectes," Agence France-Presse, Septem-ber 29, 2005). In Roulet's view the *sectes* had morphed into new configura-tions, so a new weapon was needed. Thus, MIVILUDES developed a new strategy; instead of fighting groups who were constantly challenging their definition of *secte*, they would now focus on fighting *les dérives sectaires*.[4]

Essentially, MIVILUDES's new resolve was to target those *sectes* that broke the law. Their new program was the prevention of *secte*-derived crimes and misdemeanors, and not the persecution of religious minorities *per se*. Roulet's strategy was to encourage victims to complain and train police and magistrates to assist the victims in making a deposition. He referred to *secte* leaders as "powerful people . . . that we must fight with legal tools. We must collect facts we must prosecute them with justice. . . . the sectarian fight is new and there is a lack of jurisprudence" ("Le nouveau président veut aider les victimes à dénoncer les sectes," Agence France-Presse, September 29, 2005).

Abus de faiblesse *and the About-Picard Law*

MIVILUDES was faced with a serious obstacle. There was a dearth of crimes occurring in new religions and a shortage of complaints against them by concerned citizens. The paucity of crimes undermined the justification for a state-funded organ such as MIVILUDES. Thus, MIVILUDES found a creative solution to this problem; fabricate sectarian crime by designing a law to prosecute cult leaders and disband their movements.

On June 12, 2001 the About-Picard Law was passed in the National Assembly. It created a new category of *délit* (misdemeanor) called the *abus de faiblesse* ("abuse of weakness"). This category was designed to capture the many ways that vulnerable followers might be hurt by *secte* leaders—through fraud, physical abuse, sexual exploitation, incitement to mass suicide, and withholding medical treatment or practicing medicine without a license. All these forms of social deviance were allegedly made possible through the powerful, ineluctable force of *manipulation mentale* (brainwashing). Any *secte* leaders found guilty of *"l'abus frauduleux de l'état d'ignorance ou de faiblesse"* could be imprisoned for five years and fined up to 750,000 euros in damages ("La loi About-Picard reinforce l'arsenal legislatif contre les sectes," 2004).

A deputy in the National Assembly, Catherine Picard (who later became *présidente* of UNADFI) sought to avoid the knotty problem of defining a *secte* by focusing rather on the concept of *dérives sectaires*—the "sectarian dangers" that arose from charismatic leaders' uncanny control over their followers' minds through *manipulation mentale*. The problem of finding objective criteria for "mental manipulation," however, was pointed out by the minister of justice and various lawyers. Church leaders saw the new law as a potential threat to freedom of religion. Human rights advocates dubbed the law *un délit d'opinion.*

In its final stage, a new version of the bill attempted to circumvent the problem of creating a law against brainwashing *per se*. An existing article in the criminal code already dealt with "the abuses of ignorance and weakness." Hence the wording of the law was reworked to effectively preserve the concept of brainwashing in the less inflammatory notion of *manipulation mentale*. In Articles 10 and 11 of the new law, mental manipulation was defined as "a state of psychological or physical subjection resulting from heavy or repeated pressure on a vulnerable person." Anthony and Robbins (2004) have described the French notion of *manipulation mentale* as a "third-generation version" of the brainwashing theory based on the highly questionable work of French psychiatrist Jean-Marie Abgrall.[5] Thus, the brainwashing concept, already criticized for its vagueness, was latently embedded in that ambiguous notion of *abus de faiblesse*.

The French sociologist Danièle Hervieu-Léger noted that that law "fails to define what a *secte* is from a legal point of view" but appeared to serve an "emblematic function" in that it attested to "the determination of the state to protect its citizens from dangerous *sectes*" (Hervieu-Léger, 2004:58). It is worth noting that among seven of the seventeen groups that were raided in France, allegations of *abus de faiblesse* were included in the initial charges against their leaders.[6]

The Raids

The frequency and ferocity of police raids on NRMs in France have been disturbing. Such has been noted by a local human rights group, CICNS (Center of Information and Council of the New Spiritualities), based in Montpezac de Quercy. Their observations on these types of "brutal assaults" can be found in a posting on their website, *"Assauts policiers sur les minorités spirituelles"*:

> Over the last twenty years, in an atmosphere of public ignorance and general indifference, individuals and families of voluntary associations have submitted to brutal assaults at the hands of the national or local police . . . from the simple accusation of being a "cult." Violent searches and seizures have been launched at dawn in front of traumatized children and numerous irregularities have been revealed in these *perquisitions* later. The psychological consequences of this kind of barbarous assault are one of the saddest aspects of these interventions.[7]

CICNS provides a list of 13 raids on new religious communities or spiritual healing centers between 1989 and 2011. Most of the groups on the list are small and obscure but the degree of force used in the raids has been extreme. In 1989 a raid was launched on Longo Mai, a Buddhist meditation and farming community, by the DST (*Direction de la Surveillance du Territoire*), a domestic intelligence and counterterrorism unit of the French National Police, accompanied by judiciary police, security guards, and helicopters. Another example was the 1997 raid on the Tibetan Buddhist community, Ogyen Kunzang Choling, where 150 armed gendarmes, armored vehicles, and two helicopters were deployed to conduct a surprise investigation of the residential Tibetan Buddhist school (see Palmer, 2011b for more detailed analysis).

In 2011 another raid targeted the Centre for Teaching Biodynamism, a training program that combined physiotherapy with Chinese medicine. The raid team was composed of a special antisect unit called CAIMADES (Cellule d'Assistance et d'Intervention en Matière de Dérives Sectaires) and 70 gendarmes. The heavily armed raid force descended on a small class of middle-aged and elderly women attending a garden lecture on the spiritual dimensions of physiotherapy. The physiotherapist who founded the Centre for Teaching Biodynamism was charged with *abus de faiblesse*, a pseudoscientific concept that could be applied indiscriminately to any *secte* leader.

In 2000, Terranova, a small communal group in Aveyron, was raided by 60 heavily armed gendarmes accompanied by an army brigade in full combat gear. A woman was dragged out of bed in her nightgown and thrown to the ground with a gun pointed at her head. Olivier Manitara, the spiritual leader who was branded a *"gourou,"* was grilled at length on his religious beliefs. It appears that the community was raided in part because a caravan had been parked in an *interdit* area and there was an error in a claim for Assédic (a French agency which collects and pays un-employment insurance). The group was also thought to be linked to the White Brotherhood (one of the groups on the Guyard List) simply because Manitara mentioned the White Brotherhood in one of his books. Manitara and his wife were charged and convicted of *abus de confiance*, construction without a permit, and *abus de biens sociaux* (misuse of common property or corporate assets), among other things. They were given eight-month suspended sentences and ordered to pay a minor fine. Ten members were also taken into custody and given two possible plea options: 1) "victim of a *secte*" or 2) "the *gourou*'s accomplices" ("Terranova de Montlaur," Agence France-Presse, December 19, 2003).

Space does not permit a comprehensive analysis of all the French raids in these categories. Instead, we offer a brief examination of raids on four NRMs to illustrate the difficult challenges faced by the targeted groups.

Mandarom

Between 1994 and 2001, Mandoram was the target of no less than four government raids, each motivated by a different deviance claim. Man-doram was one of the NRMs placed on the Guyard List and has been referred to by the media as "the most dangerous *secte* in France" (Palmer,

2011b:34), despite the peaceful, law abiding nature of the community. Members practice the path of Aumisme, which they believe unites all the world religions in a mission of peace. The Holy City of Mandarom is an eclectic Hindu-style ashram in the French Alps, founded by a Frenchman, Gilbert Bourdin ("Hamsah Manarah" to his devotees). Bourdin was born in Martinique and moved to France in 1962. After experiencing *samadhi* or enlightenment, he began to accept disciples and established an ashram. In 1969 he purchased land in the Alps where he and his disciples built the Holy City of Mandoram. Palmer observes that the "fierce intolerance of the French authorities toward Mandoram throughout the 1990s" might be explained "as a reaction to the group's flagrant display of alien religious symbols, or an aesthetic revulsion to Mandoram's pious display of art" (2011b:34). Indeed, this oriental folk art included an onion shaped dome of the Lotus Temple, statues of Buddha, the "Cosmic Christ," and the "Cosmoplanetary Messiah" reaching into the mountain skies.

Not surprisingly, the rationale for the first raid, on November 25, 1994, was to inspect the temples and statues for violations of the civil planning code. A judge and a unit of gendarmes paid a surprise visit on this occasion. No violations were discovered and the raid party left without incident.

The events preceding this raid are noteworthy. In 1992, the president of a local ecology activist group, Robert Ferrato, joined forces with the president of UNADFI, Janine Tavernier, to protest the building of the statues at Mandoram. They claimed that Mandoram upset the ecological balance of the mountain and demanded that their building permit be revoked. The mayor of the nearby town, Saint-Julien-du-Verdon, joined the opposition soon after. In 1994, the father of a devotee, Alain Delcourt, went on television and claimed he had lost his daughter to a "cult" and that she was living in a "concentration camp" (Palmer, 2011b:41).

The second raid was a tax fraud investigation. On January 24, 1995, 20 tax officials and 100 gendarmes stormed the monastery while roads were blocked and helicopters hovered overhead. The police searched rooms and seized documents and other items. A simultaneous *perquisition* was conducted on the Paris apartment of the head administrator of Mandarom, Dr. Christine Amory. No charges were filed but it was later learned that a list of the members of Mandoram was confiscated in the raid on Dr. Amory's apartment and given to tax authorities and then turned over to opponents, including local ADFI officials, Robert Ferrato, and a journalist, Bernard Nicolas (Palmer, 2011b:42).

A third raid was launched on June 12, 1995, to arrest the Aumiste's messianic leader, Hamsah Manarah (Bourdin), on charges of rape. Plain-clothes police arrived at the front gate of the property at 6:00 a.m., fol-lowed by 30 gendarmes in uniforms and commandos who ransacked the monastery. The residents were handcuffed and several claimed they were beaten at gunpoint. Hamsah Manarah resided in the Lotus Temple and the police broke in the door and hauled him off in chains. Eight of the resident monks were arrested in the monastery, including 12 visiting members. All those arrested were charged with complicity in a sexual misconduct case that allegedly occurred ten years earlier (Interview, Dr. Christine Amory, 2006). Hamsah Manarah was held in custody for 18 days. After his release was ordered, prosecutors appealed asking for a bail of one million francs. Hamsah Manarah was never actually tried and the rape charges were never resolved, so he lived the rest of life under a cloud of suspicion.[8] The accuser, Florence Roncaglia, claimed she was raped several times as a teen in 1984 while staying with her mother at the mon-astery. She later became the girlfriend of journalist Bernard Nicolas and they published a book together (*Mandoram: Une Victime Temoigne*). The book described the rape, among other crimes, that allegedly occurred at Mandarom. Introvigne (2004:75–76) states that Nicholas played a key role in helping Roncaglia "remember" that she had been raped, indicating that her claim was based on a "recovered memory" in therapy, a source of many false child and sex abuse allegations.

After the third raid, Dr. Jean-Marie Abgrall was appointed by the Court of Digne to investigate the doctrines and practices of the Mandoram and the allegations against Bourdin. Introvigne (2004:76) notes that this action by the court seemed to confirm that "child abuse charges were now joining the brainwashing arguments" mounted against Bourdin. Bour-din refused to meet with Abgrall several times before the arrest. But this didn't deter Abgrall from writing a psychoanalytic profile of Bourdin for the Court of Digne even though Abgrall had never met or spoken to Bour-din. Abgrall referred to Bourdin as "paranoid" and a "fraud" and described the religion of Ausmisme as a "clownesque caricature of a cult" (Palmer, 2011b:42). Abgrall later suggested in his book *La Mécanique des sectes* that Aumistes might commit mass suicide and that it would be a *"suicide à la mort du père"* (Palmer, 2011b:52). The media also carried stories com-paring Mandoram to the Order of the Solar Temple, invoking the mass suicide narrative. Nameless ex-members were quoted saying there were willing to die or commit suicide for Hamsah Manarah. Even the Waco

Branch Davidian tragedy was invoked as the mayor of Saint-Julien-du-Verdon, Roger Reybaud, was quoted in the press saying that Mandoram might shortly become a "Waco-sur-Verdon" (Palmer, 2011b:52).

A fourth raid was launched on September 8, 2001 with the intent to destroy Mandarom`s eight-meter-high statue of the Cosmoplanetary Messiah. Since 1993, the French authorities had repeatedly challenged the validity of the building permit of the statues. The Aumistes claimed that a building permit was issued on July 11, 1990, and indeed they received a certificate of compliance that reaffirmed the permit's validity in 1992. But the permit did not include the Cosmoplanetary Messiah statue. On July 1998 the Tribunal de Grande Instance in Digne declared the statue had no permit. Mandarom's chief administrator, Dr. Christine Amory, was forced to pay fines and the court ordered the destruction of the statue.

In June 2001, the prefect of les Alpes de Haute Provence asked for authorization to proceed with the demolition. On July 6, 2001, the tribunal authorized this action. On August 17, 2001, the Aumistes applied for an extension at the Court of Appeal, which was scheduled for September 10. But on September 5, 2001 the prefect paid a surprise visit, invading the monastery with 200 soldiers from the French army. The military demolition team arrived at 6 a.m. accompanied by journalists, and during the next 48 hours the French media broadcast and the public watched the military preparations for the demolition. The following morning at 5:20 a.m., the munitions were detonated and the statue exploded, toppling down the side of the mountain. The face of the Cosmoplanetary Messiah (which bore an obvious resemblance to Hamsah Manarah) fell to the ground intact. The army then pulverized it with heavy equipment.

A few weeks after the raid and destruction of the statue, Mandarom was billed for the costs involved in the demolition. On July 24, 2002, the Aumistes requested damages and interest for the abusive destruction of an edifice for which they had a valid permit. On June 22, 2006, the Tribunal Administrative of Marseille rejected the two requests. Paradoxically, the reason they gave was that the Mandarom actually had a valid permit for the statue after all. As Dr. Amory explained, "they said that the detonation was not their problem. It had been an error of the other tribunal, the correctional court. So we must apply to them instead" (Interview, Dr. Christine Amory, 2006). Since then, Aumisme has been recognized by the state as a valid religion and has been awarded the official status of a *culte*.

Amour et Miséricorde

On April 11, 2012, a tiny prayer group living in the suburbs of Dijon, which called itself Amour et Miséricorde, was raided by police investigators.[9] Four persons were taken into custody for questioning and transported to Paris for a lengthy interrogation. The secretary and spokesperson for the group was arrested. The media broadcast the fact that one of the staff happened to be a former Scientologist. He was placed *sous côntrole judiciaire.* He and Eliane Deschamps, the female founder-leader, were charged with *"abus de faiblesse aggravé"* or aggravated abuse of weakness (*Le Progrès*, 15 April, 2012).

Since 1996, Eliane Deschamps, a housewife and mother of five, living in Petit-Noir (Jura) has claimed to receive regular apparitions of the Virgin Mary for a 24-hour period on the 15th of each month. Deschamps gradually gathered a prayer group of 150 faithful Catholics, who refer to her as "La Petite Servante." Amour et Miséricorde is registered as an *association*, according to the French law of 1901. An inner circle of around 20 members live communally in Deschamps' house near Dijon. Deschamps' monthly apparitions are preceded by a 24-hour fast and constant prayer.

In 2002, the anticult group ADFI in Dijon began collecting complaints against the group. In 2004 a retired colonel, M. Doigneau (whose wife and daughters had left his home to join the prayer group, and since cut off all contact with him) filed a complaint against Eliane Deschamps for *abus de faiblesse.* The charges were dismissed in July 2007, but Doigneau then filed an appeal. After other families added their complaints to the case, the *juge d'instruction* ordered an investigation.[10] A network of interest groups formed to oppose the *secte*, composed of ex-members, concerned relatives, officials from ADFI and MIVILUDES, and the mayor of Chaussin who in an interview was investigating the possibility of demolishing Deschamps' house. (She was reacting to the row of placards placed on Deschamps' fence by group members, defending their religious freedom and proclaiming *"liberté, égalité, fraternité"*).[11]

Georges Fenech, a prominent anticultist and President of MIVILUDES, made headlines by putting the local archbishop on the spot, declaring that Amour et Miséricorde members claimed they were supported in their faith by the Archbishop of Dijon, Mgr. Minnerath. Fenech descended on the archbishop uninvited to fulminate about the dangers of the group and attempt to create countercult support. A 2008 MIVILUDES report criticizes "ecclesiatical authorities who did not seem to understand the degree of suffering involved and the dangers implied."

Fenech impugned the archbishop for *"mutisme"* and "not having the complete picture" in subsequent interviews (*Gazette de Côte d'Or*, December 11, 2008). The Archbishop, however, appeared reluctant to get involved in the dispute and refused to meet with the prayer group's critics. He was later quoted in *La Parisien* saying, "It is possible they are being bamboozled, but there is nothing serious to reproach them with" ("Une vérité difficile à établir," *L'Est Républicain*, April 10, 2013).

Amour et Miséricorde was sufficiently controversial to generate its very own anticult group. In July 2009, l'Association pour le Dialogue et la Réconciliation (ADER) was founded, composed of 180 members from across France. Its stated purpose was to help the victims of Amour et Miséricorde.[12]

Deschamps' prayer group promptly responded to the 2008 media onslaught by dissolving itself as an association. *Le Progrès* (December 18, 2008) reported the dissolution of Amour et Miséricorde that followed Fenech's visit. The group has responded to the raid and its unwelcome publicity by going underground. Today the messages from the Virgin are distributed not by e-mail, but by mail. Members change their cell numbers frequently and keep their participation in the prayer group secret.

Soon after the April 11, 2012 raid, Amour et Miséricorde reached out to the newspaper, *Le Bien public*. A story was published in which the members refuted the allegation they were a *secte* and denied being victims of "manipulation," declaring that "we are simply united in the spirit." Eliane Deschamps, when asked about her visions of Mary, was quoted saying *"Ma foi ne regarde que moi. C'est de l'ordre de l'intime"* [My faith concerns no one but me. It is intimate"] (*Le Bien public*, 2012).

The Centre for the Teaching of Biodynamism

On February 22, 2011, 70 policemen assisted by CAIMADES laid siege to the Centre for the Teaching of Biodynamism in Nyons (Drôme region). The director, Sophie Berlamont, and four of her assistants were taken into custody. The rationale for the raid was that Berlamont and her staff were suspected of "potential sectarian activity" and of "overcharging for training sessions."[13] Berlamont was later formally charged with *abus de faiblesse*.

Sophie Berlamont is a distinguished physiotherapist who worked in a hospital in Montpelier before moving to Nyons. She studied techniques from urogynaecology and kinesiology and specialized in women's health problems concerning pregnancy, menopause, and sexual dysfunctions.

She and her husband initially founded *Kinesiologie evolatif*, then *Enseignement nature*. When they divorced, Berlamont purchased a house and vineyard overlooking the Nyons valley. She created the Centre for Teaching Biodynamism in 2007, which offered courses that culled elements from Chinese medicine, reflexology, and *médicine quantique* (Interview, Sophie Berlamont in Nyons, May 22, 2012).

Over 15 years she built up a clientele of around 200 students; 180 were females between the ages of 50 and 80. The charges were not unreasonable (200 euros for a weekend, or 480 euros for a five-day course that included accommodations). Berlamont described in our interview how she and her students gathered in the courtyard to study a diagram of the human body when 72 police, dressed in blue jumpsuits and carrying handguns, leapt over the hedges that surrounded the courtyard. The CAIMADES squadron participated in the raid, which was described by Berlamont as follows:

CAIMADES is a special law enforcement [unit] from Paris created in 2009 to assist the gendarmerie in handing *sectes*. They are trained by MIVILUDES to recognize and deal with "brainwashed cult members." There were two policemen, one psychologist, one policeman trained in finance, one trained in violence. . . . There was also a dog (Interview, Sophie Berlamont, 2012)

Perquisitions were conducted simultaneously on the *Biodynamisme* center and on the homes of the four coaches, who were taken to the police station for *garde à vue* and held for 48 hours. Sophie Berlamont described how she was handcuffed and driven with a van in a motorcade to escort her. "The police searched my house expecting to find crucifixes, trappings of religion, but there is nothing." (Berlamont has no Internet at home, and this was considered a strange, *secte*-like austerity by the investigators).

The catalyst for the raid was based on information supplied by one of her former students. The actual raid was organized by MIVILUDES, whose secretary general, Hervé Mashi, told the media that Sophie Berlamont seemed to "exert mental control on the trainees and to abuse their weakness."[14]

Berlamont's lawyer later discovered that the *Biodynamisme* center had been under police surveillance for three years before the raid. The raid was initially prompted by the complaints of one of Berlamont's former students who had attended her classes for 15 years. When this former student separated from her husband and complained of being short of funds, Sophie offered her a typing job in exchange for free classes. But the woman complained to the anticult group, ADFI in Montpelier that Sophie manipulated her students into working for free.

The issue was aggravated when Sophie Berlamont became romantically involved with the woman's ex-husband and the couple started living together. The ex-member then phoned the other *stagiaires*, inviting them to complain to ADFI. After networking with ADFI and other ex-students, she continued to attend Berlamont's classes in order to encourage *stagiaires* to join the ex-member network. Several ex-members were recruited in a legal complaint filed against Berlamont and the center. According to Berlamont, "the director of ADFI . . . told the plaintiffs what to say in order to make Biodynamisme sound like a *secte*". They complained they were brainwashed, exploited financially, that Berlamont separated couples, prevented them from taking medicines, and forced them to sell their houses to give her the money.

Berlamont uses the playful *nom de plume* "Lisabelle" in her writing, which ADFI argued was a *secte* leader's charismatic title. The plaintiffs claimed Berlamont believed she was a reincarnation of Mary Magdelene (Berlamont denied this in our interview).

Berlamont's finances were found to be in order, and the court admitted she didn't seem to be making a profit; only her TVA (value-added tax) was still owed—a minor but frequent situation in France.

The *juge d'instruction*, Vergucht, found Berlamont guilty of the misdemeanor of *abus de faiblesse* according to the About-Picard Law of 2001. Berlamont was ordered to stop practicing Biodynamics, to close down her side business, her *chambre d'hôte*, and to have no communication with her students. The judgment was overturned by the appeals court in February 2012, but for a whole year the only people Berlamont saw were her companion, B, and his father. Thus she had no means of supporting herself, and depended on B and her own father, who agreed to pay for her mortgage and her legal fees. After winning her appeal, Berlamont was reindicted, and the case is pending a hearing in the *Cour de Cassation* (the highest court in France).

It is interesting to note that the kind of therapy offered by the Centre for Teaching Biodynamism, a system that blends "respectable" orthodox physiotherapy with more esoteric, Oriental healing arts would be quite common and noncontroversial in California. In France, however, it is perceived as *secte*-like. It appears the conflict originated in a former member's anger, and this internal conflict was exploited opportunistically by the anticult group ADFI, which has the legal power and means to file legal suits against so-called *"secte"* leaders on behalf of their "victims."

Berlamont is part of a network of female friends who regularly assist each other in gardening and painting their houses. Physical work was an aspect of her training course, as it is in monasteries and many religious communities. The fees for *Biodynamisme* were not excessive. But once the *"abus de faiblesse"* charge was laid against a putative *secte* leader, the "normal" voluntary patterns of work and economy found in Berlamont's *Biodynamisme* course could be easily interpreted as the abusive results of *manipulation mentale*.

Church of Scientology

Palmer (2011b:62–64) has observed that the animus of the French toward Scientology is predicated on three grounds: 1) that Scientology is a "Trojan Horse" for American imperialism, 2) that it is a not a "real" religion but a business masquerading as religion in order to bilk its gullible congregation, and 3) that the church uses masterful techniques of *manipulation mentale* and preys on the weak (*abus de faiblesse*). When we examine the government charges leading to the French raids on Scientology, it becomes clear that these sentiments are indeed driving the attacks on this particular NRM. While the raids on other NRMs in France suggest a broad range of issues (child abuse, sex abuse, sequestration, mental manipulation, non-assistance to person in danger, labor law violations, etc.), the charges against Scientology almost always begin with alleged financial or medical fraud. The roots of these charges are based on the pervasive and underlying assumption that Scientology is a faux religion and is designed to swindle or defraud members by employing psychological trickery or mental manipulation cloaked in religious language. The mere complaint by family of Scientology members, ex-members, journalists, or staff of MIVILUDES (or other ACM organizations) has been sufficient to trigger government raids. Table 9.2 shows the date, place, allegations, and type of enforcement involved in raids on the Church of Scientology. A brief survey of raids here is instructive.

In 1990, police conducted six different raids. On May 16, raids were launched on the Scientology missions in Nice and Marseilles. Thirty-nine Scientologists were arrested and charged with fraud and the illegal practice of medicine. On June 26, raids were conducted on the Scientology mission at Lyon. Staff members were arrested on the same charges of fraud and illegal practice of medicine. On July 4, raids were carried out at the Church

of Scientology and the Celebrity Center, both in Paris. Twenty members of
the church were arrested and held for questioning (*garde à vue*) involving
the similar allegations. Police confiscated a file with more than a thousand names of members of the International Association of Scientologists
(IAS), even though this organization was not under investigation.

Table 9.2 Raids on Scientology in France, 1971–2008

Year	City	Enforcement	Allegation(s)/Charge(s)
1971	Paris	Police (drug squad)	Fraud
1983	St Etienne	National police	Tax fraud
1987	Grancey	Police	Fraud
1990	Marseilles	Police	Fraud/illegal practice of medicine
1990	Nice	Police	Fraud/illegal practice of medicine
1990	Lyons	Police	Fraud/illegal practice of medicine
1990	Paris	Police	Fraud/illegal practice of medicine
1990	Lyons	*Juge d'instruction*/RG	Fraud/homicide
1990	Multiple (Church of Scientology–related companies)	Police	Fraud
1991	Paris	Police	Medical ethics/proselytizing
1992	Paris	Police	Fraud
1994	Paris	Police	Proselytizing
1999	Vincennes	Police	False advertising
2000	Paris	CNIL	Ex-member complaint
2000	Paris	CNIL	Ex-member complaint
2000	Lyons	Police	Fraud
2000	Paris	Police	False advertising
2001	Paris	Police	Fraud, misuse of funds
2002	Paris	Police	Ex-member complaint/fraud
2008	Paris	Police	False advertising
2009	Paris	CAIMADES	Complaint of family of suicide victim
		Total 21	

As the legal cases associated with these raids were under way, another major raid was being planned in response to the suicide of a Scientology member, Patric Vic. Vic had joined in Lyon in 1988 only two months prior to committing suicide by jumping out of a window. Vic's widow complained that he was pressured to take out a loan by the church in order to undergo a "purification process." Investigations were begun and on August 2, 1990, raids were conducted on both the mission center and the Church headquarters in Lyon by the Renseignement Généraux (intelligence services) accompanied by the *juge d'instruction*, Georges Fenech, who would later be named president of MIVILUDES and head the Commission to Investigate Sects and Minors.

The state's legal battle with the Church of Scientology intensified over the next several years. The Vic case symbolized the claims by opponents that Scientology was a dangerous *secte*. French media framed the story as a "cult-suicide" and played to the most sinister ACM stereotypes. In the 1996 trial of Scientology leaders, psychiatrist Jean-Marie Abgrall testified that Vic was subjected to techniques of harassment, blackmail, and guilt, exploiting the weaknesses of the young man (*abus de faiblesse*). Abgrall concluded that the methods of *manipulation mentale* employed by Scientologists were what eventually drove Mr. Vic to suicide.

Jean-Jacques Mazier, leader of the Lyon church, was convicted of fraud and involuntary homicide. He was sentenced to 18 months in prison and fined 500,000 francs. Other members were convicted of fraud. On July 28, 1997, the Court of Appeals of Lyon upheld the conviction but acquitted the other Scientologists of fraud charges. The appellate court also suspended Mazier's prison sentence. Five Scientologists were given suspended sentences of theft, complicity, or "abuse of trust." In the end, the church obtained a significant victory in the court's decision. According to the French law scholar Cyrille Duvert (2004:42), "the charges of fraud were not upheld against most of the Scientologists on trial, for the court decided they were sincere believers and [despite its controversial status] Scientology could be considered a bona fide religion." In effect, the Court of Appeals opened the door for the Church of Scientology to achieve official status as a recognized religion.

While the Vic case was being litigated, however, the state continued to launch raids on Scientology. In October 1990, companies allegedly linked to Scientology were raided as part of fraud investigations. One such company, Manhattan Langues (a language training business), was simply owned by Scientology members, but not a part of the church. In another raid in October 1991, police targeted the Paris church in pursuit of a medical doctor, Mr. Helou. The doctor was accused of "proselytizing" for Scientology in his medical practice in Reims. In January 1992, two more raids were launched on the Paris church and the Celebrity Center of Paris. Police seized computers and documents, and 30 staff members were arrested and taken into custody. Seven Scientologists were raided in their homes in the same operation. The charges involved financial fraud.

In June 1994, police raided the home of an artist who also happened to be a Scientologist. One of his students contacted a local ADFI office and filed a complaint against him for proselytizing. The artist was taken into custody and interrogated by police for 36 hours. The charges were later dismissed.

In June 1999, French police raided the Institut Aubert in Vincennes, a school that practiced Hubbard's methods of teaching. Charges were filed against the school for "advertisement lies" because the Institut did not acknowledge its link to Scientology. Authorities also charged the school's staff with "misuse of funds" because the cost of a plane ticket was paid to a Scientologist from Copenhagen who came to the school to help solve some internal problems. The police raided the homes of nine Institut teachers who were taken into custody and charged, and later raided the home of the Danish teacher and charged him with misuse of funds for receiving money for the airline ticket. As of August 2013, this case was still pending.

In May 2000, police raided the Church of Scientology in Paris based on a complaint from an ex-member, Mr. Bader. The ex-member said he continued to receive letters from the church even after he asked that his name be removed from their files. Police seized four computers and took the president of the church into custody. A month later in June, police raided the Paris church again to seize another computer they had failed to locate previously. Police also raided the Celebrity Center in Paris to search for files pertaining to the ex-member's complaint. And in the same month, police raided the Lyon church because a staff member was suspected of using the files of her personal website for the benefit of the church.

In December 2000, police conducted a raid on the Scientology publishing company, New Era France. The raid was launched after the church engaged in a publicity campaign to sell a new book. The publicity campaign included ads in a Scientology magazine distributed to bookstores and 20,000 posters advertising Hubbard's book, *Fundamentals of*

Thought. Police seized files and computers, including a list of all the New Era staff members.

In January 2002, police conducted yet another raid on the Celebrity Center in Paris based on a complaint from an ex-member, Alain Stoffen. Stoffen was a member of Scientology for 15 years and after leaving demanded that the church compensate him for the years he lost as a "brainwashed" cult member. The case was dismissed in 2006 but Stoffen appealed. The case is still pending, even though no one was ever indicted and the prosecutor asked for a dismissal in the appeal.

In December 2008, police raided the Church of Scientology in Paris and the Celebrity Center of Paris again after the mayor of Paris filed a complaint for "false advertising." The mayor had received a Scientology booklet entitled "The Way to Happiness," mailed directly to his office. Apparently, the logo of the city hall was on the cover of the booklet. The booklet was produced by the Way to Happiness Foundation (USA) and the Paris church was not aware of the mailing. Police searched computers, seized hard drives, and left without filing charges. In February 2009, police raided the home of a Scientology member linked to the Way to Happiness Foundation. They searched the premises but found nothing and left.

In June 2009, raids were conducted by the new *antisecte* squad CAIMADES on the Paris church and the Celebrity Center of Paris. It was the sixth time these two offices had been raided by government forces. The raids followed a complaint by the family of a Scientologist who committed suicide in 2006. Initially the family members tried to obtain a financial settlement with the church (€200,000). But after failing to secure the money, the family pressed officials to take action. The case was later dismissed.

The barrage of government raids targeting the Church of Scientology in France has been extraordinary. We employed a very conservative method of tabulation for these raids. In some cases, we found that there were as many as ten simultaneous raids on members' homes in conjunction with raids on the Scientology Church or its offices. Since the raids on residences were typically part of a coordinated plan targeting the institutional entities, we did not count them as additional or separate raids. Had we counted each raid on a residence, the numbers would have been much higher. It would be quite plausible to make the case that the actual number of police raids on Scientology/Scientologists in France was closer to 50.

Other Forms of State Control

The French government also waged a war against the Church of Scientology on another front, deploying agents of *l'Adminstration fiscale* and other
regulatory agencies in an effort to exercise social control over this NRM.
Akin to the U.S. Internal Revenue Service, officials with *le fisc* are empowered to conduct surprise investigations or even execute *perquisitions* (the
seizure of documents, files, and computers). We did not technically define
these government actions as "raids" except when specifically attached to
a raid team. On at least one occasion, officials from the anticult organization, UNADFI, accompanied the tax inspectors as they raided Scientology
centers in Lyon and Lille.

The deployment of tax investigators was designed to challenge Scientology's claim that it was a religion, not a business. The Church sought
tax exemptions claiming that their income from auditing, courses, books,
and printed materials were tools for religious practice. French authorities
were not persuaded and used tax inspections frequently to harass and
search for evidence of fraud. There was a sharp rise in the number of
surprise investigations by *le fisc* after the National Assembly published its
Guyard Report (the "Sects and Money" report) in 1999. The third section
of the report contains a table showing groups on the 1995 Guyard List
which were alleged to commit tax fraud. The list identifies Scientology as
well as 15 other NRMs.[15]

The use of other regulatory agencies involved compliance issues such
as building codes, health and safety codes, security or data protection,
and labor laws. Between 1990 and 2011, French authorities conducted 24
surprise investigations on Scientology churches and mission centers. The
Commission nationale de l'informatique et des libertés (CNIL), an agency designed to protect confidential information of citizens, was frequently used
by French authorities to conduct inspections of the church. In the 2000
Bader case, the church was charged with noncompliance with the data protection law by CNIL and the government attempted to use this infraction
to dissolve *l'Association de l'Église de Scientologie de l'Ile de France* (Palmer,
2011b:70–71). The case was not successful, but the CNIL trial coincided
with the National Assembly's vote on a provision of the About-Picard Law
that would allow dissolution of an organization whose aim is "exploitation
and physical or psychological subjection of persons" if members of that
association had been convicted twice (Palmer, 2011b:71). These actions
laid the groundwork for the highly publicized trial in 2009 in which the

government attempted to ban Scientology in France based on allegations of organizational fraud. The French court stopped short of banning Scientology but convicted the Church on fraud charges. The court ordered the Scientology Celebrity Center and bookshop to pay a €600,000 fine. Seven Church leaders were fined, including the head of Scientology in France, Alain Rosenberg. Rosenberg received a two-year suspended jail sentence combined with a €30,000 fine. Four of the Church leaders received suspended sentences ranging from ten months to two years, while two others were fined minor amounts. In examining the state's legal case against Scientology, one is left with the impression that the "crimes" committed the Church were fundamentally grounded in the commodification of religious symbolic products (paying for spiritual services) which *ipso facto* was defined as fraud and mental manipulation.

Conclusion

Beckford (2004:34) observes that "the complexion of anti-cult sentiment in France is . . . significantly different from that of the UK and the USA, where concern with the stability of the State rests less on the ideal of freethinking individual citizens and more on the crosscutting interdependence of social and cultural collectivities." Hervieu-Léger (2001:31) contends that the separation of religion and state in France is designed to protect the secular Republic against religion, not to protect religion against state interference, an inversion of the protection clause found in the First Amendment to the U.S. Constitution. In effect, the French believe that it is *rationality* that needs safeguarding, not religious liberty. Furthermore, "opposition to the 'intrusion' of religion into public life is all the more robust when it concerns religious organizations originating outside France or operating across borders" (Beckford, 2004:33).

In particular, French media have criticized the excessive tolerance in the United States toward "cults" (Luca, 2004:54) and warned of an "American Trojan Horse" penetrating France. French journalist Serge Faubert has described Scientology as "an agent of American imperialism," a multinational corporation that "funnels" francs and euros straight into U.S. church coffers (Palmer, 2011b:62). Another journalist, Bruno Fouchereau (2001), writing in *Le Monde diplomatique*, has argued that imperialist policies of the U.S. government and the influence of American corporations have "infiltrated France" through the *sectes*. French scholar Nathalie Luca (2004:57) notes that some NRMs such as the Unification

Church and Scientology are "well adapted to the American political and business culture" which "promotes material success as a proof of divine election" or "legitimization of a providential role." The French aversion to this perceived infiltration helps to explain some of the extraordinary actions taken against Scientology, in particular, and against NRMs more generally.

The French government's "support for the anticult cause has grown considerably stronger and more direct" in recent decades (Beckford, 2004:29). Whether or not this state-sponsored campaign will continue apace or has already peaked remains to be seen. State raids are only one measure of this dynamic, but our data suggest a slight decline in the use of raids in France after 2000, at least compared to the previous decade. This may simply signal a preference toward other forms of social control such as surprise tax investigations, regulatory inspections, or litigation. Or it may be the result of NRMs being disbanded or driven underground. Horus was disbanded in 1997 by its founder, Marie-Therèse Castano, after repeated raids on the community. Castano was imprisoned for a year for practicing "illegal medicine" and for "non-assistance to a person in danger." The Family International was driven underground after experiencing two raids on their communal homes in 1993 in Lyon and Marseille. The raids involved 200 gendarmes; 50 adults and 90 children were taken into custody. The French Raelian movement went underground in 2002–2003 after government raids and relentless media attacks. Today it has no formal presence as a voluntary association in France. Néo-Phare was officially dissolved after the About-Picard law was applied for the first time, and its leader, Arnaud Maussy, was found guilty of *abus de faiblesse* (Palmer, 2011b:187). While a few groups like Scientology and Jehovah's Witnesses have the resources to wage costly legal battles, the majority do not. Litigation can easily bankrupt a small NRM such that efforts to defend one's group against even the flimsiest of charges prove to be almost impossible. While some NRMs have banded together in an effort to protest and challenge this "new wave of discrimination" (Palmer, 2011b:24–25), their resources are no match for the French state. Under these circumstances, the state has the power to drive many *sectes* out of business, underground, or out of the country with impunity. So in the final analysis, France's "War on Sects" may simply be a war of attrition.

Exploring the Causes
and Consequences of Raids
on NRM Communities

OUR STUDY DOCUMENTS a particular form of social control of NRMs in democratic societies; one that is extreme, high-risk, overreaching, and often militarized. It is also being used more frequently. The aggregate data we collected reveal a dramatic rise in government raids beginning in the 1990s; 77 percent of raids ($N = 89$) we were able to document have occurred since 1990. We have offered a model to explain why state raids have increased exponentially since this time. We outlined and analyzed the transnational mobilization of a countermovement involving strategic framing of "cult threats" linked foremost to child abuse allegations, but also to a number of other recurring claims.[1] We identified the "brokerage" of previously unconnected networks of ACM organizations in North America, Western Europe, Australia, and elsewhere, and the forging of effective oppositional alliances or loose coalitions with state agents and media in host countries. We grounded our analysis in social movement theory, particularly the "contentious politics" approach (McAdam, Tarrow, and Tilly, 2001), to explain this transnational countermobilization that began in the United States in the 1970s but spread to other key countries through what Shupe and Darnell (2006) called "missionizing" efforts of ACM activists. We identified critical movement organizations and actors in the coordination of strategies, the designation of targets, the mobilization of resources, the attribution of threats and opportunities, and the trajectories of contention resulting from movement-countermovement conflict, including third parties and state actors.

Trajectories of contention may take many paths. Some episodes of contention are brief, while others are protracted, extended over decades or longer. In this study we examine an *ongoing stream of contention* among NRMs, the network of ACM organizations, and other third-party opponents over time. We trace the evolution of this contention as patterns of practice and strategies shifted, and both movements and countermovements expanded, taking the conflict to other parts of the world. We argue that key shifts in ACM strategy and framing, deriving from the "child abuse revolution" (Jenkins, 1998) in the 1980s, transformed the way in which opponents could effectively lobby and pressure officials to act against targeted groups. We argue that the sudden surge in state raids on NRMs beginning around 1990 corresponds to the widespread adoption of this new collective action frame (child abuse) by opponents and the "white-hot mobilization" phase (Lofland, 1979) that followed. In effect, opponents and state agents were given powerful new tools through the passage of aggressive child protection laws to investigate and exercise control over suspect religious groups.

The added ammunition provided to opponents through child abuse claims fueling the increase in government raids is supported by the data. Table 10.1 shows that 49 government raids were launched where child abuse was one of the allegations. Forty of these raids (82 percent) occurred on or after 1990. If we include two raids on The Family in Argentina in 1989 and use this date to mark the beginning of the white-hot mobilization phase, the number of raids based on child abuse allegations increases to 86 percent. This is a remarkable finding given that the bulk of raids from 1990 to 2012 took place in France, a country where a strategy of third-party claims-making regarding child abuse became much less significant given the integration of anticult organizations into government. MILS or MIVILUDES did not need the strategic framing of child abuse to investigate or raid NRMs. They already had the power to request investigations based on suspicions of tax fraud, or launch raids predicated on such rhetorical charges as "mental manipulation," *les dérives sectaire*, or *abus de faiblesse*.

In chapter 2, we offer a model (Figure 2.1) illustrating how the dynamic processes impel or hasten government raids and how the structural components interact and contribute to this outcome. We suggest that the likelihood of government raids is linked to the organized activities of "core opponents" (ACM organizations/actors, apostates, concerned relatives and/or friends of NRM converts) who form alliances to lodge claims, recruit sympathetic or opportunistic media, and pressure state agents (who may or may not become part of the alliance, but serve to carry out the partisan interests of opponents) to take action. We also note in the model that "intermediate groups," defined as independent and impartial entities (e.g., human rights organizations, civil liberties groups, ecumenical organizations, scholars of religion), are conspicuously absent in the dynamic of contention leading up to government raids. Intermediate groups are excluded, we argue, because their policies or research

Table 10.1   Raids on NRMs Where Child Abuse was One of the Allegations

Group Targeted	Year	No. of Raids
FLDS (U.S.)	1944, 1953, 2008	(3)
Doukhobors (B.C., Canada)	1953–57	(3)
Apostles of Infinite Love (Canada)	1966, 1967, 1978, 1999	(4)
The Family (Argentina, France, Spain, Australia Mexico, Italy)	1978, 1979, 1989–1993	(10)
Twelve Tribes (U.S., France, Germany)	1984, 1996–7, 2002, 2006, 2013	(8)
Branch Davidians (U.S.)	1993	(1)
Ogyen Kunzang Choling (France, Belgium)	1997	(2)
Horus (France)	1991, 1996	(2)
Nuwaubians (U.S)	2002	(1)
Order of St. Charbel (Australia)	2002	(1)
Les Gens de Bernard (France)	2007	(1)
Communauté des Béatitudes	2009	(1)
Centre for Teaching Biodynamism (France)	2011	(1)
Goel Ratzon (Israel)	2010	(1)
Agape Ministries (Australia)	2010–2011	(2)
Bratslav Sect (Israel)	2011	(1)
Alamo Foundation (U.S)	1998, 1991, 2008	(3)
Mandarom (France)	1995	(1)
Agape Ministries (Australia)	2010–11	(2)
Church of Firstborn (U.S.)	2009	(1)

Total 49

challenge intolerance toward religious minorities and tend to mitigate the claims of oppositional campaigns (Wright, 2002b). It follows from this point that the unfortunate rush to use extreme actions such as raids by law enforcement might be tempered in the future by including scholars of religion who have studied the NRMs in question. In many cases, the increased use of raids is linked to the use of unreliable and partisan sources of information by officials. A more balanced consideration of information from social scientists and religion scholars would likely yield less extreme enforcement actions.

To convey a more micro-level understanding of our model we offer a series of in-depth case studies of raided NRMs showing how the social dynamics and paths of contention play out among different actors and groups in different countries. We provide extensive, detailed accounts of the formation and mobilization of organized opponents in these cases, applying the parameters of our model. The extraordinary number of raids in France ($N = 57$) forced us into the difficult decision of consolidating all raids in one chapter, conducting a general overview of cases rather than focusing on any one single case. We took this approach because of the unique French situation in which ACM organizations have become an arm of the state and, as such, exhibit a persistent pattern in the social control of NRMs. While not ideal, we were faced with limitations of space in the writing of this book. An entire book could be devoted to raids in France and we would welcome more research on the French state of affairs. Palmer (2011b) has written elsewhere about key individual cases of government raids exclusively in France.

The data from our study here are compelling: of the 116 government raids recorded, we found evidence of well-organized opposition and activism, or in the case of France, an active and structured role of state-sponsored anticult organizations, in 81 percent of the cases ($N = 94$). As would be expected, in almost all of the raids where strong, well-organized countermobilization was evident (96 percent), they transpired on or after 1990. These data are consistent with our arguments regarding shifts in ACM strategic frame alignment and transnational mobilization that seized upon new political opportunities and threats. To be sure, we did not find in every raid incident involving organized opposition all of the structural components of our model. For example, in the Nuwaubian case discussed in chapter 6, we find no *direct* participation by ACM actors, even though there is well-defined, organized opposition. The influence of ACM actors is *indirect*, as acknowledged by Putnam County Sheriff

Howard Sills and journalist Bill Osinski. They invoke the intrinsic ACM narrative of the "violent cult" and cite such key anticult figures as Margaret Singer, Flo Conway and Jim Seigelman, and Rick Ross to help build ideological support for the raid.

Among the raids occurring before 1990, only a few involved well-organized opposition. The most significant exception is the Vermont State raid on the Twelve Tribes, discussed at length in chapter 3. It is at this juncture that a template for a shift in countermovement strategy was developed in what Swantko (1998) calls the "Kelly Plan," devised by deprogrammer Galen Kelly for the Citizens Freedom Foundation. The Kelly Plan provided a model for building a coalition of opponents and supplanting "brainwashing" with child abuse as its principal claim where there was a second generation of children in the religious community. This model eventually became an institutionalized strategy in ACM organization and can be seen in its implementation across a number of cases here and abroad beginning around 1990 (Wiseman, 2011; Wright and Richardson, 2011a).

Human Rights and Civil Liberties Violations

Having examined raids in the aggregate and their etiology in the previous chapters, we can now make some general observations on the aftermath of these raids, and their effects, long-term and short-term, on the targeted communities. The impact of these traumatic intrusions into community life is quite varied and complex, but we will limit our observations to four harmful effects we have seen repeated in different cases that might be characterized as particularly problematic: 1) human rights and civil liberties violations, 2) state-sponsored child abuse, 3) debilitation or destruction of religious communities, 4) use of excessive force through militarized raids. Some of these categories overlap and indeed, have occurred in tandem, compounding the harmful effects on religious communities.

The findings of our study should be taken in the larger context of social control efforts aimed at new or nontraditional religious movements by governments in democratic societies. In all of the countries in which these raids occurred, religious liberty and freedom of belief have legislative guarantees and traditions. Nevertheless, many of the attacks we describe were carried out while ignoring or trampling on these rights. In some cases, authorities circumvented the guarantees of religious liberty by declaring that NRMs weren't "real" religions. In nearly every case, authorities brandished the threatening label of "cult" to justify differential treatment, invoking loathsome stereotypes and relying heavily on allegations by partisan opponents. For the record, we do not object to evidence-based investigations when there are actual crimes suspected in these groups, or in any religious community for that matter. But our research suggests that sometimes merely *being* a new or nontraditional religion was seemingly criminalized.

The pseudoscientific claim of "brainwashing" or "mental manipulation" made by authorities to justify raids illustrates this point forcefully. Research has shown that it is not really the particular tactics of persuasion or processes of commitment maintenance used by NRMs that concerns their opponents, but rather the *type of group* using them (Anthony, 1990; Anthony and Robbins, 1992, 1995; Pfeiffer, 1999; Richardson, 1991, 1997). For example, the intensive commitment demands and regimented structures found in traditional Catholic religious orders certainly do not evoke allegations of "brainwashing." One would be hard-pressed to find accusations of "coercive persuasion" practiced by the Benedictines or Dominicans, or the Missionaries of Charity founded by Mother Teresa, even though these orders demand extensive personal sacrifice, devotion, selflessness, and renunciation (separation from families, relinquishing sexual control to group, disavowing material goods and property, etc.). The fact that some NRMs share the same organizational and social psychological features as some established religious orders, yet only one class of groups is condemned for "brainwashing," exposes the raw bias and selective application of brainwashing allegations.

In this context, it is a curious paradox that the Catholic Church in France has abetted the government's "War on Sects," supporting anticult legislation and actively participating in a countercult campaign (Palmer, 2011b). Duvert (2004:48) observes that some French parliamentarians close to the Catholic Church, not surprisingly, have expressed fears that "anticult theories have progressively come to be viewed as dangerous as they could be used to criticize conversions to respected traditional Catholic groups." As a case in point he notes that "a charismatic Catholic community was described as a 'cultish' group in a 1996 book by three former members . . . that raised intense debate within the Catholic Church" (Duvert, 2004:48). In other words, the untenable double standard promoted by Church-based opponents of *sectes* could collapse and be used by the state or militant anticultists as an instrument of intolerance against "respected traditional Catholic groups." This concern was realized in

2008 when the President of MIVILUDES, Georges Fenech, publicly attacked an association of lay Catholics, the French Society for the Defense of Tradition, Family, and Property, in a report, accusing them of exhibiting *secte*-like behavior. Alarmed by the repercussions of being labeled a *secte*, the lay Catholic association filed a defamation suit against Fenech. On June 1, 2012, a Paris criminal court specializing in cases concerning the press convicted Fenech of public defamation, stressing the lack of accuracy and unverified generalizations. In its ruling, the Court stressed that a state agency such as MIVILUDES should not use such vague approximations in its work (Forum for Religious Freedom in Europe, 2012).

To date, there has been no wave of government raids on Catholic churches or parishes of which we are aware. But this is not because there haven't been serious crimes committed by priests and religious leaders in the Church. Consider the sex abuse scandal concerning priests in the Catholic Church. In chapter 2, we discussed the significance of a shift in ACM strategy coinciding with the "child abuse revolution" in which the intense efforts among child protection advocates produced a moral panic. Jenkins (1998) contends that the claims-making and lobbying efforts by these special interest groups exaggerated threats of child abuse in society leading to a widespread panic regarding public concern over child protection. Organized opponents recognized that NRMs with children were vulnerable to child abuse claims since they often practiced unconventional marriage and family arrangements. We argue that the child abuse revolution and the shift in ACM strategy help to explain the sharp rise in raids on NRMs beginning in the 1990s. Yet at about the same time, reports of alleged sexual abuse of children by pedophile priests in the Catholic Church also began to surface. An organization of victims formed the Survivors Network of Those Abused by Priests (SNAP) in the United States in 1989. SNAP issued press releases and reported that the problem of priest abuse was much greater than believed or covered by the media. The Catholic Church vigorously challenged these allegations, and the media was slow to accept or investigate the charges by SNAP (Shupe, 1998). Eventually, the flood of victims' accounts became too big of a story to resist and too difficult for the Catholic hierarchy to ignore.

In 2002, the National Conference of Catholic Bishops commissioned a study by the John Jay College of Criminal Justice to investigate priest sexual abuse of children. Two years later, a report was issued by John Jay College (2004), *The Nature and Scope of Sexual Abuse of Minors by Catholic Priests and Deacons in the United States, 1950–2002*, which found that around 11,000 complaints had been filed against 4,392 priests for alleged sexual abuse of young children, mostly boys. The report states that the abuse was systemic and pervasive and that when abusive priests were discovered, the sexual abuse was often denied and concealed by the Church. These abusive priests were often transferred to other parishes to avoid detection. More complaints surfaced in other countries after the report, in Italy and Ireland. A PBS *Frontline* documentary in 2014, "Secrets of the Vatican," revealed that the number of complaints filed against the Catholic Church for sexual abuse of children by priests had risen to nearly 17,000.

In January 2014, The United Nations Committee on the Rights of the Child brought Catholic Church officials to Geneva to account for the "cover-up of decades of sexual abuse of children by clergy" (Squires, 2014). Though the Church ratified the UN Convention on the Rights of the Child in 1990, it "failed to provide progress reports for more than a decade, with victims' groups accusing the church hierarchy of fostering a culture of secrecy to hide abuse of children by priests, monks, and nuns in countries around the world" (Squires, 2014). Archbishop Silvano Tomasi, the Vatican's representative, attempted to defend the Church by arguing that the Holy See should not be held responsible for actions of clergy in separate countries outside the sovereign territory of the Vatican City State. Those priests are not functionaries of the Vatican, he claimed, but citizens of their respective countries, and hence subject to their jurisdiction. But his argument was roundly condemned as disingenuous by both the UN Committee and by victims' rights groups.

The reaction by democratic governments to the widespread sexual abuse of children by Catholic priests and the systematic cover-up by Church leaders stands in stark contrast to the alleged abuse of children by minority religions. During the same span of time, beginning with the founding of SNAP in 1989 until the present, there were no government raids on Catholic churches. Thousands of complaints of sexual abuse against the Catholic Church did not lead to paramilitary state raids on parishes to confiscate evidence, execute search warrants, or conduct show-of-force operations. Catholic parishes were not the targets of SWAT teams, armored personnel carriers, black helicopters, snipers, and militarized police in camouflage and combat gear. By comparison, we have documented 89 government raids on new or nontraditional religious communities since 1990, many of them by heavily armed paramilitary raid teams. Furthermore, many of these raids were launched on child abuse claims, as our study suggests.

In a number of cases, a *single* complaint of child abuse against a minority religion was sufficient to mobilize an entire army of law enforcement agents and child protection officials. A more vivid illustration of religious discrimination and unequal treatment is hardly imaginable.

These kinds of actions by democratic governments make a mockery of the equal protection provision in Article 7 of the Universal Declaration of Human Rights (1948):

> All are equal before the law and are entitled without any discrimination to equal protection of the law. All are entitled to equal protection against any discrimination in violation of this Declaration and against any incitement to such discrimination.

The differential treatment of NRMs is also a violation of Article 18 of the Universal Declaration of Human Rights:

> Everyone has the right to freedom of thought, conscience and religion; this right includes freedom to change his religion or belief, and freedom, either alone or in community with others and in public or private, to manifest his religion or belief in teaching, practice, worship and observance.

All of the countries where we documented raids against NRMs were signators to the Universal Declaration of Human Rights. These cherished rights and liberties enshrined in the UHDR and in the laws of Western democracies were designed specifically to protect religious minorities, not majoritarian religions, because religious minorities are most likely to be the targets of bigotry, intolerance, and discrimination.

State-Sponsored Child Abuse

In these massive raids we often see that in the name of "rescuing children," the actions of the state actually harm children. We applaud the general social axiom of protecting children and we think the state has a necessary and crucial role in this regard. But state officials too often accept uncritically the claims of partisan opponents about child abuse when there is little or no real evidence. Officials also appear to be unaware of, or ignore, the context or personal disputes out of which these complaints arise (see Bromley, 1998a). Palmer has written about raids on multiple minority religious communities where children were removed involuntarily, forced into boarding schools, robbed of their religious and ethnic heritage, exposed to extensive psychological or gynecological tests, told their parents were evil, and/or detained by the state for prolonged periods of time (Palmer, 1998, 2011a, 2011b; Palmer and Hardman, 1999a).

The Doukhobors, an Orthodox Christian anarchist community that originated in Russia and the Ukraine and settled in British Columbia in 1899, were raided by the Royal Canadian Mounted Police (RCMP) in 1953. The Doukhobors insisted on speaking their native language, refused to teach the children to read, and disavowed buying or owning property. Opponents charged that their children were poorly educated, isolated, and "brainwashed." In the raid, around 200 children were seized, separated from their parents, and loaded onto buses under the supervision of state social workers. One hundred four of the children were forcibly placed in a dormitory school at New Denver, British Columbia, for six years. The parents were not permitted to visit their children and could only speak to them through a wire fence. When the children of New Denver came of age, they brought a class-action lawsuit against the B.C. government, "alleging that they had suffered physical and sexual abuse at the hands of their teachers in the state's secular boarding school and that their families, culture, and identity had been 'stolen' from them" (Palmer, 2011a:56).

It was a cruel irony that the "rescued" children then became victims of child abuse under state supervision. A government investigation in 2002 concluded that the Doukhobor children were "wrongfully removed from their families and community, and wrongfully confined to a prison-like school" (quoted in Palmer, 2011a:56). John McClaren, a law professor at the University of Vancouver, researched the case and described the B.C. government's actions as "forced assimilation" and documented many violations of human rights as defined by the United Nations (Palmer, 2011a:56). The B.C. government never issued a formal apology to the Doukhobors for their actions. But in 2005, the children of New Denver won their class-action lawsuit and received an undisclosed financial settlement.

Ogyen Kunzang Choling (OKC) is a Tibetan Buddhist community in the French Alps and housed in a chateau known as "Chateau Soleil." On May 30, 1997, members awoke to find they were a target of a massive government raid. The raid team included 130 gendarmes from the nearby town of Castellane and 20 paramilitary GIGN[2] from Perpignon. Though authorities received no complaints about child abuse, "it appeared that one of the main purposes of the raid on OKC was to examine the thirty-two children who were enrolled in the Chateau Soleil boarding school. The raid team was accompanied by doctors, nurses, and psychologists who examined the children for signs of sexual abuse or medical neglect" (Palmer, 2011a:66). An eyewitness to the raid complained that the children were treated in a cold and callous fashion. Some of the young girls were subject to forced gynecological examinations. Investigators also reported to the press that they had uncovered "cells" in one of the buildings on the property that were constructed with soundproof walls. Journalists suspected the cells were used for the *sequestration* of children, perhaps intended to stifle children's screams. However, it was later determined that the "cells" were merely traditional Buddhist meditation chambers. At a court hearing, an expert appointed by the judge stated that it was impossible to sequester anyone inside the cells because they opened from the inside (Allard, 1997).

Authorities found no evidence of physical or sexual abuse among the children of Chateau Soleil. But the state's intrusive and coercive actions could certainly be described as a form of abuse. An attorney for the religious community, Maitre Inez Wouters, made this comment to us during an interview: "They examined all the children for abuse, and they found the children had *not* been abused—but, of course, by the end of the examination, they were!" (quoted in Palmer, 2011a:71).

In October 1991, 250 Italian police and military stormed Damanhur, a federation of spiritual communities in the Piedmont Valley north of Turin. In the predawn raid, armed officers had "pistols drawn" and "machine guns at the ready" with "helicopters hovering above" (Merrifield, 2006:186). The raid team was accompanied by drug-sniffing dogs and officials from the local government finance division, who accused the community of possible tax evasion. Members described the massive show of force as "extremely frightening"; police rounded up the adults, conducted strip searches, and searched the children's school bags. While the raid was not targeting child abuse, the children of Damanhur witnessed heavily armed agents ransacking their homes and treating their parents like terrorists. However, no evidence of criminal activity was found and no charges were ever filed.

The rationale for the raid was based on allegations by opponents, including "a religious hard-liner, Cardinal Saldarini" who was convinced that the Turin region had become a sanctuary for "Satanic" groups "dedicated to orgiastic rituals and free love" (Merrifield, 2006:183).

The Cardinal engaged in "a concerted denunciation of Damanhur as a highly suspect cult" (Merrifield, 2006:183). The campaign against Damanhur was joined by two ex-members, Filippo Cerutti and his wife, seeking financial compensation for investments, as well as journalists writing salacious stories about the community. Soon after the 1991 raid, one local newspaper printed a story with the headline, "Sex, Free Love, and Children Involved at Damanhur" (Merrifield, 2006:188). The story was based on rumors and unfounded fears. Damanhur leaders filed charges of defamation against the Ceruttis in court. But the Turin court declared that the defamation charges had no merit. In his ruling, the judge acknowledged that Mr. Cerutti exaggerated his claims, but noted that Cerutti was "an apostate, someone who leaves a group for reasons of 'faith,' and as such, he had a right to exaggerate" (Merrifield, 2006:189).

In May 1992, government raids on The Family International in Australia targeted two communities in Melbourne and Sydney. One hundred fifty-three children were seized and taken into state custody. The raid was instigated by the Department of Community Services (DCS), relying on the claims and allegations of apostates and anticult leaders. The children were forced to undergo psychological and medical/gynecological examinations. No evidence of abuse was discovered but the traumatic impacts of the raids on the children were evident. Many of the children began wetting their beds, having nightmares, and expressing fears that the incident could happen again (Nicholas, 1999). The Sydney case (in the province of Victoria) was resolved after a 31-day hearing. A settlement was reached in which the official charges of sexual abuse by the DCS were withdrawn, coupled with an agreement to allow some evaluation of the children's homeschooling and participation of the children in broader social activities (Richardson, 1999). In the Melbourne case, however, the litigation dragged on for years, ending in 1999 when the New South Wales Supreme Court declared that the police "acted lawlessly" when they raided the houses belonging to The Family (Nicholas, 1999). The Court also found the children were entitled to seek damages from the government because the search warrants used in the raids were illegal.

In chapter 4 we examined the raids on The Family International in Argentina in 1993, where 137 children were seized and placed into state custody (Honore, 1993; Nash, 1993). It is estimated that worldwide, 600 children of The Family have been examined by court-appointed officials, but no evidence of abuse has ever been found in any of these investigations. A spokesperson from the group who was present during the Argentine raids described to us how their rights were violated:

> Once the raids happen and nothing is found, then the government officials get desperate and have to find *something*. That's when corruption comes in. If they delve deep enough, they figure, they should find some sort of abuse. There is pressure on them to save face, to justify the raid, and sometimes they are tempted to manufacture "evidence." For example, one psychologist in Argentina copied a picture from a textbook on abused children and put it in our file, claiming a 7 year old from our community drew it. Luckily, someone recognized it as a forgery.
>
> The sheer magnitude of a raid, the media value of the event, turns it into chaos. The government institutions are not equipped to deal with the aftermath, so officials will cut corners. Look at the conditions of our children—that was abuse. They stuck them in a dirty warehouse. When the officials in Argentina were dealing with that magnitude of problems, they were not equipped for it, so they end up violating human rights and doing things they are supposed to be defending. (Interview with Lonnie Davis, 2012)

The most glaring case of state-sponsored child abuse was the federal raid on the Branch Davidian community in 1993. A dangerous, high-risk raid by the Special Response Team (SRT) of the Bureau of Alcohol, Tobacco and Firearms was launched despite the known presence of more than 30 children at the community residence. The ATF fired into the Mount Carmel complex through walls where children resided. Sect members and survivors provided detailed accounts of how Branch Davidian children had to duck flying bullets and lie on the floor fearful of their lives at the time of the ATF raid (Martin, 2009; Thibodeau and Whiteson, 1999). At the end of the 51-day standoff, the FBI's Hostage Rescue Team used tanks to breach the walls of Mount Carmel and fired canisters of dangerous CS gas into the structure, resulting in a catastrophic inferno that killed 76 people, including 21 children. Immediately after the tragedy, Attorney General Janet Reno told the public that she approved the CS attack because FBI officials told her that Koresh was "beating babies" (Verhovek, 1993). Incredibly, Reno maintained that her primary concern was the "welfare of the children". But it was later learned that government officials did not have evidence of any threat of ongoing child abuse inside Mount Carmel (Ellison and Bartkowski, 1995).

In April 1997, a couple who belonged to the Twelve Tribes community in France lost their baby, who had been born with a congenital heart defect. As described in chapter 3, the gendarmes arrived the next morning soon after the death was reported. The couple was arrested and charged with "non-assistance to a person in danger." Their other three children were removed from their custody and sent to live with relatives.

The same day, Tabitha's Place was besieged by the *procureur*, Jean-Pierre Dreno, 40 gendarmes, 12 doctors, a psychiatrist, and an interpreter. The doctors examined more than 80 children in the community for abuse. No evidence of abuse was found, but all the families were placed under the supervision of a children's judge in Pau and state social workers were allowed to come in at any time and visit families. Several families were threatened with the removal of their children. According to one of the leaders, "they had a problem with us not vaccinating our children and with home schooling" (quoted in Palmer, 2011b:119). In court, the Ginhoux parents were found guilty of the deprivation of medical care and food, allegedly leading to the death of the child. Stunned by the verdict, the parents appealed only to have the appeals court *increase* their sentence. While awaiting the first trial under house arrest, the couple bore another child. Authorities also took the new infant from their custody.

The Twelve Tribes were targeted by another raid in Germany in September 2013. Police in Klosterzimmern and Wornitz, towns in the Bavaria region, conducted a mass raid on the group based on allegations of physical child abuse, seizing 40 children. We described this incident briefly in chapter 1. The *Jugendamt* (Youth Services) obtained a court order for a stay of protective custody for some of the children, which remains in place today.[3] Parents have complained of how their children were neglected or abused in state institutions. A diabetic boy was rushed to hospital because his custodians did not know how to maintain the proper insulin balance and refused to listen to his mother's instructions; another boy fell down the stairs and broke his arm, and children who ran away and returned home complained of the poor diet and bleak social environment of the orphanages, convents, and juvenile delinquent homes where they had been placed. In July, the *Jugendamt* held a "*Sekte* training session" for foster parents that included the children in custody. One member of the group we spoke with described the children as "terrified" and told us that the *Jugendamt* was trying to "train them (their children) against us for the good of the German state."

Debilitation or Destruction of Religious Communities

One long-term result of intense conflict between an NRM and the state is what sociologist James Richardson calls the "deformation of NRMs" when the effort of self-defense, including exorbitant legal fees, results in diminished missionary activity and revised goals and concerns (Richardson, 1985). This concept can be extended to include the effect of state raids on new or nontraditional religious communities. The use of mass raids on NRMs can have numerous debilitating effects, including sensationalistic news coverage castigating the targeted group as a "dangerous cult," costly legal fees to mount a legal defense against charges, the creation of an inhospitable and fearful local climate, perhaps accompanied by forms of exclusion, harassment, vandalism, and adverse financial impacts on the businesses of the NRM.

We have described many of these debilitating effects in previous chapters. As result of government raids we see NRMs being impaired, weakened, or bankrupted by legal expenses, prosecuted in the media, driven underground, or otherwise forced out of the country. Members were arrested, sometimes paraded before the press, and charged with child abuse, brainwashing, financial fraud, labor violations, non-assistance to a person in danger, and a litany of other crimes, often to be acquitted or have the charges dismissed for lack of evidence at a later date. The Raelians (France), The Family International (in France and Argentina), the Apostles of Infinite Love (Canada), the Twelve Tribes (France and Germany), and other smaller religious communities have been seriously destabilized, lacking the resources to withstand the tidal wave of well-organized and well-funded state forces brought to bear on these groups in targeted campaigns.[4]

Some NRMs have been not merely debilitated but thoroughly decimated. The Centre for Teaching Biodynamism (France), Horus (France), Neo-Phare (France), Amour et Miséricorde (France), the Nuwaubians (the United States), the Nation of Yahweh (the United States), the Branch Davidians (the United States), and the Fundamentalist Latter Day Saints (Texas, the United States) were all dissolved as a result of government raids. The Nuwaubian Nation and the Nation of Yahweh (the United States) both experienced FBI raids in which RICO charges were added to the initial charges laid against their leaders. RICO gave the state the power to seize their buildings, land, and businesses, which were sold to reimburse government agencies for the expensive raids. In the case of the Fundamentalist Latter Day Saints in Eldorado, Texas, while the main community in Colorado City, Arizona, and Hildale, Utah, is still intact, the Yearning for Zion Ranch, where the FLDS built their community outside Eldorado, was seized by the State of Texas in January 2014. The state asked a judge to allow forfeiture of the property, alleging that FLDS leaders financed purchase of the YFZ Ranch through "money laundering." Under Texas law, the state can seize property used to commit or facilitate certain criminal conduct. According to authorities, when they arrived to seize the property, only eight adults were still living on the Ranch ("Texas Seizes Polygamist Group's Secluded Ranch," Associated Press, April 17, 2014). Apparently, FLDS leaders made no effort to contest the seizure of the property, as they had already exhausted their finances paid out in legal defense fees.

The Branch Davidian community was completely destroyed by a federal siege in 1993. Only a handful of sect members survived. Some were convicted of conspiracy charges and spent time in prison. Others scattered or were deported. The authors have attended several memorial or commemoration ceremonies with survivors and the family members of victims over the years, the most recent in Waco in 2013, the 20th anniversary of the deadly tragedy. At this last commemoration, photos of all the people who died at Mount Carmel were shown to the small audience. It was clearly evident to us that the lives of the survivors and their families had been deeply and irreversibly shattered. Many of those who were killed had no immediate family members living and were not afforded a burial plot by the city of Waco. In a final show of humiliation, the remains of these deceased sect members were buried in a pauper's grave.

Use of Excessive Force through Militarized Raids

The trend of police militarization in the United States in recent decades has been well documented (American Civil Liberties Union, 2014; Balko, 2013; Dunn, 1996; Haggerty and Ericson, 2001; Kraska, 2001a, Kraska 2001b; Kraska and Cubellis, 1997; Kraska and Kappeler, 1996; Skolnick and Fyfe, 1993; Wright, 2007b). The surge in American police militarization can be traced to the early years of the War on Drugs, as the Reagan administration sought to deploy the military to assist with domestic drug enforcement operations (Wisotsky, 1990). A series of new laws, beginning with the 1982 Defense Authorization Act, created amendments to the century-old Posse Comitatus Act, which prohibited military enforcement of civilian laws. Over the next decade, there was increased police-military integration in mission and function. The 9/11 terrorist attack on the World Trade Centers and the Pentagon further expanded police militarization as the threat of terrorism became an added reason for cross-training civilian police with the military. The peril of another possible terrorist attack on the United States has seemingly made permanent a comprehensive program of police-security-military integration.

Since 1990, the U.S. Department of Defense has operated the 1033 Program through the Defense Logistics Agency's Law Enforcement Support Office (LESO), which has transferred $4.3 billion worth of military property to civilian police (American Civil Liberties Union, 2014:24). This massive transfer of military equipment includes armored personnel carriers (APCs) such as the "BearCat" (Ballistic Engineering Armored Response Counter Attack) and the Mine Resistant Ambush Protected vehicle (MRAP), OH-58 helicopters for surveillance and reconnaissance, bomb suits, and forced entry tools, as well as military-grade weaponry (M-16 automatic rifles, sniper rifles, grenade launchers) to law enforcement.

One critical impact of police militarization has been the development of a "war model" (Kraska, 2001a) or "military model" of crime control (Skolnick and Fyfe, 1993:113–116). Sociologists and criminologists have described a "transformation of police culture" that casts officers as "soldiers" and suspected lawbreakers as "enemies of the state" rather than citizens with constitutional rights and protections." Radley Balko summarizes the militarization of American police as follows:

> Today in America SWAT teams violently smash into private homes more than one hundred times per day. The vast majority of these raids are to enforce laws against consensual crimes. In many cities, police departments have given up the traditional blue uniforms for "battle dress uniforms" modeled after soldier attire. Police departments across the country now sport armored personnel carriers designed for use on a battlefield. Some have helicopters, tanks, and Humvees. They carry military-grade weapons. Most of this equipment comes from the military itself. Many SWAT teams today are trained by current and former personnel from special forces units like the Navy Seals or Army Rangers. National Guard helicopters

now routinely swoop through rural areas in search of pot plants and, when they find something, send gun-toting troops dressed for battle rappelling down to chop and confiscate the contraband. But it isn't just drugs. Aggressive SWAT-style tactics are now used to raid neighborhood poker games, doctor's offices, bars and restaurants, and head shops, despite the fact that the targets of these raids pose little threat to anyone. (Balko, 2013:xi–xii)

And one could add new or nontraditional religious communities to Balko's list of raid targets. As this trend has taken hold, NRMs have become an easy target for groups labeled "dangerous cults." Exaggerated or inflated threats imputed to such groups by opponents have provided paramilitary police units with a sufficient rationale for using aggressive raid tactics.

The trend of paramilitary policing is not limited to the United States. Hill and Beger (2009:25) contend that militarized policing has expanded to other countries based on the "modern state's need to counteract the 'clandestine dimensions of globalization.'" Some famous paramilitary police forces abroad include the French Gendarmerie, the Italian Carabin-ieri, and Israel's paramilitary Border Police, Benzi Sau. Neoliberal globali-zation is thought to be the primary cause for this large-scale development, but they also suggest that "U.S. support for the use of paramilitary police in peacekeeping operations may inadvertently encourage even greater militarization of policing across the international community" (Hill and Beger, 2009:25). Hill and Beger view this growing international trend as troubling for Western democracies and warn that "the paramilitary juggernaut threatens to run roughshod over the provision of democratic policing on a global scale" (Hill and Beger, 2009:25).

While there are numerous studies that link police militarization to the drug war and the "war on terrorism," there has been much less at-tention paid to paramilitary raids on new or nontraditional religious com-munities. We have tried to address some of this deficit in the research literature by documenting and providing detailed descriptions of these raids. In France, the "War on Sects" represents the clearest example of the link between police militarization and raids on NRMs. The anticult organ MIVILUDES is a government agency tasked with investigating sec-tarian abuses and has a record of coordinating heavily armed raids with the Gendarmerie. The concentration of state resources and human capital devoted to monitoring and actively suppressing minority religions speaks volumes. As discussed in the previous chapter, the French also have created a specialized police unit called CAIMADES (Cellule d'Assistance et d'Intervention en Matière de Dérives Sectaires) designed to assist the Gendarmerie in raid operations targeting sects. CAIMADES was formed within the Central Directorate of the Judicial Police and is under the authority of the Central Office for the Prevention of Violence against People (OCRVP).

We found that almost all of the government raids on NRMs since 1990 were militarized raids ($N = 85$, or 96 percent). Thus, not only has there been a sharp increase in the number of raids on NRMs, but the raids have also become increasingly militarized. This helps to explain the persistent incidents of overreach and excessive force relative to the actual violations or crimes, as we have documented throughout the book. Predawn raids on religious communities with young children and teens awakened by armies of men in battle-dress uniforms, breaking down doors, screaming demands, and pointing military-grade weapons at unarmed family members or friends are overreach and extreme. A 2014 American Civil Liberties Union report, entitled "War Comes Home: Excessive Militarization of American Policing," made the following observation regarding paramilitary raids on residences where children were present:

> During the course of this investigation, we noted another troubling trend: the deployment of SWAT when children were present . . . As documented above, a SWAT deployment can involve significant levels of violence, including breaking down doors, shattering windows, and the detonation of explosive devices. In addition, SWAT officers also typically deploy wearing "BDUs" (battle dress uniforms), carry large semi-automatic rifles, which they sometimes point at people during deployment, and often use force, throwing people onto the floor and handcuffing them. Experiencing violent events can have serious and long-term impacts, particularly on children. (p.40)

Moreover, the militarized response by PPUs is highly disproportionate to the alleged offenses we typically find in these cases. It does not require a hundred paramilitary police armed with submachine guns, semiautomatic rifles, high-power sniper rifles, and concussion grenades to investigate a claim of child abuse, or for that matter, most of the other allegations typically made against NRMs. There may be justification for militarized raids when there are suspected weapons stockpiles. But even here, the claim by opponents or apostates often turns out to be embellished or even manufactured with the intent to pressure authorities to act, as was the case with the FLDS, Damanhur, the Nuwaubian Nation, and others. Indeed, the ACLU investigation of militarized raids reports that in nearly two-thirds of the incidents where the police expected to find weapons, there were *none to be found* (American Civil Liberties Union, 2014:33). The report goes on to conclude that "the police are not particularly good at accurately forecasting the presence of weapons" (American Civil Liberties Union, 2014:33). We find this to be especially true of raids on new or nontraditional religions where apostates and allied opponents are making unverified claims and the religious community has no history of gun violence.

Some Concluding Observations

At a macro level, it might be argued that government raids on minority religions are a reactionary impulse marshaled by entrenched power elites and defenders of the status quo to fend off forces of globalization— immigration and changing demographics, increased cultural diffusion and diversity, growing pluralism in the new religious marketplace. Peter Clarke has suggested that NRMs are a significant feature of globalization and change in the modern world.

> It is possible, if looked at from a single regional or geographical perspective only, to dismiss NRMs as marginal and inconsequential in terms of their impact on the shaping of religion in the modern world. However, not only are NRMs global in the sense of being a feature of virtually every society in the world but many are themselves, while others are becoming, global religions in their own right, and as such are major contributors . . . to the shaping of the form and content of the religion and spirituality of the modern world. (Clarke, 2006:7)

Reactionary backlash to globalization's growth of religious pluralism has been evident in a number of cases we studied. In Argentina, the raids on The Family International took place in the backdrop of a "siege mentality" exhibited by the powerful Catholic Church. As previously discussed in chapter 4, after the arrival of democracy in Argentina in 1983, nearly

3,000 new religious groups had registered with the National Register of Religion by 1990 (Rosas, 1994). The perceived threat of invading Protestant sects (mostly Pentecostal) and "cults" was cast as a crisis by dominant religious interests. Two of the principal anticult activists involved in the campaign to assail The Family International were strongly linked to the Catholic Church. José María Baamonde, working with American anticult organizations, established the SPES Foundation (Servicio Para el Esclarecimiento en Sectas, or Organization for Cult Awareness), which received funding from the Archbishop of Buenos Aires. Baamonde was one of two "cult experts" assigned to "brief" law enforcement and other officials before they conducted the 1993 raids. The other "cult expert" to work with law enforcement prior to the raids was Alfredo Silleta. Silleta was the author of book entitled *Las Sectas Invaden la Argentina* (*The Cults Invade Argentina*), which called for an urgent response to the incursion of fundamentalist sects and cults. In 1990, Silleta established FAPES (La Fundacion Argentina para el Estudio des las Sectas, or the Foundation for the Study of Sects), an anticult organization. A journalist for the newspaper *Faustino*, Silleta was an active campaigner against *las sectas* and was supported by pro-Catholic forces (Frigerio, 1993).

In France, the epicenter of government raids on NRMs, we find a similar reactionary impulse to the growth of religious pluralism. A number of scholars have observed the role of the Catholic Church in countercult and anticult activity (Beckford, 2004; Duvert, 2004; Luca, 2004; Palmer, 2011b). Palmer (2011b) notes that the most active anticult organization in the 1980s was ADFI, which networked with local parish priests combating heresy. She also describes the Catholic influence in UNADFI, citing a Vatican document from May 1986 instructing French bishops to regard new religions as a challenge to the Church. Two prominent Catholic clerics, Jean Vernette and Jacques Trousard, "worked closely with UNADFI"; Troussard was the leading expert on sects for the French National Conference of Catholic Bishops and acting chair on their committee on sects and new religions (Palmer, 2011b:14). But the reactionary element of the Church is only a part of the larger problem in France. The actions taken by secular sources—anticult organizations, media, the state—have been the more telling story.

The theme of an "invasion" by outside religious, political, and economic forces has been pervasive in the French media. French journalists in concert with anticult organizations have "promoted the notion that sects are a dangerous American import" (Goodenough, 2001). The respected newspaper *Le Monde* called the phenomenon of new *sectes* an "American Trojan Horse" invading France. French journalist, Bruno Fouchereau (2001), writing in *Le Monde diplomatique*, claims that imperialist policies of the U.S. government and the influence of American corporations have "infiltrated France" through the *sectes*. Fouchereau also has suggested that some NRMs are "front groups" conducting international espionage. In a documentary produced by Fouchereau and broadcast on France 3 television in May 2000, the mayor of Saint-Julien-du-Verdon was interviewed. The mayor reported that he had seen "cable plugs and antennas in statues belonging to a local religious movement known as Mandoram. Could this be disguised transmission devices of some foreign country, spying on the acoustic detection laboratory for submarine warfare down the mountain by Lake Castillon?" he asked (LeBlanc, 2001).

The reactionary impulse in France has not escaped critics even in France. In 2002, the best-selling nonfiction book was by political scientist Jean-Francois Revel, entitled *The Anti-American Obsession* (L'obsession anti-américaine : Son fonctionnement, ses causes, ses inconséquences). Revel condemned French anti-Americanism as both backward and dangerous, suggesting that it bordered hysteria (Introvigne, 2004:81).

The draconian response to the new religious pluralism in France, however, has had repercussions across Europe resulting in what Clarke (2006:50) calls a "single European-wide movement" prompted by anticult organizations networked in various countries. Parliamentary commissions in Germany and Belgium generated similar "blacklists" of dangerous sects and "psychogroups" in the 1990s (Fautre, 2004; Seiwert, 2004). Official government reports in Switzerland and Spain stopped short of producing blacklists but did warn of the dangers of "brainwashing" and "mental manipulation" by sects and cults (Richardson and Introvigne, 2004). More recently there is evidence to suggest that the trans-European movement, represented most forcefully in France, continues unabated through the active promotion and exportation of the *dérives sectaires* model developed by French ACM organizations. In 2011, U.S. congressional representatives and co-chairs of the House International Religious Freedom Caucus wrote a letter addressed to Prime Minister Francois Fillon expressing deep concern over sustained restrictions on religious freedom and in particular, "the French government's program against sectarian drifts and its efforts to export this 'model' to other countries."⁵ The letter goes on to state:

> We understand that MIVILUDES is currently doing exactly what MILS was criticized and disbanded for—taking certain actions abroad (exporting its model) that were perceived as contrary to religious freedom. The roots of these exporting actions go back to 2006, when the report of the Commission of Enquiry Regarding the Influence of Sects on Minors recommended strengthening MIVILUDES activities at the international level. And the recent quarterly updates of MIVILUDES describe how its leaders are actively promoting better coordination at the European level, including a European study program, a European program for sectarian drifts and replication of the About-Picard law. Further, MIVILUDES delegations have traveled and/or met with leaders of several countries, including foreign embassies, members of parliaments, and anti-sect associations.⁶

The co-chairs of the U.S. House International Religious Freedom Caucus called on the French prime minister to disband MIVILUDES and all public funding of anticult associations. Needless to say, the French did not receive the recommendations by the U.S. officials favorably and did not dissolve MIVILUDES; nor did they end funding of anticult organizations. In fact, we surmise that French officials likely saw the letter as "proof" of the conspiracy involving U.S.-based *sectes* and the Trojan Horse of American imperialism.

Lester Kurtz observes that globalization is creating a new religious syncretism, a "combination of elements from more than one religious tradition to weave a new sacred canopy that competes in the cultural marketplace" (Kurtz, 1995:191). Yet in some ways this dynamic is centuries old; a dynamic interplay between traditional faiths and the widespread experiments and transplants of emerging faiths. But globalization has accelerated this dynamic in time and space. It should not be surprising then, that "conflict between established and alternative religious communities is thereby increased, posing a significant social problem for the global village" (Kurtz, 1995:191). The world is changing, Western societies are becoming more culturally diverse and heterogeneous, and formal affiliation with traditional or established religions of the past is stagnating or shrinking. These are social conditions that are conducive to conflict;

conflict between established and alternative religions, and between NRMs and the state. It is a conflict which is often instigated or exacerbated by elite groups and gatekeepers of the status quo, who regard traditional, institutional religions as uniquely legitimate.

Government raids, as our study has indicated, are harsh instruments of social control in this ongoing conflict. Now and in the future, the scale, severity, and frequency of government raids on NRMs will likely provide important standards of measurement to gauge a nation's level of cultural assimilation, tolerance, respect for religious liberty, and equal protection.

Notes

1. "Spiritual Procreation: Alternative Patterns of Parenting in New Religions, 1990–1993," a Standard Research Grant from the Social Sciences and the Humanities Research Council.
2. "French *Sectes* in Social Context: A Study of France's Management of New Religious Movements, 2005–2008," (Standard Research Grant).
3. The title of the Palmers' SSHRC grant was "Exploring Government Raids on Unconventional Religious Communities."

CHAPTER 1

1. After the 2006 raid, the sect was allowed to continue homeschooling their children, but the new law regarding nonviolent education likely jeopardized this arrangement since the group practices corporal punishment.
2. According to Palmer and Frisk (2014), "Since 2010, a network composed of ex-members, social workers, journalists, *sekt* experts, and worried relatives ha(d) been forming, exchanging information about the fanatical, fundamentalist, patriarchal *"sekt"* where children are beaten. There was a strong Catholic and Lutheran "counter-cult" presence at the court hearings. . . . Before the raid, on August 21, there were two experts from *Sekten-Info Nordrhein-Westfalen* to support the *Jugendamt*'s application for the judge's temporary custody order. Ex-members were also present at that hearing. Since 2010, ex-members, notably the Reip family, have aired their atrocity stories in the media."
3. Mission creep refers to the expansion and routinization of paramilitary policing in which raids are used as a new tool to conduct crude forms of investigation, blurring the lines between investigation and enforcement.
4. In the months following the completion and submission of the manuscript, we documented three additional raids on NRMs. The Sahaja Yoga community in

Cabella, Italy was raided in April 2015 and 69 children were taken into custody. The Be'er Miriam seminary for women in Jerusalem was raided in May 2015. The group was accused of being a "cult." Charges included fraud, health violations, and allegedly holding a former student against her will. In June 2015, the Twelve Tribes in Sus, France, was raided again on suspicion of child abuse and "failure to comply with educational requirements." We also became aware of earlier raids that escaped our attention. Steven Gaskin's The Farm was the target of a federal raid in 1980 in Tennessee on suspicion of illicit drugs (growing marijuana), but none were found. Palmer also conducted subsequent research on the Philadelphia raid on MOVE in 1985. Though MOVE has been depicted in secular terms as a radical anarchist group, Palmer's interviews with Ramona Africa (the lone survivor of the community on Osage Avenue that was bombed in the raid) suggest that the group could be categorized as a new religious movement, and that the spiritual aspects of founder John Africa's vision have been largely ignored. His teachings were written down in *The Guideline*, the sacred text unavailable to the public that is read by current members. The group practices rituals that acknowledge the gifts of "Mother Life".

5. "Israel Detains Christian Group in Pre-millennium Sweep—The Christians Were Seized Near Jersualem's Mount of Olives," CNN, October 25, 1999; "Israel Arrests Christians Groups Accused of Planning to Harm Public Safety," ABC News, October 25, 1999.

6. The full text of this report can be found at http://www.cesnur.org/testi/ FBI_004.htm.

7. The eight raids targeted four groups—the Branch Davidians, Twelve Tribes, The Family International, and Aum Shinrikyo.

8. The FLDS, Twelve Tribes (2), and Church of the Firstborn.

9. The linking together of two or more previously unconnected social groups or sites by a unit that mediates their relations with one another and/or with other sites; see McAdam, Tarrow, and Tilly, 2001:26.

10. The term "sect" is translated more accurately as "cult." It is a pejorative, derogatory term, implying heresy or fraud.

16. Though not technically part of the 1990s, we may also consider the mass murders and suicides in March 2000 by members of the Movement for the Restoration of the Ten Commandments.

12. While French conservatives, especially those tied to the Catholic Church, have been active in the ACM, so have liberals. For example, Alain Vivien, a Socialist, was the president of CCMM and the first director of MILS.

CHAPTER 2

1. One could also include China though we do not include it in our analysis. Representatives from French ACM organizations CCMM, FECRIS, and the

governmental Mission to Fight Cults (MILS) have actively worked with Chinese officials to support governmental control of the Falun Gong and other so-called cults (see "Innocents Abroad: French Anti-Cultists, Mission Support China's Anti-Cult Campaign," at http://www.cesnur.org/2001/jan30.htm).

CHAPTER 3

1. See chapter 9 on raids in France; also short descriptions of subsequent raids at the end of this chapter.
2. Professor David G. Bromley of Virginia Commonwealth University, who has studied the American anticult movement, suggested this was why Ted Patrick chose the Vine Community Church (private communication).
3. Much of the trouble experienced by the Twelve Tribes stems from the belief in spanking children, which is based on the biblical mandate not to "spare the rod." Leaders defend the practice as a necessary discipline to ensure that children will follow a Godly path. They are insistent that they understand the distinction between abuse and spanking as a form of discipline. See Liselotte Frisk, "Twelve Tribes: Parenting and Discipline of Children, Doctrine and Practice," paper presented at annual meeting of CESNUR, Baylor University, Waco, TX, June 5–8, 2014.
4. This was hippy slang meaning something like "wise philosopher," or one who had attained enlightenment through drugs.
5. Around 1978, FREECOG was supplanted by the nationally based American anticult organization, Citizens Freedom Foundation (CFF), in the wake of the Jonestown tragedy in 1978.
6. His youngest daughter Lydia, however, was overseas in France. Cindy Mattatall was pregnant with her fifth child, had allowed the childless Spriggs to take Lydia to live with them in France. Juan accused Spriggs of kidnapping Lydia, and Cindy appeared before Judge Mahady in a series of hearings. He repeatedly asked her if she could produce Lydia, and she replied in the negative. She skipped the last hearing and made secret arrangements to fly with her children to Europe. The CFF helped Juan track down her passport number, date of departure, and address.
7. It is important to note that the Stonegate community in West Virginia and the House of Judah in Michigan are in no way connected historically, geographically, or ideologically to the NEKCC in Island Pond, or to each other.
8. This is the same argument used by the State of Texas in the 2008 raid on the Fundamentalist Latter-Day Saints (FLDS). The state had a single complaint of assault lodged by an alleged woman inside the Yearning for Zion Ranch (it turned out to be a hoax) yet seized 439 FLDS children on the premise that all the children were at risk because they lived in the community. The Texas Court of Appeals rejected the state's argument on the same grounds it was rejected by the Vermont court (see Wiseman, 2011).
9. For detailed account of Edward Dawson case see Palmer, 1999.

10. According to Rule 1902, subsection E, an ex parte hearing is necessary "only in emergency or very unusual circumstances" and only "if delay in giving notice . . . would result in serious mischief."

11. *L' histoire du petit trompeau,* a documentary film by Guillaume Joga, la communauté de Sus, Château Laroque, 64,190 Sus.

12. Interview with Elder Johan Abraham in April 1997 at Tabitha's Place.

13. *L' histoire du petit trompeau.*

14. Each adult was taxed as if they were fully employed and earning minimum wage since 1983, whereas, in fact, they had been working on a voluntary basis as communalists.

15. *L' histoire du petit trompeau.*

16. Humanity Press, April 8, 1997 (http://www.rickross.com/reference/tribes/tribes44.html).

17. This statement was reported to Palmer by Jean Swantko, who was present.

18. The names of these deputies were Philippe Vuilque, Georges Fenech, Alain Gest, and Jean-Pierre Brard.

19. The National Assembly report of December 12, 2006 reads, "the stenographer used the privileges granted to him by Article 6 of the ordinance of November 17, 1958 regarding the functioning of parliament assemblies in order to assess . . . the conditions in which home schooling was taking place."

20. The more precise title for this new initiative was *"Commission d'enquête relative a l'influence des movements a caractère sectaire et aux consequence de leurs pratiques sur la santé physique et mentale des mineurs."*

21. MIVILUDES report on the findings of the *Commission d'enquête parlementaire sur les sects et mineurs,* published April 27, 2006.

22. The Community first arrived in Germany in 1994, when they settled in Pennigbuttel.

23. Interview with Elder Ephraim at Tabitha's Place, France in June 2009.

24. For an update on the Twelve Tribes' situation in Germany, see article on German human rights website : http://foref-europe.org/2015/01/01/germany-controversy-surrounding-twelve-tribes/.

CHAPTER 4

1. There were at least two other raids in 1991 in Rosario and Cordoba but they were much smaller in scope. We concentrate here on the two larger raids.

2. The police planted cocaine in the dining room cupboard among the silverware. We were told that several Family members witnessed the incident.

3. The Spanish translation of *"la secta"* in Argentina is more akin to the English word "cult." It has a pejorative meaning.

4. One translation of SPES is "Organization for Cult Awareness," provided by Baamonde, 1994.

5. Interview with members of The Family conducted by Palmer, 1994. On file with authors.

CHAPTER 5

1. Koresh was accused of converting legal semiautomatic weapons into fully automatic weapons. With regard to the explosives charges, the ATF investigation turned up purchases of suspicious black powder and grenade shells, among other things. The investigation began in June 1992, when a UPS package delivered to the Davidians' property broke open and revealed empty pineapple grenade shells. The Davidians claimed the empty grenade shells were used to mount onto wood plaques and sell at gun shows. But the UPS driver reported the discovery to the county sheriff, Jack Harwell, who passed the information to the ATF. The ATF initiated the investigation a few weeks later.

2. According to James Tabor, the letters "consisted mostly of scriptural quotations relating to Koresh's understanding of the situation" (1995:276). Tabor criticized Miron for making his assessment without any background in church history or theology which led him to "dreadfully misinterpret" a request by Koresh to employ Tabor as a mediator in the negotiations, among other things.

3. Kiri's mother, Sheri Jewell, a Branch Davidian, and her grandmother did not believe her story. Her father, who was separated from the mother, did believe Kiri and worked with Marc Breault and other opponents to expose Koresh as a child molester.

CHAPTER 6

1. Dr. York was never charged with molestation of those particular children.

2. There is some controversy concerning Dwight York's date of birth. See Palmer, 2010b:4.

3. The possible influence of Zecharia Sitchen's *Twelfth Planet* on Dwight York's thought is discussed in Palmer, 2010b:16.

4. The spelling of Ansaar/Ansar fluctuates over the course of the movement, as does Nubian/Nuwaubian and other Arabic/Ebonic titles.

5. Personal communication. Racial issues surfaced on a number of occasions. Sheriff Sills' predecessor was quoted as saying about the Nuwaubians, "Long as they ain't messin' with my niggers, I don't care" (Osinski, 2007:125).

6. The Nuwaubians claim that Jacob turned against his father when he refused to lend him money for his music business, but Jacob told a conflicting story in his interview with Palmer in 2003 in Atlanta: "He asked *me* for money!"

7. www.heisinnocent.com. Also, see www.nuwaubianfacts.com/theconspiracy-girls.html

8. Rob Peecher describes his surveillance activities in an interview with Paul Greenhouse in *The Nuwaubian Story*, a documentary film, screened at the American Academy of Religion (AAR-EIR) at McGill University's Faculty of Religious Studies, in Montreal, Quebec, May 6–7, 2005.

9. Interview with Rob Peecher in *The Nuwaubian Story*, a documentary film by Paul Greenhouse.

10. Patrick said that "if the prosecution had simply gone with 'child molestation,' I think he would have been acquitted because there were so many children who said he didn't do it. These kids were so confused! They kept accusing each other and changing their stories. No jury would have found him guilty on the basis on those kids' testimonies" (quoted in Palmer, 2010b:126). Patrick also points out that the prosecution added the RICO charge six months after the initial charges were filed and that "RICO is extremely easy to prove because you can cite the testimony of 'unindicted co-conspirators.'" When Patrick asked if he could cross examine these witnesses, "I was told I could not because they were unindicted co-conspirators. It was like coming up against a brick wall. Who are these people? We don't know, they are simply 'unindicted co-conspirators'" (quoted in Palmer, 2010b:126). Patrick claims the prosecution's real aim was not to protect the children but rather to seize the land and expel York from the county: "The state of Georgia had an anonymous tip in 2007. If they truly believed children were being abused, they would have acted sooner, not waited three and a half years to investigate" (Palmer, 2010b:126).

CHAPTER 7

1. In some reports, the age of the accused perpetrator is 50.

2. The DFPS originally reported taking 468 children into custody but later determined that 29 of the "children" were legal adults.

3. In June 2005, Jeffs was charged in Utah with sexual assault of a minor and conspiracy to commit sexual misconduct with a minor for allegedly arranging a marriage between a 14-year-old girl and her 19-year-old cousin. Jeffs became a fugitive to avoid arrest. He was captured in Nevada in August 2006. In Utah in 2007, he was found guilty on two counts of being an accomplice to rape and sentenced to ten years in prison, but due to faulty instructions to jurors the Utah Supreme Court overturned the ruling and ordered a new trial. Jeffs was still in custody in 2008 when the state of Texas launched its raid.

4. Defense attorney Don Payne made this statement to Wright after the trial of FLDS defendant, Alan Keate. Musser's testimony had a significant impact on the jury according to Payne. The first two defendants were convicted in part because of Musser's testimony.

5. The name of the Ross Institute was recently changed to the Cult Education Institute (www.cultnews.com).

CHAPTER 8

1. The E-meter is an electrical machine that measures galvanic skin response in the auditing sessions. It was first introduced into Scientology's auditing practice

around 1951 by Volney Mathisen, who appeared at Hubbard's Research Foundation at Elizabeth, N.J., to demonstrate "a strange but intriguing box equipped with wires, handles, and a dial, which he claimed was capable of measuring thought." Mathison's name for this machine was the "psychogalvonometer," but Hubbard dubbed it the "E-Meter," and it became a standard tool in the auditing process, to assist the auditors in locating and erasing "engrams" (trace memories of traumatic events) buried in the preclear's "reactive mind."

2. According to Doherty, the majority of witnesses Anderson heard were current Scientologists who gave positive testimony, but Anderson dismissed them out of hand (personal communication).

3. It is important to note that these provisions were repealed in 1982.

4. The definition of "records" included tape recordings, registers, phonograph records, books, and documents.

5. The church was located at 1810–1820 19th Street, NW.

6. The FDA dates back to the 1930s and was once part of the Department of Agriculture. It has a wide jurisdiction, from control of cigarettes to the illegal dilution of milk (see http://www.fda.gov).

7. *United States of America, Libelant, v. An Article or Device . . . "Hubbard Electrometer" or "Hubbard E-Meter" etc., Founding Church of Scientology et al., Claimants, No. D.C. 1–63*, United States District Court, District of Columbia, July 30, 1971 (333 F. Supp. 357).

8. In 1993, after 25 years of appeal and litigation, this legal battle between the FDA and the church was finally resolved when the Church of Scientology was granted recognition as a religion in the United States.

9. The Guardian's Office was disbanded in 1983, and the bulk of its previous functions were then assigned to the Office of Special Affairs.

10. www.patheos.com/Library/Scientology.html.

11. PSI was a branch of Erhard Seminars Training or *est*.

12. Interview conducted by Susan Palmer in 2011. The interviewee preferred that we not use his/her name. We are honoring the person's request for confidentiality. The source had specific knowledge of the Toronto raid. Going forward we will identify this source only as Interview with Scientologist.

13. The Tactics and Rescue Unit (T.R.U.) is a special branch of the Ontario Police. The unit's purpose is to resolve high-risk incidents and to provide expert tactical support services in specialized areas such as hostage-taking, barricaded persons, sniper incidents, search of an armed or dangerous fugitive, execution of a high-risk warrant, and occurrences involving explosives, V.I.P. security, and prisoner escort.

14. Interview with Scientologist, 2011.

15. Interview with Scientologist, 2011.

16. Interview with Scientologist, 2011.

17. David Mayo's role in producing witnesses is described in *The Facts: The Court of Appeal for Ontario between Her Majesty the Queen and Church of Scientology and Jacqueline Matz*, CI3047, Vol. 1. p. 18, paragraph 36.

18. Emile Gilbert and Alan Buchanan had been expelled in 1982 when their attempt to splinter off Scientology in Canada was uncovered. Scientology spokespersons claim they had been caught embezzling from the church and also that they had "plotted to take over the church." Gilbert's wife, Kathy, had served in the Guardian's Office and left with her husband. She was told by prosecutors that if she testified against the church, she would be granted immunity. Kathy Gilbert, knowing she would implicate Marion Evoy and Bryan Levman, started the domino effect which brought Evoy, Levman, and another former GO member, Diane Fairfield, all on board as witnesses against the church under immunity agreements (Interview with Scientologist, 2011).

19. Interview with Scientologist, 2011.

20. Interview with Scientologist, 2011.

21. She was later expelled from the church by the Ethics Mission in 1983.

22. Interview with Scientologist: "Jane Kember was the Guardian Worldwide, and under her direction the Guardians became involved in illegal tactics. They were very secretive and didn't answer to anyone else in the church, but reported directly to Kember. The church of Toronto had no way for monitoring actions of Guardian Officers. In 1983 the GO was disbanded, because it had gone off the rails; it had its own policy. A watchdog committee was set up to make sure this never happened again. There was a tremendous cover-up by the GO to the CoS; they were claiming persecution, planting evidence, etc. But the GO was a law unto itself. David Miscavage came to the U.S. as one of LRH's messengers to defend LRH who had been named in several of the GO's lawsuits. He found that the legal suits were not properly handled. Jane Kember had a plant steal documents from the attorney general's office. They found a cover note from her explaining the documents in the L.A. raid. The GO was protecting their own people, Mary Sue Hubbard and Jane Kember, but not defending the reputation of LRH! Messengers were sent to the U.K. to find out what was going on with the legal suits. They discovered a big mess in the GO, so Mary Sue and Jane were removed and the GO was disbanded. They both went to prison."

23. On December 2, 1991, the raid was declared illegal and all of the seized materials were returned to the church. The raid was deemed illegal because the police failed to limit what was seized. The warrant only covered relevant evidence but the police took everything, including all of the 854 parishioners or "preclear" folders. The undercover OPP plant, Barb Taylor, who had infiltrated the GO, had neglected to inform the police which folders to seize.

CHAPTER 9

1. In a report dated March 8, 2007, Ms. Asma Jahangir sent a communication to the French government to ask questions about the way they were dealing with the Plymouth Brethren. In her observations to the French government,

she noted that the concepts of "religion" and "belief" must be understood in a broad sense. "The Special Rapporteur urges the government to make sure that the mechanisms in charge of the management of these religious groups or belief communities deliver a message based on tolerance, freedom of religion or belief, and the principle according to which people's actions can only be judged through appropriate judicial proceeding." Moreover, "she recommends to the government to monitor more closely the prevention actions and campaigns which are carried out all over the country by private entities or organizations sponsored by the state, especially in the school education system, to avoid any suffering of the children of members of such groups."

2. France's intelligence service, the security branch of the police force. The "RG," as it is called, is similar to the CIA in the United States or CSIS in Canada.

3. See www.Zooey.wordpress.com/2008/02/02/french-justice-and-jacques-guyard.

4. Palmer's interview with Nathalie Luca, Director of Research at EHESS, 2001.

5. Abgrall offers up his theory of mental manipulation in his book, *La Mécanique des Sectes* (1996), which was translated into English as *Soul Snatchers: The Mechanics of Cults* (1999). Anthony and Robbins (2004) systematically deconstruct the theory as "pseudoscientific."

6. The groups are in question are Scientology, La Patriarche, Centre for Teaching Biodynamism, Raelian Movement, Communauté des Béatitudes, Amour et Miséricorde, and Tabitha's Place (Twelve Tribes). Also, leaders of groups that were not raided, for example Arnaud Mussy of Néo-Phare, were also charged with *abus de faiblesse*.

7. Accessed online at www.sectes-infos.net/Assauts.htm. Translation from French by Susan Palmer.

8. At Bourdin's hearing on the rape charge in 1995, the reliability of the witness Florence Roncaglia was seriously challenged. Asked by the defense if she had seen Bourdin's naked body, she replied "yes." Asked if she noticed any distinguishing marks on his body, she replied "No, it was normal like any other man." At that point, Bourdin cast off a garment revealing the "garish writhing of tattoos of arcane symbols that covered every inch of his chest, belly, back, and shoulders" (Palmer, 2011b:48). Needless to say, the people in the courtroom were stunned. Roncaglia also didn't know the exact dates or places where she was allegedly raped.

9. Investigators of the research section of the gendarmerie of Dijon.

10. UNADFI Bulletin No. 118 June 2013. "The first trial in which charges were laid against the community for sectarian harm/cult abuse resulted in the dismissal of the charges due to insufficient evidence. The families launched an appeal."

11. Video: "Une secte au Village?" Posted at www.wat.tv *Info/magazine TF1*, February 15, 2009.

12. Accessed online at www.unadfi.org/Une-association-pour-venir-en-aide, April 9, 2013.

13. "Deviations of MIVILUDES: Raid of 70 Policemen on a Biodynamism Centre." Accessed online at http://www.freedomofconscience.eu/2011/03/deviations-of-miviludes/#sthash.oxo8GqR2.dpuf.
14. Found on CICNS website at www.sectes-infos.net/communiques_presse_187_desc.
15. The other groups on the list include Au Coeur de la Communication (ACC), Dianova—Le Patriarche, Energo Chromo Kinèsis (ECK), Fédération d'Agrément des Réseaux, Human Universal Energy, ISKCON (Krishna), Mandarom, Mahikari, Rael, ORKOS, Prima Verba, Soka Gakkai, Jehovah's Witnesses, and Tradition Famille Propriété.

CHAPTER 10

1. While child abuse allegations became a more powerful claim under new laws allowing opponents to exploit a moral panic involving child endangerment, allied opponents continued to rely on previous charges of brainwashing, mind control, forced labor, mass suicide, stockpiling weapons, and sexual abuse.
2. GIGN stands for the Groupe d'Intervention de la Gendarmerie Nationale. It is part of the French Gendarmerie's elite special operations counterterrorism and hostage rescue unit.
3. A German law passed in 2000 outlawed corporal punishment. The Twelve Tribes continued to spank their children, believing it to be a biblical mandate. A journalist surreptitiously recorded a spanking and alerted authorities, who then responded by raiding the community and seizing the children.
4. We might also mention MOVE in this regard. The group was the target of a militarized raid by state police when its row house was bombed on May 13, 1985. After evacuating the neighborhood, the MOVE house was surrounded by "five hundred police armed with military and commercial explosives (C-4 and Tovex), automatic and semi-automatic weapons, sharpshooter rifles, two M-60 machine guns, UZIs, shotguns, a silenced .22-caliber rifle and a Lahti antitank weapon" (Wagner-Pacifici, 1994:16). Philadelphia mayor Wilson Goode ordered a Pennsylvania State Police helicopter to drop two satchels of explosives onto the rooftop of the row house, an action that killed 11 members (including 5 children) and destroyed 61 houses in the adjacent neighborhood. Palmer contends that MOVE's religious and spiritual aspects have been ignored. Based on her interviews with surviving members and on conversations with Anthony T. Fiscella, a doctoral candidate at Lund University, Sweden, who is writing his Ph.D dissertation on MOVE, it certainly could be argued that MOVE is a new religious group. It was founded by Vincent Leapheart (John Africa) in 1972 when it was dubbed the Christian Movement for Life. He was a mystic who propounded a radical ethic of biocentrism in which animals were humanity's equals, in terms of rights and spiritual status. His followers still perform

rituals to acknowledge the gifts of "Mother Life." John Africa's teachings are encapsulated in *The Guideline*. In this book, which is regarded as sacred and is hidden from the public, the spiritual vision and philosophy of natural law of founder John Africa was written down by one of his followers, Don Glassey.

5. Copy of official letter signed by co-chairs Trent Franks (R-Arizona) and Heath Shuler (D-North Carolina), on file with authors.

6. Ibid.

References

Adams, Brooke. 2008. "People Who Have Left Sect Go to Texas to Help." *Salt Lake City Tribune*, April 7.

Allard, Philippe.1997. "Vaste operacion policiere dirigee contre l'OKC." *Non aux sectes*, May 30.

Altglas, Veronique.2008. "Updating the Study of the French Cult Controversy." Paper presented at the INFORM Conference, London School of Economics, London, April 16.

Altglas, Vernonique. 2010. "Laïcité Is What Laïcité Does: Rethinking the French Cult Controversy." *Current Sociology* 58 (3):489–510.

American Civil Liberties Union. 2014. "War Comes Home: Excessive Militarization of American Policing." Accessed online at https://www.aclu.org/feature/war-comes-home.

Ammerman, Nancy T. 1995. "Waco, Federal Law Enforcement, and Scholars of Religion," pp.282–298 in Stuart A. Wright (ed.), *Armageddon in Waco*. Chicago: University of Chicago.

Anthony, Dick. 1990. "Religious Movements and Brainwashing Litigation," pp.295–344 in Thomas Robbins and Dick Anthony (eds.), *In Gods We Trust*. New Brunswick, NJ: Transaction.

Anthony, Dick. 1999. "Pseudoscience and Minority Religion: An Evaluation of the Brainwashing Theories of Jean-Marie Abgrall." *Social Justice Research* 12: 421–56.

Anthony, Dick and Thomas Robbins. 1992. "Law, Social Science, and the 'Brainwashing' Exception to the First Amendment." *Behavioral Sciences and the Law* 10:5–30.

Anthony, Dick and Thomas Robbins. 1994. "Brainwashing and Totalitarian Influence," pp.457–71 in *Encyclopedia of Human Behavior*, Vol. 1. San Diego: Academic Press.

Anthony, Dick and Thomas Robbins.1995. "Negligence, Coercion, and the Protection of Religious Belief." *Journal of Church and State* 37:509–536.

Anthony, Dick and Thomas Robbins. 2004. "Psuedoscience versus Minority Religion: An Evaluation of the Brainwashing Theories of Jean-Marie Abgrall," pp.127–150 in James T. Richardson (ed.), *Regulating Religion: Case Studies from around the Globe*. New York: Kluwer.

Anthony, Paul. 2005. "Shrouded in Secrecy: Former Members of Eldorado Sect Speak of Abusive, Closed Society, Fanaticism." *San Angelo Standard-Times*, March 27. Accessed online at http://nlnewsbank.com/nl-search/we/Archives?.

Aristequi, M.C. 1996. "Du vinaigre et du miel." *Sud Ouest*, January 2.

Atak, Jon. 1990. *A Piece of Blue Sky: Scientology, Dianetics and L. Ron Hubbard Exposed*. New York: Lyle Stuart Books.

Atchouel, Guillaume. 2006. "Dix-huit enfants coupes du monde a Tabitha's Place." *Le Figaro*, November 23.

Baamonde, José María. 1994. "The Experience of the SPES Foundation: Some Remarks on the Different Attitudes toward New Religious Movements in Argentina and Europe." *Cultic Studies Journal* 11 (1):56–65.

Bainbridge, William Sims. 2002. *The Endtime Family: The Children of God*. Albany: SUNY Press.

Balko, Radley. 2013. *Rise of the Warrior Cop: The Militarization of America's Police Forces*. New York: Public Affairs.

Barker, Eileen. 1984. *The Making of a Moonie*. London: Blackwell.

Barker, Eileen. 1988. "Defection from the Unification Church: Some Statistics and Distinctions," pp.166–184 in David G. Bromley (ed.), *Falling from the Faith*. Newbury Park, CA: Sage.

Barry, Ellen. "His Dream Became Their Nightmare." *Los Angeles Times*, January 22, 2004.

Bass, Ellen and Laura Davis. 1988. *Courage to Heal*. New York: Harper Collins.

Bazilchuk, Nancy.2000. "The Raid Revisited: Island Pond Community Heals Wounds from 1984." *The Burlington Free Press*, June 18.

Beckford, James A. 1985. *Cult Controversies: The Societal Response to New Religious Movements*. London: Tavistock.

Beckford, James A. 1994. "The Mass Media and New Religious Movements." *ISKCON Communication Journal* 4:17–24.

Beckford, James A. 2004. "Laicite, Dystopia, and the Reaction to New Religious Movements in France," pp.27–40 in James T. Richardson (ed.), *Regulating Religion: Case Studies from around the Globe*. New York: Kluwer.

Beckford, James A. and Melanie Cole. 1988. "British and American Responses to New Religious Movements." *Bulletin of the John Rylands University Library of Manchester* 70 (3):209–224.

Bennion, Janet. 2004. *Desert Patriarchy*. Tucson: University of Arizona Press.

Bennion, Janet. 2008. *Evaluating the Effects of Polygamy on Women and Children in Four North American Mormon Fundamentalist Groups*. Lewiston, NY: Edwin Mellen.

Bennion, Janet. 2011. "History, Culture, and Variability of Mormon Schismatic Groups," pp.101–124 in Cardell K. Jacobson and Lara Burton (eds.), *Modern Polygamy in the United States*. New York: Oxford University Press.

Beresford, David.1980a. "Snow White's Dirty Tricks." *The Guardian*, Feb. 7.

Beresford, David.1980b. "Sect Framed Journalist over 'Bomb Threats.'" Feb. 9, *The Guardian*.

Bernardelli, Giorgio. 2013. "Patriarchate of Constantinople Wages War against Rebel Monks on Mount Athos." *Vatican Insider*, July 29.

Best, Joel. 1990. *Threatened Children: Rhetoric and Concern about Child–Victims*. Chicago: University of Chicago Press.

Beverly, James. n.d. "Kingdom Concerns: A Critique of the Northeast Kingdom Community Church." (flyer).

Bilodeau, Katherine. 1994. "The Media's Role in the Island Pond Church Story." *The Chronicle*, June 22.

Blades, Kent. 1990. "Cult Defector Killed by Mother." *The Guardian* (Clark's Harbour, N.S.), June 12, p.1.

Blanco, Eduardo. 1994a. "El Gobierno, Alberto Piotti and Antonio Cafiero." *La Maga*, May 4, p.45.

Blanco, Eduardo. 1994b. "Jose Maria Baamonde, Director de SPES: 'Se puede manipular a una persona.'" *La Maga*, May 4, p.46.

Blaney, Betsy and Michelle Roberts. 2008. "Cyanide Document Found at Texas Compound." Associated Press, April 12.

Borowick, Claire. 1994. "Falsely Accused and Jailed in Argentina. *PEN: Persecution Endtime News*, Special Edition, March, 3:1–8.

Bozeman, John M. and Susan J. Palmer. 1997. "The Northeast Kingdom Community Church of Island Pond, Vermont: Raising Up a People for Yahshua's Return." *Nova Religio* 12 (2):181–190.

Bradley, Martha Sonntag. 1993. *Kidnapped from That Land: The Government Raids on the Short Creek Polygamists*. Salt Lake City: University of Utah.

Bradley, Martha Sonntag. 2011. "A Repeat of History: A Comparison of the Short Creek and Eldorado Raids on the FLDS," pp.3–40 in Cardell K. Jacobson and Lara Burton (eds.), *Modern Polygamy in the United States*. New York: Oxford University Press.

Brauthwaite, Chris. 1983. "Island Pond Cult Loses Custody Fight, Business." *The Chronicle* (Orleans County, VT), May 25.

Braithwaite, Chris. 1984. "Cultism and Child Abuse: Cases of Convergence." *The Cult Observer* (September):3–6.

Breault, Marc and Martin King. 1993. *Inside the Cult*. New York: Signet.

Bright Dr., Frederick, n.d. Recorded interview with Abigail Washington. Accessed online at www.youtube.com/watch?v=HFnUoBIajiU.

Bromley, David G. 1998a. *The Politics of Religious Apostasy*. Westport, CT: Praeger.

Bromley, David G. 1998b. "Sociological Perspectives on Apostasy: An Overview," pp.3–16 in David G. Bromley (ed.), *The Politics of Religious Apostasy*. Westport, CT: Praeger.

Bromley, David G. 1998c. "The Social Construction of Contested Exit Roles: Defectors, Whistleblowers, and Apostates," pp.19–48 in David G. Bromley (ed.), *The Politics of Religious Apostasy*. Westport, CT: Praeger.

Bromley, David G. and Edward Breschel. 1992. "General Populations and Institutional Elite Support for Social Control of New Religious Movements: Evidence from National Survey Data." *Behavioral Sciences and the Law* 10 (1):39–52.

Bromley, David G. and Anson D. Shupe. 1981. *Strange Gods: The Great American Cult Scare*. Boston: Beacon Press.

Bromley, David G. and Anson D. shupe. 1994. "The Modern American Anti-Cult Movement: A Twenty Year Retrospective," pp. 3–32 in Anson Shupe and David Bromley (eds.), *Anticult Movements in Cross-Cultural Perspective*. New York: Garland.

Bromley, David G., Anson D. Shupe, and G. C. Ventimiglia.1979. "Atrocity Tales, the Unification Church, and the Social Construction of Evil." *Journal of Communication* (Summer):42–53.

Bromley, David G. and Edward D. Silver. 1995. "The Davidian Tradition: From Patronal Clan to Prophetic Movement,"pp. 43–74 in Stuart A. Wright (ed.), *Armageddon in Waco*. Chicago: University of Chicago.

Brown, J. David. 1996. "The Professional Ex-: An Alternative for Exiting the Deviant Career," pp.439–447 in Earl Rubington and Martin Weinburg (eds.), *Deviance: The Interactionist Perspective*. Boston: Allyn & Bacon.

Bryner, Jenna. 2008. "Texas Group: Religious Sect or Cult?" http://MSNBC. com, April 19. Accessed online at www.msnbc.com/id/24032149/print/1/ displaymode/1098.

Campbell, Angela. 2009. "Bountiful Voices." *Osgoode Hall Law Journal* 47:183–234.

Carney, T. 1993. "Children of God; Harbingers of Another (Child Law) Reformation?" *Criminology Australia* 5:2–5.

Celizic, Mike. 2008. "Woman Describes 'Escape' from Polygamy." MSNBC. com, April 8. Accessed online at www.msnbc.com/id/24009286/print/1/ displaymode/1098/.

CESNUR. 2001. "Innocents Abroad: French Anti-Cultists, Mission Support China's Anti-Cult Campaign." Jan. 30. Accessed online at http://www.cesnur.org/2001/ jan30.htm.

Chaffanjon, Charlotte. 2008. "'Vers une nouvelle commission d'enquête parlementaire sur les sectes.'" *Le Point*, February 29.

Chaintrier, Jean-Paul Bearn. 1988. "Le secte de Sus.'" *Sud Ouest*, November 5.

Chancellor, James. 2000. *Life in The Family: An Oral History of the Children of God*. Syracuse: Syracuse University Press.

Claridge, Thomas. 1992a. "Police Files Were Target, Trial Told." *Globe and Mail*, 23 April.

Claridge, Thomas. 1992b. "Church Guilty in Spy Case." *Globe and Mail*, June 27.

Claridge, Thomas. 1997. "Court Rejects Scientology's Religious Freedom Argument." *Globe and Mail*, 19 April.

Clarke, Peter. 2006. *New Religions in Global Perspective*. New York: Routledge.

Coleman, Lee. 1989. "Medical Examination for Sexual Abuse: Have We Been Misled?" *Issues in Child Abuse Accusations* 1 (3):1–9.

Coleman, Lee. 1994. Declaration of Lee Coleman, M.D., December 13. Submitted to the New South Wales Supreme Court. Document on file with authors.

Coleman, Lee and Patrick E. Clancy. 1990. "False Allegations of Child Sexual Abuse." *Criminal Justice* (Fall):14–20, 43–47.

Coser, Lewis. 1954. "The Age of the Informer." *Dissent* 1:249–254.

Cowan, Douglas. 2003. "Confronting the Failed Failure: Y2K and Evangelical Eschatology in Light of the Passed Millennium." *Nova Religio* 7 (2):71–85.

CNN Transcript, Anderson Cooper, May 16, 2008. Accessed online at http://transcripts.cnn.com/TRANSCRIPTS/0805/16/acd.html.

Cragun, Ryan T., Michael Nielsen, and Heather Clingenpeel. 2011. "The Struggle for Legitimacy: Tensions between the LDS and FLDS," in Stuart A. Wright and James T. Richardson (eds.), *Saints under Siege*. New York: New York University Press.

Darroch, Wendy. 1992. "Ex-Scientologist Tells of Pilfering OPP Files." *Toronto Star*, May 1.

Dawson, Edward. 1994. "Taking Our Children: The Testimony of Edward Dawson of the Northeast Kingdom Community Church." Unpublished manuscript, June 13.

Demara, Bruce. 1992. "Scientology Testimony Marked by Jargon." *Toronto Star*, 23 April.

DeNavas-Walt, Carmen, Bernadette D. Proctor and Jessica C. Smith. 2013. Income, Poverty, and Health Insurance Coverage in the United States: 2012. Current Population Reports, September. Washington, DC: U.S. Census Bureau.

Doherty, Bernard. 2014. "Sensational Scientology! The Church of Scientology and Australian Tabloid Television." *Nova Religio* 17 (3):38–63.

Doberty, Bernard. 2015. "Colonial Justice or Kangaroo Court? Public Controversy and the Church of Scientology in 1960s Australia." *Alternative Sprituality and Religion Review* (in press).

Donnelly, Jack. 1998. *International Human Rights*. Boulder: Westview.

Driggs, Ken. 2011. "Twenty Years of Observations about the Fundamentalist Polygamists," pp.77–100 in Cardell K. Jacobson and Lara Burton (eds.), *Modern Polygamy in the United States*. New York: Oxford University Press.

Dunn, Timothy. 1996. *Militarization of the U.S.-Mexico Border, 1978–1992*. Austin: University of Texas Press.

Dunphy, Bill. 1992a. "Ex-Scientology Boss Testifies." *Toronto Sun*, 23 April.

Dunphy, Bill. 1992b. "Ex-Cult Member: Mounties Targeted as Enemy." *Toronto Sun*, May 13.

Dunphy, Bill. 1992c. "Ex-Scientology Boss Testifies: She Ran the Agents." *Toronto Sun*, April 23.

Dunphy, Bill. 1992d. "Spies Stole Key Files." *Toronto Sun*, May 3.

Dunphy, Bill. 1992e. "Scientology Trial: 800 Fired by Spy Network." *Toronto Sun*, June 5.

Duvert, Cyrille. 2004. "Anti-Cultism in the French Parliament: Desperate Last Stand or an Opportune Leap Forward? A Critical Analysis of the 12 June 2001 Act," pp.41–52 in James T. Richardson (ed.), *Regulating Religion: Case Studies from around the Globe*. New York: Kluwer.

Eckenrode, Vicky. 2001. "Mystery Circles Georgia's Clan of Nuwaubians." *Atlanta Chronicle*, February 25.

Ellison, Christopher G. and John P. Bartkowski. 1995. "'Babies Were Being Beaten': Exploring Child Abuse Allegations at Ranch Apocalypse," pp.111–152 in Stuart A. Wright (ed.), *Armageddon in Waco*. Chicago: University of Chicago.

England, Mark and Darlene McCormick. 1993. "The Sinful Messiah." *Waco Tribune-Herald*, February 27.

Evans, Christopher Evans. 1974. *Cults of Unreason*. London: Farrar Straus & Giroux.

Evans, Martha Bradley. 2011. "The Past as Prologue: A Comparison of the Short Creek and Eldorado Polygamy Raids," pp. 25–50 in Stuart A. Wright and James T. Richardson (eds.), *Saints under Siege*. New York: New York University Press.

Fautre, Willy. 2004. "Belgium's Anti-Sect Policy, " pp.113–126 in James T. Richardson (ed.), *Regulating Religion: Case Studies from around the Globe*. New York: Kluwer.

"FBI Heaps Ridicule on Koresh," *Houston Chronicle*, April 17, 1993, p.1A.

FBI Report. 1993. "The Ansaru Allah Community, also known as The Nubian Islamic Hebrews, The Tents of Kedar." U.S. Department of Justice, Federal Bureau of Investigation, Domestic Security/Terrorism.

Floyd, John and Bill Sinclair. 2009. "The Unrelenting March against the FLDS." Accessed online at http://texascriminaldefense.com/comments/July09/27ahtml.

Forum for Religious Freedom in Europe. 2012. "President of French Anti-religious Organization MIVILUDES Convicted by Criminal Court in Paris." Accessed online at http://foref-europe.org/2012/06/28/president-of-french-anti-religious-organization-miviludes-convicted-by-criminal-court-of-paris/.

Foster, Lawrence. 1981. *Religion and Sexuality: The Shakers, the Mormons, and the Oneida Community*. Champagne: University of Illinois.

Foster, Lawrence. 1984. "Career Apostates: Reflections on the Works of Jerald and Sandra Tanner." *Dialogue: Journal of Mormon Thought* 17 (2):35–60.

Fouchereau, Bruno. 2001. "Les sectes, cheval de Troie des Etats-Unis en Europe." *Le Monde Diplomatique*, May, p.1.

Freedberg, Sydney P. 1994. *Brother Love: Murder, Money, and a Messiah*. New York: Pantheon.

Freidman, Emily. 2008. "Sect Members: Brainwashed or Believers?" ABC News, April 16. Accessed online at www.rickross.com/reference/polygamy/polygamy832.html.

Frigerio, Alejandro. 1993. "'La invasion de las sectas': El debate sobre nuevos movimientos religiosos en los medio de communicacion en Argentina." *Sociedad y Religion* 10:24–51.

Frink, Sandra. 2009. "Women, the Family, and the Fate of the Nation in American Anti-Catholic Narratives, 1830–1860." *Journal of the History of Sexuality* 18 (2): 237–264.

Galanter, Marc. 1989. *Cults: Faith, Healing and Coercion.* New York: Oxford.

Garrett, Robert T. 2008. "Colorado Woman May Be Caller Who Sparked CPS Sweep, Officials Say." *Dallas Morning News*, April 19.

Garrison, Omar V. 1974. *The Hidden Story of Scientology.* New York: Citadel Press.

Goldman, Miriam. 1995. "Continuity in Collapse: Departures from Shiloh." *Journal for the Scientific Study of Religion* 34 (3):342–353.

Goldstone, Jack A. 2003. *States, Parties, and Social Movements.* New York: Cambridge University Press.

Goodenough, Patrick. 2001. "French Anti-Sect Law: Christian Lawyers Prepare for Action." CBS News, June 4. Accessed online at www.cbsnews.com.

"Governor Perry Signs SB 6 into Law." 2005. *Eldorado Success*, June 9.

Green, Glenn. 1989. "Oral Memoirs." Institute for Oral History, Waco: Baylor University.

Gunn, T. Jeremy. 2003. "The Complexity of Religion and the Definition of Religion in International Law." *Harvard Human Rights Journal* 16 (2003):189–215.

Haggerty, Kevin D. and Richard V. Ericson. 2001. "The Military Technostructures of Policing," pp.43–64 in Peter B. Kraska (ed.), *Militarizing the American Criminal Justice System.* Boston: Northeastern University Press.

Hall, John R. 1995. "Public Narratives and the Apocalyptic Sect: From Jonestown to Mt. Carmel," pp.205–235 in Stuart A. Wright (ed.), *Armageddon in Waco.* Chicago: University of Chicago.

Hall, John R. and Philip Schuyler. 1998. "Apostasy, Apocalypse and Religious Violence: An Exploratory Comparison of People's Temple, the Branch Davidians and the Solar Temple," pp.141–170 in David G. Bromley (ed.), *The Politics of Religious Apostasy.* Westport, CT: Praeger.

Hall, Stuart, Chris Critcher, Tony Jefferson, John Clarke, and Brian Roberts. 1978. *Policing the Crisis.* London: MacMillan.

Hallechuk, Rick. 1990. "Scientology Church Gets Ruling Today." *Toronto Star*, September 21.

Hammon, Heber B. and William Jankoviak. 2011. "One Vision: The Making, Unmaking, and Remaking of a Fundamentalist Polygamous Community," pp.45–71 in Cardell K. Jacobson and Lara Burton (eds.), *Modern Polygamy in the United States.* New York: Oxford University Press.

Barbara Grizutti. 1984. "The Children and the Cult." *New England Monthly*, December.

Hanna, Bill. 2008. "Temple used for sex with young girls, officials say." *Fort Worth Star-Telegram*, April 9.

Harrison, Barbara Grizutti. 1993. "Bad Faith." *Mirabella*, August.

Hassan, Steven. 1988. *Combatting Mind Control*. Rochester, VT: Park Street.

Heller, Matthew. 2004. "Flora's War: Flora Jessop Knows What It's Like to Flee an Insular and Polygamous World." *Los Angeles Times Magazine*, August 1.

Hertic, Nancy. 1978. "Church to Sell Its Yellow Delis, Other Properties and Relocate." *Chattanooga Times*, March 26.

Hervieu-Léger, Danièle. 2001. "France's Obsession with the Sectarian Threat." *Nova Religio* 4 (2):249–257.

Hervieu-Léger, Danièle. 2004. "France's Obsession with the Sectarian Threat," pp.40–59 in Phillip C. Lucas and Thomas Robbins (eds.), *New Religious Movements in the 21ˢᵗ Century*. New York: Routledge.

Hexham, Irving. 2001. "New Religions and the Anticult Movement in Canada." *Nova Religio* 4 (2):281–288.

Hill, Daniel G. 1980. "Mind Development Groups, Cults and Sects in Ontario." Toronto: Toronto Government Printing Office, June.

Hill, Stephen and Randall Beger. 2009. "A Paramilitary Juggernaut." *Social Justice* 36 (1):25–40.

Hoffman, J. 1984. "Island Pond Raid, 10 Years Later." *Sunday Rutland Herald and Sunday Times Argus* (Barre-Montepelier, VT), June 9.

Homer, Michael. 1999. "The Precarious Balance between Freedom of Religion and the Best Interests of the Child," pp.187–209 in Susan J. Palmer and Charlotte Hardeman (eds.), *Children in New Religions*. New Brunswick: Rutgers University Press.

Honore, Carl. 1993. "'Explicit' Sex in Sect Tapes." *Houston Chronicle*, September 3, p.25A.

Hunsicker, Brent. 2008. "Who Is Willie Jessop?" ABC4News.com, June 6.

Hylton, Hillary. 2008. "The Future of the Polygamist Kids." *Time*, April 15. Accessed online at www.time.com/time/printout/0,8816,1730471,00.html.

International Helsinki Federation for Human Rights. 1999. Report to the OSCE Supplementary Human Dimension Meeting on Freedom of Religion, Vienna, March 22. Accessed online at http://www.ihf-hf.org/.

Interview with Catherine Matteson, Waco, Texas, June 1993. On file with authors.

Interview with Elder Ephraim at Tabitha's Place, May 29, 2009. On file with authors.

Interview with Jacob York, August 19, 2003. On file with authors.

Interview with Linda Werlein, July 2008. On file with authors.

Interview with Sheriff Howard Sills, August 14, 2003. On file with authors.

Introvigne, Massimo. 1995. "The Secular Anti-Cult and the Religious Counter-cult Movements: Strange Bedfellows or Future Enemies?" Pp.32–54 in Eric Towler (ed.), *New Religions and the New Europe*. Aarhus, Denmark: Aarhus University Press.

Introvigne, Massimo. 2001. "Blacklisting or Greenlisting? A European Perspective on the New Cult Wars." *Nova Religio* 2:47–59.

Introvigne, Massimo. 2004. "Holy Mountains and Anti-Cult Ecology: The Campaign against the Aumist Religion in France," pp.73–83 in James T. Richardson (ed.), *Regulating Religion: Case Studies from Around the Globe*. New York: Kluwer.

Investigation into the Activities of Federal Law Enforcement toward the Branch Davidians. Thirteenth Report by the Committee on Government Reform and Oversight Prepared in Conjunction with the Committee on the Judiciary Together with Additional and Dissenting Views, August 2, 1996.

Investigative Proposal Regarding Island Pond. n.d. Kingston, NY: Galen Kelly Associates. Document on file with authors.

Jacobson, Cardell K. and Lara Burton (eds.), *Modern Polygamy in the United States*. New York: Oxford University Press.

Jenkins, Philip. 1992. *Intimate Enemies: Moral Panics in Contemporary Great Britain*. New York: Aldine de Gruyter.

Jenkins, Philip. 1998. *Moral Panic: Changing Concepts of the Child Molester in Modern America*. New Haven: Yale University Press.

Jessop, Carolyn. 2008. "One Woman's Harrowing Tale of Escaping the Texas Polygamist Sect." *Daily Mail*, April 21. Accessed online at www.dailymail.co.uk/femail/article-559132.

Jessop, Carolyn with Laura Palmer. 2008. *Escape*. New York: Broadway Books.

Jessop, Flora and Paul T. Brown. 2009. *Church of Lies*. New York: Jossey-Bass.

Johnson, Daniel Carson. 1998. "Apostates Who Never Were: The Social Construction of *Absque Facto* Narratives," pp.115–138 in David G. Bromley (ed.), *The Politics of Religious Apostasy*. Westport, CT: Praeger.

Johnson, Kirk. 2008. "Texas Polygamy Raid May Pose Risk." *New York Times*, April 12.

Kaihla, Paul and Ross Laver. 1993. *Savage Messiah*. New York: Doubleday.

Kavanaugh, Jean. 1992. "Conviction Frightening for Religions, Lawyer Says." *Toronto Star*, June 29.

Kraska, Peter B. 2001a. "Crime Control as Warfare," pp.14–25 in Peter B. Kraska (ed.), *Militarizing the American Criminal Justice System*. Boston: Northeastern University Press.

Kraska, Peter B. 2001b. *Militarizing the American Criminal Justice System*. Boston: Northeastern University Press.

Kraska, Peter B. and Louis J. Cubellis. 1997. "Militarizing Mayberry and Beyond: Making Sense of American Paramilitary Policing." *Justice Quarterly* 14 (Dec.):607–629.

Kraska, Peter B. and Victor E. Kappeler. 1996. "Militarizing American Police: The Rise and Normalization of Paramilitary Units." *Social Problems* 44 (1):1–18.

Kurtz, Lester. 1995. *Gods in the Global Village*. Thousand Oaks, CA: Pine Forge Press.

Labaton, Stephen. 1993. "Scientologists Granted Tax Exemption by the U.S." *New York Times*, November 14.

Langford, Terri. 2009. "Hundreds of Children Die Despite CPS Involvement." *Houston Chronicle*, October 22, p.A6.

Langford, Terri and Emily Ramshaw. 2010. "Kids at Facilities in Texas Choked, Stripped, Beaten." *Houston Chronicle*, June 6.

Langone, Michael D. 1993a. *Recovery from Cults: Help for Victims of Psychological and Spiritual Abuse*. New York: W.W. Norton.

Langone, Michael D. 1993b. "Introduction," pp.1–15 in Michael D. Langone (ed.), *Recovery from Cults*. New York: W.W. Norton.

Lassette, Tom. 1999. "Tensions Simmer around Black Sect in Georgia." *New York Times*, June 29.

LeBlanc, Benjamin-Hugo. 2001. "No Bad Sects in France." *Religion in the News* 4 (3):1–7.

Lee, Helene. 2003. *The First Rasta*. 2003. Chicago: Lawrence Hill Books.

"Les enfants proies de plus et plus faciles pour les sectes" Paris (Reuters) December 19, 2006.

Le Parisien, November 23, 2006.

"Les membres d'Amour et Miséricorde livrent leur vérité." *le Bien public*, May 18.

Levine, Saul. 1984. *Radical Departures: Desperate Detours to Growing Up*. New York: Harcourt, Brace & Jovanovich.

Lewis, James R. 1986. "Reconstructing the 'Cult' Experience." *Sociological Analysis* 47 (2):151–159.

Lewis, James R. 1992. "'Poisonous Tenets': Religious Insanity in Nineteenth Century Anglo-American Medical Theory." *Syzygy* 1 (2):173–84.

Lewis, James R. 1995. "Self-Fulfilling Stereotypes, the Anticult Movement, and the Waco Confrontation," pp.95–110 in Stuart A. Wright (ed.), *Armageddon in Waco*. Chicago: University of Chicago.

Lewis, James R. 2006. *The Order of the Solar Temple: The Temple of Death*. Hampshire, UK: Ashgate.

Lewis, James R. 2009. *Scientology*. New York: Oxford University Press, 2009.

Lifton, Robert J. 1961. *Thought Reform and the Psychology of Totalism: A Study of "Brainwashing" in China*. New York: W.W. Norton.

Lofland, John. 1979. "'White Hot Mobilization: Strategies of a Millenarian Movement,'" pp.157–166 in Mayer N. Zald and John D. McCarthy (eds.), *The Dynamics of Social Movements*. Cambridge, MA: Winthrop.

Luca, Nathalie. 2004. "'Is There a Unique French Policy of Cults? A European Perspective,'" pp.53–72 in James T. Richardson (ed.), *Regulating Religion: Case Studies from around the Globe*. New York: Kluwer.

MacKaye, William R. 1973. "Church Gets Back Books, E-Meters." *Washington Post*, October 24.

Malcairne, Vanessa and John D. Burchard. 1992. "Investigations of Child Abuse/ Neglect Allegations in Religious Cults: A Case Study in Vermont." *Behavioral Sciences and the Law* 10:75–88.

Marro, Anthony.1977. "Federal Agents Raid Scientology Church; Offices in Two Cities Are Searched for Allegedly Stolen IRS Files." *New York Times*, July 8.

Marshall, John.1980 "Hubbard Still Gave Orders, Records Show." *The Globe and Mail*, Jan. 24.

Martin, Paul. 1996. "Pitfalls to Recovery." *AFF News* 2 (1):1–3.

Martin, Sheila. 2009. *When They Were Mine: Memoirs of a Branch Davidian Wife and Mother*. Edited by Catherine Wessinger. Waco: Baylor University Press.

Mauss, Armand. 1998. "Apostasy and the Management of Spoiled Identity," pp.51–74 in David G. Bromley (ed.), *The Politics of Religious Apostasy*. Westport, CT: Praeger.

Maychuk, Matt, Don Dutton, and John Ferri. 1984. "Scientology Office Stormed by Police, Documents Seized." *Toronto Star*, March 4.

Mayer, Jean-Francois. 1996. *Les Mythes du Temple Solaire*. Geneva: Georg Editeur.

McAdam, Doug. 1999. *Political Process and the Development of Black Insurgency, 1930–1979*, 2nd ed. Chicago: University of Chicago.

McAdam, Doug. 2003. "Beyond Structural Analysis: Toward a More Dynamic Understanding of Social Movements," pp.281–298 in Mario Diani and Doug McAdam (eds.), *Social Movements and Networks*. New York: Oxford University Press.

McAdam, Doug, Sidney Tarrow, and Charles Tilly. 2001. *Dynamics of Contention*. New York: Cambridge University Press.

McCain, Robert Stacy. 2002. "Nuwaubian Nightmare." *Washington Times*, June 2. Accessed online at www.wwrn.org/articles/6687/?&section=nuwaubian-nation.

Melton, J. Gordon. 1997. *The Children of God: "The Family*. Salt Lake City: Signature Books.

Melton, J. Gordon. 2000. *Scientology*. Salt Lake City: Signature Books.

Melton, J. Gordon. 2002. "A Contemporary Ordered Religious Community: The Sea Organization," pp.45–80 in Derek H. Davis and Barry Hankins (eds.), *New Religious Movements and Religious Liberty in America*. Waco: Baylor University Press.

Merrifield, Jeff. 2006. *Damanhur: The Story of the Extraordinary Italian Artistic and Spiritual Community*. Second edition. Santa Cruz, CA: Hanford Mead.

Miller, Donald E. 1983. "Deprogramming in Historical Perspective," pp.15–28 in David G. Bromley and James T. Richardson (eds.), *The Brainwashing/Deprogramming Controversy*. Lewiston, NY: Mellen.

Mitchell, Kirk. 2008. "Details Emerging on Calls that May Have Sparked Raid," *Salt Lake City Tribune*, April 20, p.A17.

Morgan, Lucy. 1999. "Critics Public and Private Keep Pressure on Scientology." *St. Petersburg Times*, March 29.

Moritz, John. 2008. "'Texans' Tab for YFZ Roundup Tops $14 Million." *Fort Worth Star-Telegram*, June 14.

Moser, Bob. 2002. "'Savior' in a Strange Land." Southern Poverty Law Center: *Intelligence Report* (Fall). Accessed online at www.splcenter.org/intelreport/article.jsp?pid=88.

Murray, Alan. 1978a. "Friends, Foes, Give Opinions of Vine Christian Community." *The Chattanooga Times*, January 16.

Murray, Alan. 1978b. "Tax Question Is Answered for Church." *The Chattanooga Times*, January 18.

Murray, Alan. 1978c. "Vine Elders Concede Church has Authoritarian Character." *The Chattanooga Times*, January 19.

Nash, Nathaniel C. 1993. "Argentines Say a Sex Cult Enslaved 268 Children." *New York Times*, September 3, p.1A.

Nathan, Debby. 1991. "Satanism and Child Molestation: Constructing the Ritual Abuse Scare," pp.75–94 in James T. Richardson, Joel Best, and David G. Bromley (eds.), *The Satanism Scare*. New York: Aldine.

Nathan, Debby and Michael Snedeker. 1995. *Satan's Silence: Ritual Abuse and the Making of a Modern American Witch Hunt*. New York: Basic Books.

Neil, Martha. 2008. "Texas Changed Marriage Age to Restrict Rights of Polygamy Ranch Residents." *ABA Journal*, May 2.

Neilsen, Kirsten. 2007. *Cult Scare: The Firsthand Account of the Shocking Kidnapping of Kirsten Neilsen*. Island Pond, VT: Parchment Press.

Nellis, William. 1983. "100 Officers Raid Scientology Centre." *The Globe and Mail*, March 4.

Newsome, Brian. 2008. "Springs Woman Suspected of Hoax Call Says Father Abused Her." *Colorado Springs Gazette*, April 21.

Nicholas, Grace.1999. "Seizure of Sect Children Ruled Unlawful." *Sydney Morning Herald*, April 1.

Noesner, Gary. 2010. *Stalling for Time: My Life as an FBI Hostage Negotiator*. New York: Random House.

Olsen, Paul J. 2006. "The Public Perception of 'Cults' and New Religious Movements." *Journal for the Scientific Study of Religion* 45 (1):97–106.

Osinski, Bill. 2002. "Legislator Intervenes in Nuwaubian Case." *Atlanta Journal-Constitution*, August 31.

Osinski, Bill. 2007. *Ungodly: The True Story of Unprecedented Evil*. Macon: Indigo.

Pagliarini, Marie Anne. 1999. "The Pure Woman and the Wicked Catholic Priest: An Analysis of Anti-Catholic Literature in Antebellum America." *Religion and American Culture* 9 (1): 97–128.

Palmer, Susan J. 1994. Interview notes. Document on file with author.

Palmer, Susan J. 1998. "Apostates and Their Role in the Construction of Grievance Claims against the Northeast Kingdom/Messianic Communities," pp.191–208 in David G. Bromley (ed.), *The Politics of Religious Apostasy*. Westport, CT: Praeger.

Palmer, Susan J. 1999. "Frontiers and Families: The Children of Island Pond," pp.153–171 in Palmer, Susan A. and Charlotte Hardeman (eds.), *Children in New Religions*. New Brunswick: Rutgers University.

Palmer, Susan J. 2001. "Peace, Persecution, and Preparations for Yahshua's Return: The Case of the Messianic Communities 'Twelve Tribes,'" pp.59–80 in Stephen Hunt (ed.), *Christian Millenarianism: From the Early Church to Waco.* London: Hurst.

Palmer, Susan J. 2002. "Field Notes: France's Anti-Sect Wars." *Novo Religio* 6 (1):174–182.

Palmer, Susan J. 2006. "Cult Fighting in Middle Georgia." *Religion in the News* 9 (1). Accessed online at https://trincoll.edu/depts./crsp/rinvol9/Cult%Fighting %in%Middle%Georgia/.

Palmer, Susan J. 2010a. "The Twelve Tribes: Preparing the Bride for Yahshua's Return" *Nova Religio* 13 (3):59–80.

Palmer, Susan J. 2010b. *The Nuwaubian Nation: Black Spirituality and State Control.* Surrey, UK: Ashgate.

Palmer, Susan J. 2011a. "Rescuing Children? Government Raids and Child Abuse Allegations in Historical and Cross-Cultural Perspective," pp.51–79 in Stuart A. Wright and James T. Richardson (eds.), *Saints under Siege.* New York: New York University Press.

Palmer, Susan. J. 2011b. *The New Heretics of France: Minority Religions, la République, and the Government-Sponsored "War on Sects."* New York: Oxford University Press.

Palmer, Susan J. and Charlotte Hardman. 1999a. *Children in New Religions.* New Brunswick: Rutgers University.

Palmer, Susan J. and Charlotte Hardman. 1999b. "Introduction: Alternative Childhoods," pp.1–10 in Susan J. Palmer and Charlotte Hardman (eds.), *Children in New Religions.* New Brunswick: Rutgers University.

Palmer, Susan J. and Lisotta Frisk. 2014. "Update on the Raid on the Children of the Twelve Tribes in Germany." Article posted on the CESNUR webpage at http://www.cesnur.org/2014/12tribes.htm.

Palmer, Susan and Steve Luxton. 1998. "The Ansaru Allah Community: Postmodern Narration and the Black Jeremiah," pp.353–370 in Peter Clarke (ed.), *New Trends and Developments in the World of Islam.* London: Luzac Oriental.

Patrick, Ted with Tom Dulack. 1976. *Let Our Children Go!* New York: Dutton.

Peecher, Rob. 2002. "DFACS Takes Custody of 5 Nuwaubian Children." *Macon Telegraph*, May 10.

Peecher, Rob. 2003. "Lawyers Argue Details in York Case." *Macon Telegraph*, January 18.

Perkins, Nancy. 2008. "Texas Officials Deny Ex-FLDS Members Involved in Search Warrant." *Deseret News*, April 19. Accessed online at http://findarticles.com/p/articles/mi_qn4188/is_2008419/ai_n25352.

Perry, Bruce D. 1994. "Destructive Childrearing Practices by the Children of God." Report to the Health and Community Services, Melbourne, Australia, March 28. Document on file with authors.

Perry, Bruce D. and Maia Szalavitz. 2007. "Stairway to Heaven: Treating Children in the Crosshairs of Trauma." *International Cultic Studies Association E-Newsletter* 6 (3). Accessed online at http://wwwicsahome/infoserrve_articles/perry_szalavitz_trauma_eno603.htm.

Pfeifer, Jeffrey E. 1999. "Perceptual biases and mock juror decision-making: Minority religions in court." *Social Justice Research*, 12, 409–419.

Philips, Abu Ameenah Bilal. 1988. *The Ansar Cult in America*. New Delhi, India: Islamic Book Service.

Phinney, Matt. 2005. "Religious Sect out in Eldorado Causing Unrest in the Community." *San Angelo Standard-Times*, March 27. Accessed online at http://nl-newsbank.com/nl-search/we/Archives?

Pinzur, Matthew. 2000. "The Nuwaubians: Who Are These People?" *Macon Telegraph*, May 15.

Pitts, William L. 1995. "Davidians and Branch Davidians: 1929–1987," pp.20–42 in Stuart A. Wright (ed.), *Armageddon in Waco*. Chicago: University of Chicago.

"Polygamist Sect Kids to Undergo DNA Tests." 2008. CBS News, April 18. Accessed online at http://cbsnews.com/stories/2008/04/18/national/.

Possamai, Adam and Alphia Possamai-Inesedy. 2009. "Scientology Down Under," pp.345–364 in James R. Lewis (ed.), *Scientology*. New York: Oxford University Press.

Priest, Lisa. 1991. "Trial Set to Begin on Charges against Church of Scientology." *Toronto Star*, April 24.

Report on Discrimination against Spiritual and Therapeutical Minorities in France. 2000. Centre d'Information et de Conseil des Nouvelles Spiritualités.

Richardson, James T. 1985. "The Deformation of New Religions: Impacts of Societal and Organizational Factors," pp.163–175 in Thomas Robbins, William Shepherd, and James McBride (eds.), *Cults, Culture, and the Law*. Chico, CA: Scholars Press.

Richardson, James T. 1991. "Cult/Brainwashing Cases and the Freedom of Religion." *Journal of Church and State* 33:55–74.

Richardson, James T. 1992. "Public Opinion and the Tax Evasion of Reverend Moon." *Behavioral Sciences and the Law* 10:53–63.

Richardson, James T. 1993. "Definitions of Cult: From Sociological-Technical to Popular-Negative." *Review of Religious Research* 34:348–356.

Richardson, James T. 1995. "Manufacturing Consent about Koresh: A Structural Analysis of the Role of Media in the Waco Tragedy," pp.153–176 in Stuart A. Wright (ed.), *Armageddon in Waco*. Chicago: University of Chicago.

Richardson, James T. 1997. "Sociology and the New Religions: "Brainwashing," the Courts and Religious Freedom," pp.115–137 in Phillip Jenkins and Stephen Kroll-Smith (eds.), *Witnessing for Sociology*. New York: Praeger.

Richardson, James T. 1999. "Social Control of New Religions: From Brainwashing Claims to Child Sex Abuse Accusations," pp.172–186 in Susan J. Palmer and Charlotte E. Hardman (eds.), *Children in New Religions*. New Brunswick: Rutgers University.

Richardson, James T. 2000. "Discretion and Discrimination in Legal Cases Involving Controversial Religious Groups and Allegations of Ritual Abuse," pp.111–132 in Rex Ahdar (ed.), *Law and Religion*. Aldershot, UK: Ashgate.

Richardson, James T. 2004a. *Regulating Religion: Case Studies from Around the Globe*. New York: Kluwer.

Richardson, James T. 2004b. "Regulating Religion: A Sociological and Historical Introduction," pp.1–22 in James T. Richardson (ed.), *Regulating Religion: Case Studies from around the Globe*. New York: Kluwer.

Richardson, James T., Joel Best, and David G. Bromley. 1991. *The Satanism Scare*. New York: Aldine.

Richardson, James T. and David G. Bromley. 1983. *The Brainwashing/Deprogramming Controversy*. New York: Edwin Mellen.

Richardson, James T. and Massimo Introvigne. 2001. "Brainwashing Theories in European Parliamentary and Administrative Reports on "Cults" and "Sects."" *Journal for the Scientific Study of Religion* 40:143–168.

Richardson, James T. and Massimo Introvigne. 2004. "Brainwashing Theories in European Parliamentary and Administrative Reports on Cults and Sects," pp.151–178 in James T. Richardson (ed.), *Regulating Religion: Case Studies from around the Globe*. New York: Kluwer.

Richardson, James T. and Massimo Introvigne. 2007. "New Religious Movements, Countermovements, Moral Panics, and the Media," pp.91–114 in David G. Bromley (ed.), *Teaching New Religious Movements*. New York: Oxford.

Richardson, James T. and Tamatha L. Schreinert. 2011. "Political and Legislative Context of the FLDS Raid in Texas," pp.221–241 in Stuart A. Wright and James T. Richardson (eds.), *Saints under Siege*. New York: New York University Press.

Richardson, James T. and Baren van Driel. 1984. "Public Support for Anti-cult Legislation." *Journal for the Scientific Study of Religion* 23 (4): 412–19.

Richardson, James T. and Baren van Driel. 1997. "Journalists' Attitudes toward New Religious Movements." *Review of Religious Research* 39:116–136.

Riera, Daniel and Eduardo Blanco. 1994a. "Alfredo Silleta: 'Yo hablo el viernes y el sabado se arma quilombo.'" *La Maga*, May 4, p.44.

Riera, Daniel and Eduardo Blanco. 1994b. "El 'lavado de cerebro,' una teoria de dudoso valor cientifico." *La Maga*, May 4, p.47.

Rizzo, Russ. 2008. "Seeking Sarah: Colorado Caller Is 'Person of Interest.'" Salt Lake City Tribune, April 19, p.4A.

Robbins, Thomas. 1988. *Cults, Converts and Charisma*. Newbury Park, CA: Sage.

Rosas, Faustino. 1994. "Political Background and Religious Conflict Due to Rapid Growth of Christian 'Sects.'" *El Informador Publico*, January, pp.1,15.

Ross, Rick. 2003. "Cult News from Rick Ross," July 17. Accessed online at www.cultnews.com/cat?=105.

Ross, Joan Carol and Michael D. Langone. 1988. *Cults: What Parents Should Know*. Weston, MA: American Family Foundation.

Saether, George William. 1975. "Oral Memoirs." Institute for Oral History. Waco: Baylor University.

Schein, Edgar. 1961. *Coercive Persuasion: A Socio-psychological Analysis of the "Brainwashing" of American Civilian Prisoners by the Chinese Communists*. New York: W.W. Norton.

Schreinert, Tamatha L. and James T. Richardson. 2011. "Pyrrhic Victory? An Analysis of the Appeal Court Opinions Concerning the FLDS Children," pp.242–264 in Stuart A. Wright and James T. Richardson (eds.), *Saints under Siege*. New York: New York University Press.

Seiwert, Hubert. 2004. "The German Enquete Commission on Sects: Political Conflicts and Compromises," pp.85–102 in James T. Richardson (ed.), *Regulating Religion: Case Studies from around the Globe*. New York: Kluwer.

Selway, Deborah. 1992. "Religion in the Mainstream Press: The Challenge of the Future." *Australian Religious Studies Review* 5:18–24.

"Shooting Deaths." *Orlando Sentinel*, May 9, 1990.

Shupe, Anson D. 1998. *Wolves within the Fold: Religious Leadership and Abuses of Power*. New Brunswick, NJ: Rutgers.

Shupe, Anson D. and David G. Bromley. 1980. *The New Vigilantes: Deprogrammers, Anti-cultists and New Religions*. Los Angeles: Sage.

Shupe, Anson D. and David G. Bromley. 1994. *Anti-Cult Movements in Cross-Cultural Perspective*. New York: Garland.

Shupe, Anson D. and Susan Darnell. 2006. *Agents of Discord: Deprogramming, Pseudo-Science and the American Anticult Movement*. New Brunswick: Transaction.

Shupe, Anson D. and Jeffrey K. Hadden. 1995. "Cops, News Copy and Public Opinion: Legitimacy and the Social Construction of Evil in Waco," pp.177–202 in Stuart A. Wright (ed.), *Armageddon in Waco*. Chicago: University of Chicago.

Silleta, Alfredo. 1984. *La secta Moon: Como destruir la democracia*. Buenos Aires: Editor.

Silleta, Alfredo. 1986. *Las sectas invaden la Argentina*. Buenos Aires: Contrapunto.

Silleta, Alfredo. 1992. *Sectas: Cuando el paraiso es un inferno*. Buenos Aires: Meridion.

Singer, Margaret T. with Janja Lalich. 1995. *Cults in Our Midst: The Hidden Menace in Our Everyday Lives*. San Francisco: Jossey-Bass.

Skolnick, Jerome H. and James J. Fyfe. 1993. *Above the Law: Police and the Excessive Use of Force*. New York: Free Press.

Skonovd, Norman L. 1983. "Leaving the Cultic Religious Milieu," pp.91–105 in David G. Bromley and James T. Richardson (eds.), *The Brainwashing/Deprogramming Controversy*. New York: Edwin Mellen.

Smith, John L. 2008. "Affidavits Paint a Disturbing Picture of Texas Child Protective Services." *Las Vegas Review Journal*, June 3. Accessed online at www.reviewjournal.com.

Snow, David A. and Robert Benford. 1992. "Master Frames and Cycles of Protest," pp.135–55 in Aldon D. Morris and Carol McClurg Mueller (eds.), *Frontiers in Social Movements*. New Haven, CT: Yale University Press.

Snow, David A, Burke E. Rochford, Steven Worden, and Robert Benford. 1986. "Frame Alignment Process, Micromobilization and Movement Participation." *American Sociological Review* 51 (4):464–481.

Soneira, Jorge. 1993. "El Debate Sobre Las 'Sectas en Argentina,'" pp.35–48 in Alejandro Frigerio (ed.), *Nuevos movimientos religiosos y ciencias sociales*. Buenos Aires: Centro Editor de America Latina.

Spina, Julio. 1994. "La historia de la causa contra La Familia." *La Maga*, May 4, p.46.

Squires, Nick. 2014. "Vatican Taken to Task by UN on Child Abuse: Will the Church Change?" Accessed online at http://www.csmonitor.com/World/Europe/2014/0116/Vatican-taken-to-task-by-UN-on-child-abuse.-Will-the-church-change-video.

Stephens, Robert. 1983. "Scientologists Sue over Search." *Globe and Mail*, June 24.

Swantko, Jean. A. 1998. "An Issue of Control: Conflict between the Church in Island Pond and the State Government." Paper presented at the 14th World Congress of Sociology, Montreal.

Swantko, Jean A. 2004. "The Twelve Tribes Messianic Communities, the Anti-Cult Movement, and Governmental Response," pp.179–200 in James T. Richardson (ed.), *Regulating Religion: Case Studies around the Globe*. New York: Kluwer Academic/Plenum Publishers.

Swantko, Jean A. 2009. "State-Sanctioned Raids and Government Violations of Religious Freedom." Paper presented at the annual meeting of CESNUR, Salt Lake City, June.

Tabor, James D. 1995. "Religious Discourse and Failed Negotiations: The Dynamics of Biblical Apocalypticism in Waco," pp.263–281 in Stuart A. Wright (ed.), *Armageddon in Waco*. Chicago: University of Chicago.

Tarr, James. 2013. "Laws for Firearms: Best State for Gun Owners in 2013." Accessed online at www.gunsandammo.com/2013/03/14/ga-ranks-the-best-state-for-gun-owners-in-2013/.

Tarrow, Sidney. 1994. *Power in Movement*. New York: Cambridge University Press.

Taslimi, Cheryl Rowe, Ralph W. Hood Jr., and P. J. Watson. 1991. "Assessment of Former Members of Shiloh: The Adjective Check List 17 Years Later." *Journal for the Scientific Study of Religion* 30 (3):306–311.

Tavris, Carol. 1986. "The Truth About Sexual Abuse." *Vogue*, May.

"Texas Authorities Defend Sect Raid." 2008. NBC News,com, April 10. Accessed online at http://www.nbcnews.com/id/24014376/ns/us_news-crime_and_courts/t/texas-authorities-defend-polygamous-sect-raid/#.U2FdlXxOUiQ.

Thibodeau, David with Leon Whiteson. 1999. *A Place Called Waco: A Survivor's Story*. Washington, DC: Public Affairs.

Tilly, Charles. 1978. *From Mobilization to Revolution*. Reading, MA: Addison-Wesley.

Tobias, Madeleine Landau and Janja Lalich. 1994. *Captive Hearts, Captive Minds*. Alameda, CA: Hunter House.

Torpy, Bill. 2004a. "Sect Leader Framed, Daughter Says: Brother Had 'Vendetta' She Tells Jury." *Atlanta Journal-Constitution*, January 21.

Torpy, Bill. 2004b. "York Trial Hits Third Week: Key Ruling Expected Today." *Atlanta Journal-Constitution*, January 19.

Trott, Jon and Michael Hertenstein. 1992. "Selling Satan: The Tragic History of Michael Warnke." *Cornerstone Magazine* 21 (98):7–9.

Tully, Stephen. 2005. *Research Handbook on Corporate Legal Responsibility*. Cheltenham, UK: Edward Elgar Publishing.

Urban, Hugh B. 2006. "Fair Game: Secrecy, Security and the Church of Scientology in Cold War America." *Journal of the American Academy of Religion* 74 (2):356–389.

U.S. Department of Justice. 1993. *Report to the Deputy Attorney General on the Events at Waco, Texas, February 28 to April 19, 1993*. Redacted version, October 8. Washington, DC: U.S. Government Printing Office.

U.S. Department of Treasury. 1993. *Report of the Department of Treasury on the Bureau of Alcohol, Tobacco, and Firearms Investigation of Vernon Wayne Howell, Also Known as David Koresh*. Washington, DC: U.S. Government Printing Office.

Van Eck Duymaer van Twist, Amanda. 2015. *Perfect Children: Growing Up on the Religious Fringe*. New York: Oxford University Press.

Verhovek, Sam Howe. 1993. "In Shadow of Texas Siege, Uncertainty for Innocents." *New York Times*, March 8.

Wagner-Pacific, Robin. 1994. *Discourse and Destruction: The City of Philadelphia versus MOVE*. Chicago: University of Chicago.

Wall, Elissa with Lisa Pulitzer. 2008. *Stolen Innocence*. New York: William Morrow Books.

Wallis, Roy A. 1977. *The Road to Total Freedom: A Sociological Analysis of Scientology*. New York: Columbia University Press.

Wallis, Roy A. 1982. "Charisma, Commitment and Control in a New Religious Movement," pp.73–140 in Roy A. Wallis (ed.), *Millennialism and Charisma*. Belfast: Queens University Press.

Walters, Joanna. 2006. "Fears of New Waco as FBI Hunt for Svengali Leader of Polygamy Cult." *London Observer*, August 24. Accessed online at www.childbrides.org/abuses_Afternet_behind_the_cloak_of_polygamy.html.

Warnke, Michael. 1991. *Schemes of Satan*. Tulsa: Victory House.

Weber, Max. 1947. *The Theory of Social and Economic Organization*. Edited with an introduction by Talcott Parsons. New York: Free Press.

Weber, Max. 1968. *Max Weber on Charisma and Institution Building*. Edited by S.N. Eisenstadt. Chicago: University of Chicago.

Weber, Paul. 2012. "Texas out to Seize Warren Jeffs' Polygamist Ranch." Associated Press, November 28, 2012. Accessed online at http://bigstory.ap.org/article/texas-out-seize-warren-jeffs-polygamist-ranch.

"We Fear Another Waco." 2004. *The Independent* (UK), February 19.

Wessinger, Catherine. 2009. "Deaths in the Fire at the Branch Davidians' Mount Carmel: Who Bears Responsibility?" *Nova Religio* 13 (2):25–60.

Williams, George Hunston. 2000. *The Radical Reformation*. Kirksville, MO: Truman State University Press.

Winslow, Ben.2006. "New Film by Ex-Wife Takes Aim at FLDS." *Deseret News*, August 27.

Winslow, Ben. 2008. "Hilsdale and Colorado City Worry over Texas Raid." *Deseret News*, April 5.

Wiseman, Jean Swantko. 2011. "Strategic Dissolution and the Politics of Opposition: Parallels in the State Raids on the Twelve Tribes," pp.201–220 in Stuart A. Wright and James T. Richardson (eds.), *Saints under Siege*. New York: New York University Press.

Wisotsky, Steven. 1990. *Beyond the War on Drugs*. New York: Prometheus Books.

World Services. 1995. *The History of The Family, 1968–1994*. Zurich, Switzerland: World Services.

Wright, Stuart A. 1984. "Post-involvement Attitudes of Voluntary Defectors from Controversial New Religious Movements." *Journal for the Scientific Study of Religion* 23 (2):172–182.

Wright, Stuart A. 1987. *Leaving Cults: The Dynamics of Defection*. Washington, DC: Society for the Scientific Study of Religion.

Wright, Stuart A. 1988. "Leaving New Religious Movements: Issues, Theory and Research," pp.143–165 in David G. Bromley (ed.), *Falling from the Faith: The Causes and Consequences of Religious Apostasy*. Beverly Hills: Sage.

Wright, Stuart A. 1991. "Reconceptualizing Cult Coercion and Withdrawal: A Comparative Analysis of Divorce and Apostasy." *Social Forces* 70 (1):125–145.

Wright, Stuart A. 1995a. *Armageddon in Waco: Critical Perspectives on the Branch Davidian Conflict*. Chicago: University of Chicago.

Wright, Stuart A. 1995b. "Construction and Escalation of a Cult Threat: Dissecting Moral Panic and Official Reaction to the Branch Davidians," pp.75–94 in Stuart A. Wright (ed.), *Armageddon in Waco*. Chicago: University of Chicago.

Wright, Stuart A. 1997. "Media Coverage of Unconventional Religion: Any 'Good News' for Minority Faiths?" *Review of Religious Research* 93 (2):101–115.

Wright, Stuart A. 1998. "Exploring Factors That Shape the Apostate Role," pp.95–114 in David G. Bromley (ed.), *The Politics of Religious Apostasy*. New York: Praeger.

Wright, Stuart A. 1999. "Anatomy of a Government Massacre: Abuses of Hostage-Barricade Protocols during the Waco Standoff." *Terrorism and Political Violence* 11 (2):39–68.

Wright, Stuart A. 2002a. "A Critical Analysis of Evidentiary and Procedural Rulings in the Branch Davidian Civil Trial," pp.101–113 in Derek Davis (ed.), *New Religious Movements and Religious Liberty in America*. Waco: Baylor University Press.

Wright, Stuart A. 2002b. "Public Agency Involvement in Government-Religious Movement Confrontations," pp.102–122 in David G. Bromley and J. Gordon Melton (eds.), *Cults, Religion and Violence*. New York: Cambridge University Press.

Wright, Stuart A. 2005. "Explaining Militarization at Waco: Construction and Convergence of a Warfare Narrative," pp.75–97 in James R. Lewis (ed.), *Controversial New Religions*. New York: Oxford University Press.

Wright, Stuart A. 2007a. "The Dynamics of Movement Membership: Joining and Leaving NRMs," pp.187–210 in David G. Bromley (ed.), *Teaching New Religious Movements*. New York: Oxford University Press.

Wright, Stuart A. 2007b. *Patriots, Politics and the Oklahoma City Bombing*. London and New York: Cambridge University Press.

Wright, Stuart A. 2009. "Revisiting the Branch Davidian Mass Suicide Debate." *Nova Religio* 13 (2):4–24.

Wright, Stuart A. 2011. "Deconstructing Official Rationales for the Texas State Raid on the FLDS," pp.124–149 in Stuart A. Wright and James T. Richardson (eds.), *Saints under Siege*. New York: New York University Press.

Wright, Stuart A. and Helen R. Ebaugh. 1993. "Leaving New Religions," pp.117–138 in David G. Bromley and Jeffrey K. Hadden (eds.), *Handbook of Cults and Sects in America*. Greenwich: JAI Press.

Wright, Stuart A. and Jennifer Lara Fagen, 2011. ""Texas Redux: A Comparative Analysis of the FLDS and Branch Davidian Raids," pp.150–177 in Stuart A. Wright and James T. Richardson (eds.), *Saints under Siege*. New York: New York University Press.

Wright, Stuart A. and James T. Richardson. 2011a. *Saints under Siege: The Texas State Raid on the Fundamentalist Latter Day Saints*. New York: New York University Press.

Wright, Stuart A. and James T. Richardson. 2011b. "Introduction," pp.1–24 in Stuart A. Wright and James T. Richardson (eds.), *Saints under Siege*. New York: New York University Press.

Wright, Stuart A. and James T. Richardson. 2014. "The Fundamentalist Latter Day Saints after the Texas State Raid: Assessing a Post-Raid Movement Trajectory." *Nova Religio* 17 (4):38–48.

LEGAL CASES AND DOCUMENTS

Affidavit for Search and Arrest Warrant, No. M-08-001 S, The State of Texas, County of Schleicher, April 3, 2008.

Family and Children's Services of King County v. E.F. Dawson, 12 R.F.L. (3d) 104 (N.S.C.A. 1988).

Federal Court of Appeals of San Martin, Case N 81/89, December 13, 1993. Transcript translated from Spanish on file with authors.

Gregoire v. Gregoire, 1983. Family Abuse Hearing, District Court of Vermont, Chittenden Circuit Unit 2, Burlington, May.

In Re: C.C., 22-6-84 Osj (Vermont District Court, Unit III, 1984). Unreported Juvenile Court opinion of Judge Frank Mahady, available at www.twelvetribes.com, as Appendix B of "An Issue of Control: Conflict between the Church at Island Pond and State Government," by Jean Swantko.

In re Texas Department of Family and Protective Services. 255 S. W. 3d 613 (Tex.), 2008.

Original Petition for Protection of Children, District Court of Schleicher County, Western District of Texas, 51st J.D., Cause 2902, 2008.

U.S. District Court. 1993. Application and Affidavit for Search Warrant, W93-15M. Western District of Texas. Filed February 26.

Index